JANE AUSTEN: *Emma* David Lodge
JANE AUSTEN: *'Northanger Abbey'* & *'Persuasion'* B.C. Southam
JANE AUSTEN: *'Sense and Sensibility'*, *'Pride and Prejudice'* & *Mansfield Park'*
  B.C. Southam
BECKETT: *Waiting for Godot* Ruby Cohn
WILLIAM BLAKE: *Songs of Innocence and Experience* Margaret Bottrall
CHARLOTTE BRONTË: *'Jane Eyre'* & *'Villette'* Miriam Allott
EMILY BRONTË: *Wuthering Heights* Miriam Allott
BROWNING: *'Men and Women'* & *Other Poems* J.R. Watson
CHAUCER: *Canterbury Tales* J.J. Anderson
COLERIDGE: *'The Ancient Mariner'* & *Other Poems* Alun R. Jones &
  William Tydeman
CONRAD: *'Heart of Darkness'*, *'Nostromo'* & *'Under Western Eyes'* C.B. Cox
CONRAD: *The Secret Agent* Ian Watt ·
DICKENS: *Bleak House* A.E. Dyson
DICKENS: *'Hard Times'*, *'Great Expectations'* & *'Our Mutual Friend'* Norman Page
DICKENS: *'Dombey and Son'* & *'Little Dorrit'* Alan Shelston
DONNE: *Songs and Sonets* Julian Lovelock
GEORGE ELIOT: *Middlemarch* Patrick Swinden
GEORGE ELIOT: *'The Mill on the Floss'* & *'Silas Marner'* R.P. Draper
T.S. ELIOT: *Four Quartets* Bernard Bergonzi
T.S. ELIOT: *'Prufrock'*, *'Gerontion'*, *'Ash Wednesday'* & *Other Shorter Poems*
  B.C. Southam
T.S. ELIOT: *The Waste Land* C.D. Cox & Arnold P. Hinchliffe
T.S. ELIOT: *Plays* Arnold P. Hinchliffe
HENRY FIELDING: *Tom Jones* Neil Compton
E.M. FORSTER: *A Passage to India* Malcolm Bradbury
WILLIAM GOLDING: *Novels 1954–64* Norman Page
HARDY: *The Tragic Novels* R.P. Draper
HARDY: *Poems* James Gibson & Trevor Johnson
HARDY: *Three Pastoral Novels* R.P. Draper
GERARD MANLEY HOPKINS: *Poems* Margaret Bottrall
HENRY JAMES: *'Washington Square'* & *'The Portrait of a Lady'* Alan Shelton
JONSON: *Volpone* Jonas A. Barish
JONSON: *'Every Man in his Humour'* & *'The Alchemist'* R.V. Holdsworth
JAMES JOYCE: *'Dubliners'* & *'A Portrait of the Artist as a Young Man'* Morris Beja
KEATS: *Odes* G.S. Fraser
KEATS: *Narrative Poems* John Spencer Hill
D.H. LAWRENCE: *Sons and Lovers* Gamini Salgado
D.H. LAWRENCE: *'The Rainbow'* & *'Women in Love'* Colin Clarke
LOWRY: *Under the Volcano* Gordon Bowker
MARLOWE: *Doctor Faustus* John Jump
MARLOWE: *'Tamburlaine the Great'*, *'Edward the Second'* & *'The Jew of Malta'*
  John Russell Brown
MARLOWE: *Poems* Arthur Pollard
MAUPASSANT: *In the Hall of Mirrors* T. Harris
MILTON: *Paradise Lost* A.E. Dyson & Julian Lovelock
O'CASEY: *'Juno and the Paycock'*, *'The Plough and the Stars'* & *'The Shadow of a*
  Gunman' Ronald Ayling
EUGENE O'NEILL: *Three Plays* Normand Berlin
JOHN OSBORNE: *Look Back in Anger* John Russell Taylor
PINTER: *'The Birthday Party'* & *Other Plays* Michael Scott
POPE: *The Rape of the Lock* John Dixon Hunt
SHAKESPEARE: *A Midsummer Night's Dream* Antony Price
SHAKESPEARE: *Antony and Cleopatra* John Russell Brown

SHAKESPEARE: *Coriolanus* B.A. Brockman
SHAKESPEARE: *Early Tragedies* Neil Taylor & Bryan Loughrey
SHAKESPEARE: *Hamlet* John Jump
SHAKESPEARE: *Henry IV Parts I and II* G.K. Hunter
SHAKESPEARE: *Henry V* Michael Quinn
SHAKESPEARE: *Julius Caesar* Peter Ure
SHAKESPEARE: *King Lear* Frank Kermode
SHAKESPEARE: *Macbeth* John Wain
SHAKESPEARE: *Measure for Measure* C.K. Stead
SHAKESPEARE: *The Merchant of Venice* John Wilders
SHAKESPEARE: *'Much Ado About Nothing' & 'As You Like It'* John Russell Brown
SHAKESPEARE: *Othello* John Wain
SHAKESPEARE: *Richard II* Nicholas Brooke
SHAKESPEARE: *The Sonnets* Peter Jones
SHAKESPEARE: *The Tempest* D.J. Palmer
SHAKESPEARE: *Troilus and Cressida* Priscilla Martin
SHAKESPEARE: *Twelfth Night* D.J. Palmer
SHAKESPEARE: *The Winter's Tale* Kenneth Muir
SPENSER: *The Faerie Queene* Peter Bayley
SHERIDAN: *Comedies* Peter Davison
STOPPARD: *'Rosencrantz and Guildenstern are Dead', 'Jumpers' & 'Travesties'*
  T. Bareham
SWIFT: *Gulliver's Travels* Richard Gravil
TENNYSON: *In Memoriam* John Dixon Hunt
THACKERAY: *Vanity Fair* Arthur Pollard
TROLLOPE: *The Barsetshire Novels* T. Bareham
WEBSTER: *'The White Devil' & 'The Duchess of Malfi'* R.V. Holdsworth
WILDE: *Comedies* William Tydeman
VIRGINIA WOOLF: *To the Lighthouse* Morris Beja
WORDSWORTH: *Lyrical Ballads* Alun R. Jones & William Tydeman
WORDSWORTH: *The 1807 Poems* Alun R. Jones
WORDSWORTH: *The Prelude* W.J. Harvey & Richard Gravil
YEATS: *Poems 1919–35* Elizabeth Cullingford
YEATS: *Last Poems* Jon Stallworthy

Issues in Contemporary Critical Theory Peter Barry
Thirties Poets: 'The Auden Group' Ronald Carter
Tragedy: Developments in Criticism R.P. Draper
Epic Ronald Draper
Poetry Criticism and Practice: Developments since the Symbolists A.E. Dyson
Three Contemporary Poets: Gunn, Hughes, Thomas A.E. Dyson
Elizabethan Poetry: Lyrical & Narrative Gerald Hammond
The Metaphysical Poets Gerald Hammond
Medieval English Drama Peter Happé
The English Novel: Developments in Criticism since Henry James Stephen Hazell
Poetry of the First World War Dominic Hibberd
The Romantic Imagination John Spencer Hill
Drama Criticism: Developments since Ibsen Arnold P. Hinchliffe
Three Jacobean Revenge Tragedies R.V. Holdsworth
The Pastoral Mode Bryan Loughrey
The Language of Literature Norman Page
Comedy: Developments in Criticism D.J. Palmer
Studying Shakespeare John Russell Brown
The Gothic Novel Victor Sage
Pre-Romantic Poetry J.R. Watson

Thirties Poets: 'The Auden Group'

A CASEBOOK

EDITED BY

RONALD CARTER

First published 1984 by
THE MACMILLAN PRESS LTD
Houndmills, Basingstoke, Hampshire RG21 2XS
and London
Companies and representatives
throughout the world

ISBN 0–333–29328–2 hardcover
ISBN 0–333–29329–0 paperback

A catalogue record for this book is available
from the British Library.

Printed in Hong Kong

Reprinted 1989, 1992

CONTENTS

2 Poets and Wars

3 Poetry and the Thirties

GENERAL EDITOR'S PREFACE

The Casebook series, launched in 1968, has become a well-regarded library of critical studies. The central concern of the series remains the 'single-author' volume, but suggestions from the academic community have led to an extension of the original plan, to include occasional volumes on such general themes as literary 'schools' and genres.

Each volume in the central category deals either with one well-known and influential work by an individual author, or with closely related works by one writer. The main section consists of critical readings, mostly modern, collected from books and journals. A selection of reviews and comments by the author's contemporaries is also included, and sometimes comments from the author himself. The Editor's Introduction charts the reputation of the work or works from the first appearance to the present time.

Volumes in the 'general themes' category are variable in structure but follow the basic purpose of the series in presenting an integrated selection of readings, with an Introduction which explores the theme and discusses the literary and critical issues involved.

A single volume can represent no more than a small selection of critical opinions. Some critics are excluded for reasons of space, and it is hoped that readers will pursue the suggestions for further reading in the Select Bibliography. Other contributions are severed from their original context, to which some readers may wish to turn. Indeed, if they take a hint from the critics represented here, they certainly will.

A. E. DYSON

A NOTE ON EDITIONS

It has not been possible to relate every poem cited or every extract used to its precise position in the canon of each individual author. As is mentioned in the Introduction, the poets concerned did 'return' with a critical eye to their poetry of this period, and readers should be alert to this. For example, Stephen Spender's 'Vienna' and W. H. Auden's 'Spain' only appear in texts by special permission of their authors. Each has in a way dissociated himself from his poem by not reprinting it in subsequent, post-1940 editions of their respective *Collected Poems*.

All the poets have made some textual or verbal changes to earlier material, though some have been less thorough-going than others. Louis MacNeice, for example, writes thus in the Preface to his volume of *Collected Poems* (1949): 'In preparing this book for the press I have also resisted the temptation to make many revisions, since I feel that after three or four years from the date of writing a poet should leave even not-so-well alone.'

On the other hand, in the case of W. H. Auden, the issue is a particularly complex one. The view expressed in the Preface to his *Collected Shorter Poems* (1966) is that of Valéry, whom Auden quotes as saying: 'A poem is never finished, it is only abandoned.' Readers are referred to the Select Bibliography for further information as well as for a review of different available editions of Auden's poetry.

The general line taken by critics who are faced with alternative versions is to work as far as possible from the earliest 1930s editions, since it is those poems which can be taken to be more significant from a period point of view.

R.C.

INTRODUCTION

There are a number of problems and pitfalls in preparing a critical anthology of this kind. Before discussing the nature of the selection made, it would be well for the selector to point out the limitations that such a choice brings with it.

Inherent in the title of this Casebook are three potential limitations. One is that four poets (and, for the most part, no more than four) are seen to represent the poetry produced in a single decade and are thus labelled 'Thirties Poets'. It is commonly recognised, certainly, that W. H. Auden, C. Day Lewis, Stephen Spender and Louis MacNeice are the figures who came to prominence in the poetry of those years. But this label should not be taken to imply that justice could not also be done to the poetic achievements of their contemporaries. Furthermore, all four poets have produced an important body of work after the close of that decade. Although the emphasis in this book is largely restricted to their work in those years, they would not want to be, and should not be, solely regarded as 'Thirties' poets.

Another problem is that the use of the term 'Group' would be misleading if it suggested that the poets concerned thought of themselves as a particular 'school of poetry', with a unified set of aims, principles and poetic means, and a consciously preformulated aesthetic. As Day Lewis pointed out in his autobiography, *The Buried Day*, at no time did the group come together to produce any common manifesto. In fact, it was not until 1947 that Day Lewis, Spender and Auden even met in the same room together. And, as Auden has put it:

From a literary point of view, the customary journalistic linkage of the names Auden, Day Lewis, MacNeice and Spender is, and always was, absurd. Even when we seemed to share some common concern – political let us say – our approaches to it, our sensibilities and techniques were always different.[1]

A third potential limitation is brought about by the suggestion that 'the Auden Group' was dominated to such an extent by Auden that the distinctive character of the other poets becomes submerged. Although I have followed majority critical opinion in recognising Auden's pre-eminence as a talent and an influence, not all critics would submit that Auden is the most significant or the best poet of the group.

There is no easy answer to the charges that selectivity produces distortion. I can only alert the reader to them, stress that they should be borne in mind when using the anthology, and strongly recommend that the Select Bibliography be consulted for fuller critical amplification of those areas and questions which must be omitted from detailed treatment here.

What, then, are the principles which inform the selection made for this Casebook? One of the main aims I have sought is that the poets should be heard as far as possible in their own voices. The two sections of Part One are taken up with extracts from their own critical writings produced in the Thirties, and with comments on each other's work seen both in the context of its time and, in some instances, retrospectively. The first section allows us to perceive something of their attitude to poetry in those years and indicates that, while no manifesto was produced, there is a certain uniformity in the issues and questions raised. The second section, apart from providing useful critical insight, underlines the point that there was among the group a closeness of appreciation and mutual interest which was formed in the Thirties (in some cases – e.g., Auden and MacNeice – as a result of poetic collaboration) but which also continued long after that time. It is largely from their writing on poetry that extracts have been drawn, but it should be remembered that their writings in these years cover a wide range of topics, and that overt interest in political philosophy (Day Lewis) and psychology (Auden) will be necessarily reflected in their concern for poetry. Consultation of *The English Auden* (1977)[2] will give an idea of the eclectic interests of just one of the group in these years. Although the nature of their views of poetry prevents such a conclusion, the section captions of Part One – 'The Poets on Poetry' and 'The Poets on Each Other' – should not tempt us into believing this group of poets to be either introverted or exclusively concerned with purely aesthetic questions.

In Part Two I have attempted to present a range of critical reaction by the poets' contemporaries which is both synoptic and focused on individual writers. Christopher Isherwood may stand as representative of other writers who were intimate with the Auden Group; and Michael Roberts, himself a poet, was foremost among those critics who were proselytisers for their early work. Francis Scarfe's book, from which excepts on MacNeice and Day Lewis are taken, is one of the first studies to attempt a sustained critical examination of the poetry of the Thirties.[3]

Part Three continues the attempt to reconcile studies of the individual poets with criticism which recognises a degree of corporateness in the achievement. But in its first section the main emphasis is on the individual poets. This section – 'Individual Assessments' – contains extracts from criticism spanning some twenty-five years, and it is hoped that the material it includes will enable the reader to make a sufficiently detailed evaluation of the poets' singular achievements. The focus for most of the extracts here is on the Thirties poetry of the poets concerned, although for purposes of illuminating comparison, and to allow proper assessment of poetic development, change and continuity, some discussion of post-Thirties poems is included.

It is, of course, impossible properly to cover in this way the manifold nature of the poets' work. The attention given in most of the extracts in section 1 of Part Three is, therefore, largely to formalistic aspects. A number of the essays contain a high proportion of practical criticism of poems. From this base of consideration of how individual poems or sequences of poems work, some generalisations can be drawn. Where authors do not draw them, or where the exigences of editing leave some relevant aspects unrevealed, readers may wish to establish their own connections with the more general material elsewhere in the book or in the references in the Select Bibliography. Space precludes too detailed a consideration of intellectual, social and cultural background, important as it is, but close, sensitive reading of the poets' work is a necessary first base for study, and this major section in the volume seeks to provide such a framework.

The criticism ranges from early and influential work on Auden by Richard Hoggart (see the Bibliography for later studies by him), through not wholly enthusiastic voices (Graham Hough), to more recent work which incorporates close attention to the functions of language and image (Justin Replogle, Terence Brown), and to approaches which challenge previous assessments – here exemplified by Geoffrey Thurley's appreciation of Spender which seeks to unbalance Auden from his pivotal position in 'the Auden Group'.

Section 2 of Part Three – 'Poets and Wars' – may be seen as a link passage between the particular and the general themes, discussing three of the poets (Spender, Auden and Day Lewis) as individual writers but in the general context of the political and cultural crisis of Spanish Civil War and the movement toward world conflict at the end of the decade. Aspects of the 'political commitment' among members of the group and their contemporaries are touched on by contributors elsewhere in the selection. But the reader will probably find it convenient to have Samuel Hynes's contribution singled out in this way, both in regard to its inherent merits and also as an appropriate way, given its distinctive subject and its collective treatment, of making the transition from 'Individual Assessments' to 'Poetry and the Thirties'. (The principles of selection and the limitations of space and structure in the Casebook have not permitted fuller citation of Hynes's seminal study, *The Auden Generation*.[4] The excerpts in the 'Poets and Wars' section are editor-devised morsels from a much greater whole. Hynes's book is especially useful for the way in which it links critical discussion of the literature with the significant socio-political contours of the decade.)

In sum, it is hoped that the view which emerges of the poets in the first two sections of Part Three is broadly balanced, offers perspectives, is positively critical, and is rooted in the kind of text study which encourages cross-comparison and inter-evaluation.[5]

The concluding section of Part Three – 'Poetry and the Thirties' – follows what is taken to be a productive suggestion in Bernard Bergonzi's *Reading the Thirties*.[6] This is that there is often something 'transindividual' about literary periods: that such factors as collective styles and corporate preoccupations can be discerned when writers are studied as groups. Bergonzi's own essay on the 'Audenesque' features in the style of the poets both in this and in subsequent decades examines the linguistic organisation and structure of the 'code' which Auden 'devised, without intending to', but which enabled other poets to 'express their fears and anxieties and hopes through a period of sustained historical crisis'.[7] The other essays in this section – by Francis Hope and Martin Dodsworth – are from a similar perspective and adopt a socio-historical and stylistic viewpoint respectively. The section should provide a basis for discussing the poets of the Thirties in a rather broader context than that of the 'Macspaunday' phenomenon – as MacNeice, Spender, Auden and Day Lewis were collectively labelled by the poet Roy Cambell.

II THE AUDEN GROUP: SOME ASPECTS OF THEIR POETRY IN THE THIRTIES

Auden, MacNeice, Spender and Day Lewis came to poetic maturity within the context of a decade the character of which is well-defined by Michael Roberts who, as an editor, was responsible for publishing some of their earliest verse:

Those of us who grew up to manhood in the post-war years remember how, in that period, it seemed to us there was no finality. We learned to question every impulse until we became so self-conscious, so hag-ridden by doubts, indecisions, uncertainties that we lost all spontaneity, and, because we learned to account for the actions of others, we learned neither to praise nor blame them. It was not any one thing which caused this scepticism: it appeared in various guises – the theory of relativity breaking up our neat mechanical world, science learning to doubt whether it could approach any finality, psychoanalysis discovering how many actions, apparently spontaneous, were rigidly determined; and beyond all this a feeling that the middle-class world, the world of the nineteenth century, was definitely breaking up, and that it would be replaced in the near future by a world of communism or big business.[8]

This 'context' gave rise to fundamental literary questions to which the poets responded collectively and uniquely. Many of their essays of the time attempt theoretical discussion of these questions; their poetry constantly reflects the effort to realise some practical resolution of them. The questions are ones which had been put before, but in these years they were forced on all writers with a particular intensity and urgency. Questions such as: can or should a poet stand above the contemporary struggle going on around him? Should he put his talent at the service of specific causes? If he does the latter, what *kind* of poetry does he write? What is the relationship between political poetry, propaganda and art? How can literature become an effective moral force? If – as Louis MacNeice pleads in the Preface to his book on *Modern Poetry* (see Part One, section 1) – poetry should become 'impure', that is 'conditioned by the poet's life and the world around him', then what place is there for the private world of the poet?

These and related questions were not put as part of some kind of generational ideology, nor all in one single year by the same group of poets, nor were they always framed in quite this way, but they do form a common basis to the thinking about poetry undertaken by poets in these years and they do constitute, as it were, a Thirties 'poetic' providing a common structure and theme in many of the key poems of the age. As Robin Skelton has put it: 'What gives the best of the period's poetry its unmistakable quality seems to be the way in which feelings of private and of communal insecurity are fused together, so that the personal lyrical anguish informs the political statement.'[9]

Or, as Samuel Hynes writes of Auden's poem 'Summer Night': 'It places the traditionally private feelings of lyric poetry in the public world of history. . . . Auden's poem is a parable of the pressure of immediate events upon private lives.'[10] In Hynes's view the nature of such interrelation of private and public worlds is at the centre of debates on poetry in the Thirties and becomes a definitive characteristic of the poetry itself.

Consideration of such questions led to a relatively uniform challenge of assumptions about the nature of poetry. It led to concerted literary actions which examined the very basis of literariness and action. It is no coincidence that Wilfred Owen is invoked by several poets as a kind of presiding example of the need to bring poetry into closer, more democratic contact with people and with basic human and moral concerns. Auden's interest in working with traditional poetic forms, his assumption that poetry has an audience to whom it is important to be accessible, his editorship of *The Oxford Book of Light Verse*,[11] MacNeice's proclamation of the desired ordinariness of the poet,[12] the nature of Day Lewis's hopes for poetry being, among other things, 'socially important' (see Part One, section 1) – all these testify to a widespread awareness that, especially in the context of an increasingly scientific and impersonal age, poetry cannot afford to be either narrowly aesthetic, or purely lyrical, or too difficult. (See Richard Hoggart's essay herein for further discussion.)

Two words used by Hynes and Skelton require further definition in this connection: '*political* statement' and 'parable'. Although the term politics is frequently employed in association with these poets (and indeed enters their poetry and statements in a number of cases in terms of particular theories and allegiances), the 'politics' of these poets as poets – and they were not a homogeneous group with reference to either consistency or kind of political belief – is perhaps most generally defined as a recognition of the truth of two famous statements by Wilfred Owen: firstly, that 'the poetry is in the pity'; and secondly, that 'All a poet can do to-day is to warn. That is why the true poets must be truthful.' This meant, as Spender put it (see Part One, section 1), that the poet 'is dealing with reality and establishing the significance of his emotional reactions to reality, by stating what are the conditions within which he experiences these emotions'. For most poets of the Thirties those conditions were the 'chaos of values which is the substance of our environment' (see Auden and Day Lewis, Part One, section 1).

Such responses to an age in which the contradictions, inequalities and insecurities of what was felt by many to be a sick capitalist society were becoming more overt, may be termed political but in the sense of attempting to evoke sympathetic identification with the problems produced by the conditions rather than directly proposing courses of action. There was a basic prevalence of political feelings rather than political ideas, a sense of fatality, disorientation and loneliness which in itself has no clear political implications at first. As Day Lewis, the most 'committed' of the group, put it in 1934: 'We shall not begin to understand post-war poetry until we realise that the poet is appealing above all for the creation of a society in which the living contact between man and man may again become possible.'[13]

The extent of political involvement is recognised, too, by Spender in his contribution to the Auden Double Number of *New Verse* in 1937:

From the point of view of the working-class movements the ultimate criticism of Auden and the poets associated with him is that we haven't deliberately and consciously transferred ourselves to the working class. The subject of his poetry is the struggle, but the struggle seen, as it were, by someone who whilst living in one camp, sympathises with the other; a struggle in fact which is also taking place within the mind of the poet himself, who remains a bourgeois.[14]

What poets felt they could do was to diagnose the sickness, to atomise, to classify, to try to chart an imaginative territory in which the personal and public problems could be dramatised. There is often something allegorical or parabolic in such procedures.[15] Crucially, the 'parable' allows a poet to warn without being didactic or crudely propagandising. It also led to a common fund of images and symbols for example, mountains, frontiers, journeys over alien territories, industrial and technological collapse, battles between opposing sides – many of which became *actual* in the course of the decade, and, to a considerable extent, to the evolution of common styles. David Lodge notes that the period was one characterised by the development of journalistic-reporting and metonymic styles:[16] the fusion or co-existence of such procedures with the parabolic method gives rise to the need for a careful consideration of the function of poetic imagery. Rather than being employed – as in the case of Eliot and many modernist writers – to suggest areas often resistant to conscious formulation, such imagery should serve to clarify and make concrete[17] even if it were almost to take on the character of myths. As a particular example, journeys or travel – however directionless – become the framework for a parabolic form (with landscape and incident doing the work of fable and myth), and it is interesting to note, not simply the number of times reference is made to this by critics in this Casebook, but also how frequently the writers in this period turned to the genre of travel literature.[18]

Finally, important though the debates and struggles with forms and styles were, and however pertinent the poet's self-consciousness about his role to the actual poetry, such questions cannot be isolated from the external events to which in several important respects they are a response. Poets felt that many of the myths and poetic means inherited from their immediate predecessors would not do because it was a new situation with which they were dealing. 'From 1931 onwards, in common with many other people, I felt hounded by external events', wrote Stephen Spender.[19] Even if one result can be the assumption of a public role to which the personal self does not wholly accede,[20] the topical, contemporaneous response to immediate social reality ('Consider *this* and *in our time*') is a recurring feature of the poetry of the period. As Bernard Bergonzi's contribution reminds us, it is perhaps no accident that the personification of 'History' is one of the most common poetic processes. The sense of an impersonal, inexorable active force (or, in the case of Fascism, positively evil force) over which the individual has little control, but to which he feels compelled to respond, is a determining feature of the poetic landscape of the Thirties, perhaps because it is his weakness and culpability which gives rise to the process in the first place.

III CRITICAL REPUTATIONS

It is difficult in this short space adequately to review the developing critical reputation of four poets, but reference to the Bibliography reveals that since 1975 there has been something of a renaissance of critical interest in the Auden group and in writing generally in the Thirties. Of the four poets, the reputations of Day Lewis and Spender have grown evenly. In general it is their traditional qualities rather than anything markedly 'Thirties' about their verse which have been adjudged most enduring. Indeed, Spender has put on record his sense of strangeness at being classified as a poet of the Thirties (see Part One, section 2). Spender has not been a prolific writer and has to date published only one volume since his *Collected Poems* (1953).[21] Geoffrey Thurley in his essay here argues the case that Spender has in his view been wrongly taken as a 'scapegoat' for all that is least successful about Thirties verse. Thurley refocuses and reinforces attention on the qualities of immediacy and actuality in Spender's poetry, his undifferentiated emotional engagement with his material and his preference for evoking states.[22] In comparison with Auden, for example, Thurley sees Spender as a poet who undergoes experience and particularises it poetically rather than as one who detaches himself from it or turns it into a generalisable instance.

Perhaps Spender was initially misunderstood as a result of his more popular poems (such as 'The Express' or 'The Pylons') working to categorise him as a poet concerned to make poetry about or out of modern industrial landscape. In fact, in his early poetry he might be better regarded as simply exploring the poetic possibilities of such material 'as a young man of neo-Romantic sensibility faced with a situation in which it was impossible to go on writing overtly neo-Romantic poetry'.[23] Spender's continuing concern to filter experience through a unitary poetic 'I' is nowhere better illustrated than in his war poems which have generally been singled out by critics as especially praiseworthy. It is interesting in this respect to read Samuel Hynes's sensitive discussion herein of the contrasting approaches of Spender and Auden in their poems of the Spanish Civil War.

In the case of Day Lewis, it is his Hardyesque lyricism rather than his political poetry which has been felt by critics to be of most significance. Poems of personal meditation, about ordinary domestic events, or those devoted to childhood reminiscence are seen to be part of a lyrical vein which was always present in his early Thirties poetry but which, as both Maxwell and Hynes note in their contributions here, comes increasingly to dominate his poetry since the publication of *Overtures to Death and Other Poems* in 1938. His 'political' verse has usually been regarded as imitative of Auden, both stylistically and often in terms of image and motif, but many feel it is characterised by excessive imagistic abstraction and lacks the clarity of parabolic or allegorical contour so frequently found in Auden's poetry of the same period. But as one contemporary reviewer put it: '. . . he is a borrower of an ingenous and unaffected type'.[24]

Samuel Hynes (in an article of 1973) neatly crystallises much contemporary opinion of Day Lewis's poetry: 'Day Lewis's efforts to write like Auden fail both as imitations and as poems; but his poems in the Hardy tradition succeed, and though they remind us of Hardy, they retain their own individuality, they are not imitations but new poems.' Hynes continues, writing of the well-known poem, 'Cornet Solo': '. . . it has Day Lewis's own mark upon it. Its tone is softer, its irony less relentless, its movement less crabbed than a Hardy version would be; it belongs, not to Hardy, but to the tradition.'[25]

Day Lewis's narrative expertise should be noted, too. In a poem like 'The Nabara' (1938), which has been widely praised, his handling of traditional forms is allied to a celebration of authentic heroism in a way which contrasts with the more lyrical, committed or abstract intellectual foci on the same subject by his contemporaries.

Louis MacNeice's reputation has grown steadily since the Thirties. Auden's view of his poetry in his 'Memorial Address' for MacNeice reflects a strand common to much MacNeice criticism:

Of all the poets of his generation and mine, I would say that Louis MacNeice had the least cause for self-reproach and his example denies to the rest of us the excuse that, in the historical circumstances under which we grew up, the temptations to fake feelings were unusually strong. . . . Louis MacNeice's work is a proof that they could be resisted.[26]

Although some critics (including Spender – see Part One, section 2) have tended to see a 'brilliant' surface in MacNeice, others have detected, in his frequent refusal to explore the poetic consequences generated by a line of feeling or an idea, a depth of creative 'scepticism' which results in equilibrium. The equilibrium means he is often neutral, sometimes wary about life and its implications, perhaps sometimes guilty of lapsing into purely aesthetic or an aridly speculative resolution of difficulties in experience;[27] but this same balance is also seen to involve a suspicion of moralising or any belief that he is given special access to the truth. His 'evasive honesty', as G. S. Fraser (in his contribution here) puts it in an apt oxymoron, is seen now to be the most enduring characteristic; and the accompanying excellent study by Terence Brown explores the nature of this tension in terms of metaphysics, image, tone and syntax.

Ian Hamilton's perceptive account of MacNeice's poetry[28] reflects well the doubts about MacNeice, and acknowledges the common critical consensus concerning his decline in the early Fifties – see Auden (Part One, section 2) and Fraser on *Ten Burnt Offerings* (1952) and *Autumn Sequel* (1954). But his typical strengths are seen in terms of: 'a passive liveliness to the sheer plentitude and variety of human experience', 'brilliant passages of social reportage' and his belief that the poet 'must write out of experience which was generally available and interesting'.

As is the case with the other poets in the 'group', critical debate concerning the relationship between the poet and the experiencing 'I' is also central to the development of views of W. H. Auden's poetry. But in Auden's case the relationship is a much more complex one and has in the last decade been more openly acknowledged and analysed as such. For many critics of Auden – from early reviews by Leavis[29] to the kind of position adopted by Thurley in his essay on Spender – the cumulative effect of many poems is that of an extremely clever but generalising intelligence only rarely capable of making experiences felt in any direct and unmediated way. Richard Hoggart is not alone, in fact, in detecting 'uncertainties of tone'. In attempting to detect pattern in life (such critics ask), in exploring analogues or models for social and moral action, is the subject too easily abstracted by the clinical uninvolvement of the poet? Is the sheer range and heterogeneity of Auden's forms and styles a reflection of inconsistency of commitment, both emotional and intellectual? Is there an unexplained and therefore fundamentally dishonest shift in the kind of poetry written by Auden in the Thirties and that written after his removal to America? [30] The range of textual emendations to this early poetry has served also to increase suspicion.[31] In her essay here on Auden's 'reticence', Barbara Hardy seeks to refute such claims by showing how in many of his poems, from one of the very earliest 'The Letter' through to 'In Praise of Limestone' (a much admired poem written in 1947), there is a characteristic structure within which Auden deliberately withholds direct emotional expression until the final lines where the feeling is all the more powerfully realised for having emerged by indirect means.

Or, alternatively, perhaps we should abandon both the essentially modernist notion that a poem should not mean but be, and also the more traditional Romantic conception that the only valid poetic index is that of the felt self at the centre of each poem, and instead come to see what Auden and Day Lewis (cf. Part One, section 1), describe as the opposition of the 'self as subject' and 'the self as object'. This means accepting that the voice or voices in some 1930s poetry may not always be readily and consistently equatable with that of the poet; that the views it expresses may be dramatised explorations of them, an objective sounding out rather than a signal of personal adherence or commitment to them. The deliberate withholding of one's position may be recognised, not as a failure of self-realisation, but as a kind of integrity in the face of multiplying external pressures which do not allow of a unitary or homogenous view of reality. Such an approach may further make us regard questions of the expression of political belief in a more critical spirit.[32] This view of Auden's 'personae', with its resultant and often *comic* mixing of poetic styles,[33] is argued convincingly and influentially by Justin Replogle in his *Auden's Poetry* (1969), from which an excerpt is made for this Casebook. The same general position is argued with clarity by Edward Mendelson, Auden's literary executor.[34]

What is clear is that each member of the Auden group responded to the various voices heard in the Thirties in his own unique and individual way. It is not surprising that paradoxes and tensions emerge which are not easily explained. A start has been made, but in certain areas some of the critical tools required to account fully for the intricate relations between styles, poetic meanings and social realities have still to be developed. The poetry of the Thirties is very much a fertile ground for further exploration.

NOTES

1. W. H. Auden, 'Louis MacNeice: Memorial Impressions', *Encounter*, XXI, no. 5 (November, 1963), p. 48.

2. W. H. Auden, *The English Auden: Poems, Essays and Dramatic Writings*, ed. E. Mendelson (London, 1977); see also Stephen Spender, *The Thirties and After* (London, 1978).

3. For another example, see J. Southworth, *Sowing the Spring: Studies in British Poets from Hopkins to MacNeice* (Oxford, 1940). The book contains chapters on Day Lewis, Spender and MacNeice.

4. Samuel Hynes, *The Auden Generation: Literature and Politics in the 1930s* (London, 1976).

5. It is regretted, however, that space could not be found for demonstrating critics' changing views in debates over single poems. A good example would be the many detailed studies of Louis MacNeice's poem 'Snow'. See, for example, R. C. Cragg ' "Snow", A Philosophical Poem: A Study in Critical Procedure', *Essays in Criticism*, 3 (Oct. 1953), pp. 425–33. This evoked replies from M. A. M. Roberts, D. J. Enright, F. W. Bateson, and S. W. Dawson in volume 4. See also Marie Boroff 'What a Poem is, for instance "Snow" ', *Essays in Criticism*, 8 (Oct. 1958), pp. 393–404; and C. B. Cox and A. E. Dyson, *Modern Poetry: Studies in Practical Criticism* (London, 1963), pp. 85–9.

6. B. Bergonzi, *Reading The Thirties* (London, 1978), p. 6.

7. Ibid., p. 59.

8. Michael Roberts, *Critique of Poetry* (London, 1934), p. 238.

9. Robin Skelton, Introduction to *Poetry of the Thirties* (Harmondsworth, 1964), p. 36.

10. Hynes, op. cit., p. 135.

11. Auden edited the first *Oxford Book of Light Verse* in 1938. He was not unrealistic about the relationship between poet and audience in his own age. As he says in his Introduction: 'Burns . . . came from . . . a genuine

community where the popular traditions in poetry had never been lost. In consequence Burns was able to write directly and easily about all aspects of life, the most serious as well as the most trivial. He is the last poet of whom this can be said.'

12. MacNeice sounds more optimistic: 'My own prejudice, therefore, is in favour of poets whose worlds are not too esoteric. I would have a poet able-bodied, fond of talking, a reader of the newspapers, capable of pity and laughter, informed in economics, appreciative of women, involved in personal relationships, actively interested in politics, susceptible to physical impressions.' But he did not expect such conditions to be realised in the near future. See *Modern Poetry*, p. 198.

13. C. Day Lewis, *A Hope for Poetry* (Oxford, 1934), p. 38.

14. Stephen Spender, 'Oxford to Communism', *New Verse*, 26–27 (Nov. 1937), p. 10.

15. See Auden's statements on this question in Part One, section 1, below. For further discussion, see Louis MacNeice, *Varieties of Parable* – The Clark Lectures, 1963 – (Cambridge, 1965), and Stephen Spender, 'Fable and Reportage', *Left Review*, 2 (Nov. 1936).

16. D. Lodge, *The Modes of Modern Writing: Metaphor, Metonymy and the Typology of Modern Literature* (London, 1977), pp. 188–211.

17. See W. H. Auden, review of R. M. Rilke's 'Duino Elegies', *The New Republic*, 6 (1939), for a fuller statement of this use of imagery as part of a kind of psychic or moral geography.

18. See also Hynes, op. cit., pp. 227–31.

19. Stephen Spender, *World Within World* (London, 1951), p. 137.

20. Writing retrospectively, Auden provides us with an interesting perspective on this: 'Looking back, it seems to me that the interest in Marx taken by myself and my friends . . . was more psychological than political; we were interested in Marx in the same way that we were interested in Freud, as a technique of unmasking middle class ideologies, not with the intention of repudiating our class, but with the hope of becoming better bourgeois. . . .' – 'Authority in America', *The Griffin* (March 1955). For an explicit account of role-playing, see Christopher Isherwood, *Christopher and His Kind* (London, 1977), pp. 247–8. See also note 14 above.

21. The volume is entitled *The Generous Days* (London 1971).

22. Anticipating perhaps Louis MacNeice's definition of 'impure poetry', Day Lewis draws attention to Spender's 'pure' poetry and says of him that he '. . . is unlike most of his contemporaries in that he relies for poetic effect considerably on the associational value of his words'. See C. Day Lewis, *A Hope for Poetry* (Oxford, 1934), pp. 89–93.

23. Arnold Kettle, *Poetry and Politics* (Open University Press, 1976), p. 54. See also C. B. Cox and A. E. Dyson, *Modern Poetry*, op. cit., pp. 80–4 for a discussion of Spender's 'The Landscape Near an Aerodrome', a poem which incorporates much imagery of contemporary industrial society.

24. 'Day Lewis, A Minor Prophet', review of *A Time to Dance* and *Collected Poems 1929–1933* in *New Verse*, 11 (Oct. 1934), pp. 18–19.

25. Samuel Hynes, 'The Single Poem of C. Day Lewis', in D. Abse (ed.) *Poetry Dimension Annual 5* (London, 1973), pp. 75–81.

26. W. H. Auden, 'A Memorial Address', in T. Brown and A. Reid (eds.), *Time Was Away: The World of Louis MacNeice* (Dublin, 1974), p. 8.

27. As early as 1934, Day Lewis in his *Hope for Poetry* (p. 82) is referring to MacNeice's 'humorous but armed neutrality'. For a less sympathetic view of this poetic stance, see Stephen Wall, 'Louis MacNeice and the Line of Least Resistance', *The Review*, no. 11–12 (1964), pp. 91–4.

28. Ian Hamilton, 'Louis MacNeice', *A Poetry Chronicle* (London, 1973), pp. 30–6.

29. F. R. Leavis, 'Auden, Bottrall and Others', *Scrutiny*, III, 1 (June 1934), pp. 70–83.

30. See particularly the criticisms of Randall Jarrell, 'Changes of Attitude and Rhetoric in Auden's Poetry', *Southern Review*, VIII (Autumn 1941), pp. 326–49. For an account of continuities in Auden's poetry see R. A. Carter, 'Auden Forty Years On: *City Without Walls*', *Agenda*, 16, 2 (Summer, 1978), pp. 63–71.

31. Interesting analyses of these questions are to be found in A. E. Rodway and F. W. Cook, 'An Altered Auden', *Essays in Criticism*, VIII, 3 (July 1958), pp. 303–19, and substantially in J. Warren Beech, *The Making of The Auden Canon* (Minneapolis, 1957).

32. See note 20.

33. For an excellent discussion of Auden's comic-ironic relationship with his material, particularly as reflected in style and language, see John Holloway, 'The Master as Joker', *Art International*, XIII, 1 (Jan. 1969), pp. 17–20. Note also Spender's comment (1951) on Auden's 'serious insistence on unseriousness' (see Part One, section 2, below).

34. E. Mendelson, 'Introduction' to *W. H. Auden: Selected Poems* (London, 1979).

PART ONE

The Poets

1. THE POETS ON POETRY

W. H. Auden & C. Day Lewis (1927)

'Private spheres out of a public chaos'

Did it serve no other purpose, this volume [*Oxford Poetry*] should at least offer a rebutment of the tendency, shared by many serious-minded and a few single-minded persons, contemptuously to credit Oxford with 'the undergraduate mind'. We confess ourselves able neither to comprehend such an abstraction nor to surmise what increment may result from the fitting of any intellectual caption to so many diverse heads. Our minds are sparse enough, in all conscience: they must not also be held obnoxious to the charge of uniformity.

On the other hand, the chaos of values which is the substance of our environment is not consistent with a standardisation of thought, though, on the political analogy, it may have to be superseded by one. All genuine poetry is in a sense the formation of private spheres out of a public chaos; and therefore we would remind those who annually criticise us for lack of homogeneity, first, that on the whole it is environment which conditions values, not values which form environment; second, that we must hold partly responsible for our mental *sauve-qui-peut* that acedia and unabashed glorification of the subjective so prominent in the world since the Reformation. . . .

A tripartite problem remains, and may be stated thus:

(*a*) The psychological conflict between self as subject and self as object, which is patent in the self-consciousness and emotional stultification resultant from the attempt to synchronise within the individual mind the synthesis and the analysis of experience. Such appears to be the prime development of this century, our experiment in the 'emergent evolution of mind'. Emotion is no longer necessarily to be analysed by 'recollection in tranquillity': it is to be prehended emotionally and intellectually at once. And this is of most importance to the poet; for it is his mind that must bear the brunt of the conflict and may be the first to realise the new harmony which would imply the success of this synchronisation.

(*b*) The ethical conflict: a struggle to reconcile the notion of Pure Art, 'an art completely isolated from everything but its own laws of operation, and the object to be created as such,[1] with those exigencies which its conditions of existence as a product of a human mind and culture must involve, where the one cannot be ignored nor the other enslaved.

(*c*) The logical conflict, between the denotatory and the connotatory sense of words, which is the root-divergence of classic and romantic; between, that is to say, an asceticism tending to kill language by stripping words of all association and a hedonism tending to kill language by dissipating their sense under a multiplicity of associations.

In what degree this problem is realised and met in these pages, the individual reader must decide. Those who believe that there is anything valuable in our youth as such we have neither the patience to consider nor the power to condone: our youth should be a period of spiritual discipline, not a self-justifying dogma. As for the intelligent reader, we can only remind him, where he experiences distaste, that no universalised system – political, religious or metaphysical – has been bequeathed to us; where pleasure, that it is but an infinitesimal progression towards a new synthesis – one more of those efforts as yet so conspicuous in their paucity.

SOURCE: Introduction to *Oxford Poetry* (Oxford, 1927).

NOTE

1. Jacques Maritain, 'Poetry and Religion', *New Criterion*, v, 1.

W. H. Auden & John Garrett   (1935)

'Definition and Diagnosis'

Of the many definitions of poetry, the simplest is still the best: 'memorable speech'. That is to say, it must move our emotions, or excite our intellect, for only that which is moving or exciting is memorable, and the stimulus is the audible spoken word and cadence, to which in all its power of suggestion and incantation we must surrender, as we do when talking to an intimate friend. We must, in fact, make exactly the opposite kind of mental effort to that we make in grasping other verbal uses, for in the case of the latter the aura of suggestion round every word through which, like the atom radiating lines of force through the whole of space and time, it becomes ultimately a sign for the sum of all possible meanings, must be rigorously suppressed and its meaning confined to a single dictionary one. For this reason the exposition of a scientific theory is easier to read than to hear. No poetry, on the other hand, which when mastered is not better heard than read is good poetry.

All speech has rhythm, which is the result of the combination of the alternating periods of effort and rest necessary to all living things, and the laying of emphasis on what we consider important; and in all poetry there is a tension between the rhythm due to the poet's personal values, and those due to the experiences of generations crystallised into habits of language such as the English tendency to alternate weak and accented syllables, and conventional verse forms like the hexameter, the heroic pentameter, or the French Alexandrine. Similes, metaphors of image or idea, and auditory metaphors such as rhyme, assonance and alliteration help further to clarify and strengthen the pattern and internal relations of the experience described. . . .

A great many people dislike the idea of poetry as they dislike over-earnest people, because they imagine it is always worrying about the eternal verities.

Those, in Mr Spender's words, who try to put poetry on a pedestal only succeed in putting it on the shelf. Poetry is no better and no worse than human nature; it is profound and shallow, sophisticated and naïve, dull and witty, bawdy and chaste in turn.

In spite of the spread of education and the accessibility of printed matter, there is a gap between what is commonly called 'highbrow' and 'lowbrow' taste, wider perhaps than it has ever been.

The industrial revolution broke up the agricultural communities, with their local conservative cultures, and divided the growing population into two classes: those whether employers or employees who worked and had little leisure, and a small class of shareholders who did no work, had leisure but no responsibilities or roots, and were therefore preoccupied with themselves. Literature has tended therefore to divide into two streams, one providing the first with a compensation and escape, the other the second with a religion and a drug. The Art for Art's sake of the London drawing-rooms of the '90s, and towns like Burnley and Rochdale, are complementary.

Nor has the situation been much improved by the increased leisure and educational opportunities which the population to-day as a whole possess. Were leisure all, the unemployed would have created a second Athens.

Artistic creations may be produced by individuals, and because their work is only appreciated by a few it does not necessarily follow that it is not good; but a universal art can only be the product of a community united in sympathy, sense of worth, and aspiration; and it is improbable that the artist can do his best except in such a society. . . .

The 'average' man says: 'When I get home I want to spend my time with my wife or in the nursery; I want to get out on to the links or go for a spin in the car, not to read poetry. Why should I? I'm quite happy without it.' We must be able to point out to him that whenever, for example, he makes a good joke he is creating poetry, that one of the motives behind poetry is curiosity, the wish to know what we feel and think, and how, as E. M. Forster says, can I know what I think till I see what I say, and that curiosity is the only human passion that can be indulged in for twenty-four hours a day without satiety.

The psychologist maintains that poetry is a neurotic symptom, an attempt to compensate by phantasy for a failure to meet reality. We must tell him that phantasy is only the beginning of writing; that, on the contrary, like psychology, poetry is a struggle to reconcile the unwilling subject and object; in fact, that since psychological truth depends so largely on context, poetry, the parabolic approach, is the only adequate medium for psychology.

The propagandist, whether moral or political, complains that the writer should use his powers over words to persuade people to a particular course of action, instead of fiddling while Rome burns. But Poetry is not concerned with telling people what to do, but with extending our knowledge of good and evil, perhaps making the necessity for action more urgent and its nature more clear, but only leading us to the point where it is possible for us to make a rational and moral choice.

SOURCE: extracts from the Introduction to Auden and Garrett's *The Poet's Tongue: An Anthology* (London, 1935), pp. v–ix.

W. H. Auden (1935)

'Literature and Psychology'

. . . I do not intend to take writers one by one and examine the influence of Freud upon them. I wish merely to show what the essence of Freud's teaching is, that the reader may judge for himself. I shall enumerate the chief points as briefly as possible:

1. The driving force in all forms of life is instinctive; a libido which of itself is undifferentiated and unmoral, the 'seed of every virtue and of every act which deserves punishment'.

2. Its first forms of creative activity are in the ordinary sense of the word physical. It binds cells together and separates them. The first bond observable between individuals is a sexual bond.

3. With the growth in importance of the central nervous system with central rather than peripheral control, the number of modes of satisfaction to which the libido can adapt itself become universally increased.

4. Man differs from the rest of the organic world in that his development is unfinished.

5. The introduction of self-consciousness was a complete break in development, and all that we recognise as evil or sin is its consequence. Freud differs both from Rousseau who denied the Fall, attributing evil to purely local conditions ('Rousseau thought all men

good by nature. He found them evil and made no friend'), and also from the theological doctrine which makes the Fall the result of a deliberate choice, man being therefore morally responsible.

6. The result of this Fall was a divided consciousness in place of the single animal consciousness, consisting of at least three parts: a conscious mind governed by ideas and ideals; the impersonal unconscious from which all its power of the living creature is derived but to which it was largely denied access; and a personal unconscious, all that morality or society demanded should be forgotten and unexpressed.*

7. The nineteenth-century doctrine of evolutionary progress, of man working out the beast and letting the ape and tiger die, is largely false. Man's phylogenetic ancestors were meek and sociable, and cruelty, violence, war, all the so-called primitive instincts, do not appear until civilisation has reached a high level. A golden age, comparatively speaking (and anthropological research tends to confirm this), is an historical fact.

8. What we call evil was once good, but has been outgrown, and refused development by the conscious mind with its moral ideas. This is the point in Freud which D. H. Lawrence seized and to which he devoted his life:

> Man is immoral because he has got a mind
> And can't get used to the fact.

The danger of Lawrence's writing is the ease with which his teaching about the unconscious, by which he means the impersonal unconscious, may be read as meaning, 'let your personal unconscious have its fling' – i.e., the *acte gratuite* of André Gide. In personal relations this itself may have a liberating effect for the individual. If the fool would persist in his folly he would become wise. But folly is folly all the same and a piece of advice like 'Anger is just – Justice is never just', which in private life is a plea for emotional honesty, is rotten political advice, where it means 'beat up those who disagree with you'. Also Lawrence's concentration on the fact that if you want to know what a man is, you must look at his sexual life, is apt to lead many to believe that pursuit of a sexual goal is the only necessary activity.

---

* The difference between the two unconscious minds is expressed symbolically in dreams; e.g., motor-cars and manufactured things express the personal unconscious; horses, etc., the impersonal.

9. Not only what we recognise as sin or crime, but all illness, is purposive. It is an attempt at cure.

10. All change, either progressive or regressive, is caused by frustration or tension. Had sexual satisfaction been completely adequate, human development could never have occurred. Illness and intellectual activity are both reactions to the same thing, but not of equal value.

11. The nature of our moral ideas depends on the nature of our relations with our parents.

12. At the root of all disease and sin is a sense of guilt.

13. Cure consists in taking away the guilt feeling, in the forgiveness of sins, by confession, the re-living of the experience, and absolution, the understanding of its significance.

14. The task of psychology, or art for that matter, is not to tell people how to behave, but by drawing their attention to what the impersonal unconscious is trying to tell them, and by increasing their knowledge of good and evil, to render them better able to choose, to become increasingly morally responsible for their destiny.

15. For this reason psychology is opposed to all generalisations; force people to hold a generalisation and there will come a time when a situation will arise to which it does not apply. Either they will force the generalisation, the situation, the repression, when it will haunt them, or they will embrace its opposite. The value of advice depends entirely upon the context. You cannot tell people what to do, you can only tell them parables; and that is what art really is, particular stories of particular people and experiences, from which each according to his immediate and peculiar needs may draw his own conclusions.

16. Both Marx and Freud start from the failures of civilisation, one from the poor, one from the ill. Both see human behaviour determined, not consciously, but by instinctive needs, hunger and love. Both desire a world where rational choice and self-determination are possible. The difference between them is the inevitable difference between the man who studies crowds in the street, and the man who sees the patient, or at most the family, in the consulting-room. Marx sees the direction of the relations between outer and inner world from without inwards, Freud vice versa. Both are therefore suspicious of each other. The socialist accuses the psychologist of caving in to the status quo, trying to adapt the neurotic to the system, thus depriving him of a potential revolutionary; the psychologist retorts that the

socialist is trying to lift himself by his own boot tags, that he fails to understand himself, or the fact that the lust for money is only one form of the lust for power – and so that after he has won his power by revolution he will recreate the same conditions. Both are right. As long as civilisation remains as it is, the number of patients the psychologist can cure are very few, and as soon as socialism attains power, it must learn to direct its own interior energy and will need the psychologist.

Conclusion

Freud has had certain obvious technical influences on literature, particularly in its treatment of space and time, and the use of words in associational rather than logical sequence. He has directed the attention of the writer to material such as dreams and nervous tics hitherto disregarded; to relations as hitherto unconsidered as the relations between people playing tennis; he has revised hero-worship.

   He has been misappropriated by irrationalists eager to escape their conscience. But with these we have not . . . been concerned. We have tried to show what light Freud has thrown on the genesis of the artist and his place and function in society, and what demands he would make upon the serious writer. There must always be two kinds of art: escape-art, for man needs escape as he needs food and deep sleep; and parable-art, that art which shall teach man to unlearn hatred and learn love . . . .

   SOURCE: extract from 'Psychology and Art Today', in Geoffrey Grigson (ed.), *The Arts Today* (London, 1935), pp. 13–20.

Louis MacNeice   (1934)

'Reply to an Enquiry'

An Enquiry:
   1. Do you intend your poetry to be useful to yourself or others?
   2. Do you think there can now be a use for narrative poetry?

3. Do you wait for a spontaneous impulse before writing a poem; if so, is this impulse verbal or visual?

4. Have you been influenced by Freud and how do you regard him?

5. Do you take your stand with any political or politico-economic party or creed?

6. As a poet what distinguishes you, do you think, from an ordinary man?

MacNeice's Reply

1. Mainly to myself; but I find it a very helpful detour to try to make my poems intelligible and interesting to others.

2. Yes. Narrative poetry should, logically, supersede the novel.

3. Sometimes a spontaneous impulse (its nature varies); often I have a vague feeling of deficiency which I try to fill out with a poem; this first deliberate and tentative poem is often followed quickly by a second poem which shapes itself and is usually better than No. 1.

4. Not to my knowledge. I feel that most of those artists who use him as a sanction misrepresent him. He will be more helpful when they reorientate him.

5. No. In weaker moments I wish I could.

6. Dissatisfaction with accepted formulas. But most of the time one is not a poet and is perfectly satisfied.

SOURCE: from *New Verse*, no. 11 (Oct. 1934), pp. 2 and 7.

Louis MacNeice   (1938)

'Critic and Entertainer'

I have been asked to commit myself about poetry. I have committed myself already so much *in* poetry that this seems almost superfluous. I think that the poet is only an extension – or, if you prefer it, a concentration – of the ordinary man. The content of poetry comes out of life. Half the battle is the selection of material. The poet is both critic and entertainer. He should select subjects therefore which (*a*) he is in a position to criticise, and (*b*) other people are likely to find interesting. The poet at the moment will tend to be moralist rather than aesthete. But his morality must be honest; he must not merely retail other people's dogma. The world no doubt needs propaganda, but propaganda (unless you use the term, as many do, very, very loosely indeed) is not the poet's job. He is not the loud-speaker of society, but something much more like its still, small voice. At his highest he can be its conscience, its critical faculty, its grievous instinct. He will not serve his world by wearing blinkers. The world today consists of specialists and intransigents. The poet, by contrast, should be synoptic and elastic in his sympathies. It is quite possible therefore that at some period his duty as a poet may conflict with his duty as a man. In that case he can stop writing; but he must not degrade his poetry even in the service of a good cause; for bad poetry won't serve it much anyway. It is still, however, possible to write honestly without feeling that the time for honesty is passed.

SOURCE: 'A Statement' in *New Verse*, nos 31–32 (Autumn, 1938), p. 7.

Louis MacNeice   (1938)

'Impure Poetry'

This book [*Modern Poetry*] is a plea for *impure* poetry; that is, for poetry conditioned by the poet's life and the world around him.

I have not attempted here to give a full survey of contemporary poetry. There are many poets, and a few good poets, whom I have not mentioned. I am putting a personal point of view, but one with which, I feel, many readers of poetry will sympathise.

The poet, I consider, is both critic and entertainer (and his criticism will cut no ice unless he entertains). Poetry today should steer a middle course between pure entertainment ('escape poetry') and propaganda. Propaganda, the extreme development of 'critical' poetry, is also the defeat of criticism. And the mere slogan-poet contradicts his name – *poiétes*, a 'maker'. The poet is a maker, not a retail trader. The writer today should be not so much the mouthpiece of a community (for then he will only tell it what it knows already) as its conscience, its critical faculty, its generous instinct. In a world intransigent and over-specialised, falsified by practical necessities, the poet must maintain his elasticity and refuse to tell lies to order. Others can tell lies more efficiently; no one except the poet can give us poetic truth.

SOURCE: Preface to *Modern Poetry: A Personal Essay* (Oxford, 1938, 2nd edn, 1968).

Louis MacNeice   (1941)

'Poetry and Propaganda'

. . . The propaganda poets claim to be realists – a claim which can only be correct if realism is identical with pragmatism. Truth, whether poetic or scientific, tends as often as not to be neither simple nor easily intelligible, whereas the propagandist is bound by his function to give his particular public something that they can easily swallow and digest. Realism, in the proper sense of the word, takes account of facts regardless of their propaganda value, and records not only those facts which suit one particular public but also those facts which suit no one. The propagandist may have his 'truth' but it is not the truth of the scientist or of the realist; it is even further removed from these than poetic truth is. He is only interested in changing the world; any use of words therefore which will lead to that end – lies, distortions, or outrageous over-simplifications – will, from his point of view, be true. This again is a tenable position but it does not prove either that the poet will write better poetry by substituting propagandist truth for poetic truth or even that it is the poet's duty as a man to write propaganda poetry. Even if the poet believes in the *end* of the propagandist, he can have legitimate doubts whether that end will be in the long run usefully served by a prostitution of poetry. Poetry is to some extent, like mathematics, an autotelic activity; if bad poetry or bad mathematics is going to further a good cause, let us leave this useful abuse of these arts to people who are not mathematicians or poets. . . .

SOURCE: extract from *The Poetry of W. B. Yeats* (Oxford, 1941), pp. 214–15.

C. Day Lewis   (1934)

'Between Two Fires'

It is a truism that a sound society makes for sound individuals, and sound individuals instance a sound society. For the post-war poet, living in a society undeniably sick, that truism has turned into a dilemma. We have seen him on the one hand rendered more acutely conscious of individuality by the acceptance of current psychological doctrines; and on the other hand, rendered both by poetic intuition and ordinary observation acutely conscious of the present isolation of the individual and the necessity for a social organism which may restore communion. He looks to one side and he sees D. H. Lawrence, the extreme point of individualism in this century's literature, its zenith or its nadir: he admits the force of Lawrence's appeal, but he has watched him driven from continent to continent, driven ill and mad, a failure unable to recreate a satisfactory social group from the nucleus of his own individuality. He looks to the other side and he sees Communism, proclaiming – though with a different meaning from Lawrence's – 'revolution for life's sake,' the most whole-hearted attempt ever made to raise the individual to his highest power by a conditioning of his environment: yet here too he notices the bully and the spy, and wonders if any system can expel and survive that poison.

So there arises in him a conflict; between the old which his heart approves and the new which fructifies his imagination; between the idea of a change of heart that should change society and the idea of a new society making a new man; between individual education and mass economic conditionment. At which end should one begin? The poet, you will say, has no business to be trespassing: if he will wander into other people's fields, he must take the consequences. But it is not

as simple as that. The poet, besides being a poet, is also a man, 'fed
with the same food, hurt with the same weapons' as other men. Where
there is hope in the air, he will hear it; where there is agony about, he
will feel it. He must feel as a man what he reveals as a poet. It is as
absurd to tell him that he must only feel strongly about natural
scenery as it is to call every 'nature-poet' an escapist. Nor is it right for
us to say that the poet should be concerned only with eternal facts,
with summer and winter, birth, marriage and death. These are the
mountain-peaks, the final and everlasting limits of his known world,
but they are always the background against which stand out and are
measured temporal things – the rise and fall of cities, the year's
harvest, the moment's pain. To-day the foreground is a number of
fluid, confused and contradictory patterns. Standing at the end of an
epoch, the poet's arms are stretched out to opposite poles, the old life
and the new; that is his power and his crucifixion.

> Come down, come down, you suffering man,
> Come down, and high or low
> Follow your fancy and go with us
> The Way that we should go.
>
> That cannot be till two agree
> Who long have lain apart:
> Traveller, know, I am here to show
> Your own divided heart.   (C. Day Lewis)

Standing as a man between two worlds, he stands as a poet between
two fires. On the one hand the Communist tells him that he is no
better than a dope-peddler unless he 'joins the revolution,' that he is
unhappy and ineffective because he is trying to live in two worlds at
once, and that (although the achievements of 'bourgeois' art are
undeniable and to be respected) the function of artists at the present
crisis is to help lead men out of the bourgeois position towards the
proletarian, to be propagandists for the new world. On the other
hand, the bourgeois critic rebukes him for allowing a sympathy with
Communism to drive him into a kind of writing that at any rate
sounds very like propaganda, asserting that an ideology is only useful
to the poet in so far as it is felt and that ideas, whether revolutionary or
reactionary, must never be more to the poet than the raw material out
of which his poetry is formed.

They are both right up to a point. Yet the bourgeois critic must
remember that there is no reason why poetry should not also be

propaganda; the effect of invocation, of poetry, and of propaganda is to create a state of mind; and it is not enough to say that poetry must do unconsciously what propaganda does consciously, for that would be to dismiss all didactic poetry from that of the Bible downwards. All one can say is that propaganda verse is to be condemned when the didactic is achieved at the expense of the poetic: poetry, in fact, whatever else it may or may not be, must be poetry – a sound, if obvious, conclusion. In this context we may instance the reception of Auden's recent work 'The Dance of Death'. It is compared unfavourably with his earlier books largely on the ground that it is propaganda: but the *Poems* [1930] and *The Orators* [1932] were full of propaganda too; they told the Englishman, particularly the middle-class Englishman, in a variety of subtle ways, that he is half-dead. And if a powerful writer insists for long enough that you are half-dead, why, then, you begin to realise or believe it; the insistent suggestion puts you in that frame of mind: poetry has been propaganda. So 'The Dance of Death,' if it is to be criticised, must be criticised as poetry and not for being propaganda.

Poems and *The Orators* are didactic from an individualist psychological standpoint. 'The Dance of Death' is an attempt at didactic writing from a Marxian standpoint. If it fails, the failure must be imputed to the fact that the classless society is not established in England, for we have seen that social satire requires an established system from which to work: the poet cannot satirise the present in the uncertain light of the future. Should Communism come to be the settled system in England, we might then expect a great renaissance of satire. And that must be our first answer to the Communist critic. The poet is a sensitive instrument, not a leader. Ideas are not material for the poetic mind until they have become commonplaces for the 'practical' mind. On the other hand, when the Communist tells the poet that he must 'join the revolution', he is right in the sense that there can be no divorce for the Marxist between theory and practice, and that only revolutionary activity can make a revolutionary poet. Nothing, however, is to be gained by accusing the poet of employing each poem as a solution of his own difficulties, of drugging himself and thus unfitting himself through his poetry to be a happy class-warrior. The poet is made like that, he has to protest; and while it is true, in a sense, that each poem solves its own conflict, it is only a temporary solution; his agonies of mind are drugged, perhaps, but not ended. Again, too much has been made of the adverse effect of so-called 'revolutionary' poetry upon a potentially revolutionary public. Spender has written: 'The people who had read these poems would linger over certain aspects of materialism, they would forget, in the course of their meditations, the social revolution. . . . From the point of view of the revolutionary propagandist art plays amongst the more intelligent and less satisfied members of the leisured classes the same rôle as charity plays amongst the poor. Where there should be friction leading to a final break-down it oils the machine and enables it to go on running.' That is the conventional Communist attitude, too: but it is by no means all the truth. The drug-fiend will get drugs somewhere: if he finds his poppy and mandragora in poetry, you must blame his habit, not the poet. But a poetry sympathetic to Communism can strike home to sounder hearts than these: it can awaken interest, kindle indignation that may spread wildfire, not flicker out in private; it can cause conversions and hasten a decline. The revolutionary poet is not a leader: he stands, like a mirror at the crossroads, showing the traffic, the danger, the way you have come and the ways you may go – 'your own divided heart'. He must give courage by reflecting your own courage, and forward revolution by reflecting your own will to it. . . .

We may go further and say that, if a poet is going to be receptive of political ideas, it is essential for him as a man to feel strongly about them. For this strong 'human' emotion, working upon ideas, makes them a more tractable material for poetry; the poetic faculty will, in fact, have to deal – not with an abstract idea – but with an idea suffused and moulded by emotion; and that is a common subject for poetry. What is really undesirable is that the poet should have dealings with political ideas as a poet without first having feelings about them as a man: for direct contact between the poetic function and abstract ideas can give birth only to rhetoric. The man must pass the idea through the medium of his emotion before the poet can get to work upon it.

'We make out of the quarrel with others rhetoric', Yeats has said, 'but of the quarrel with ourselves, poetry.' This conception of the quarrel with ourselves has, I believe, a twofold significance. It conveys first the idea of spiritual doubt as a poetic agent (we have seen this conflict at work in Gerard Manley Hopkins). And secondly it expresses the opposition between the divided selves of the poet, his poetic self and his 'human' self, a conflict of which Yeats has always been acutely aware. Yeats's own magnificent political poems –

'Easter 1916', for instance, or 'Sixteen Dead Men' – are sufficient proof that a deep feeling about political ideas and events is not necessarily synonymous with that 'quarrel with others' which produces only rhetoric. Unsuccessful propaganda verse *is* an example of this kind of rhetoric: it is the result of the poet trying to convince others without having experienced either uncertainty or conviction himself; or else, of his not being a poet: the 'quarrel with others' must, for the poet, be expressed in terms of the quarrel with himself. And failure to do this accounts for the failure of much so-called revolutionary verse.

It accounts, also, to a certain extent, for its frequent vagueness. It is not asked that poetry should offer naked argument and skeleton plans. But English revolutionary verse of to-day is too often neither poetry nor effective propaganda for the cause it is intended to support. Its vague *cris-de-cœur* for a new world, its undirected and undisciplined attack upon the whole world-broad front of the status quo, are apt to produce work which makes the neutral reader wonder whether it is aimed to win him for the communist or the fascist state. Here again the influence of D. H. Lawrence assists to confuse the issue. We find, for instance, in Auden's preoccupation with the search for 'the truly strong man', Lawrence's evangel of spiritual submission to the great individual: 'All men say they want a leader. Then let them in their souls submit to some greater soul than theirs.' And though this does not necessarily contradict communist theory, it is likely in practice to give a fascist rather than a communist tone to poetry.

There are, however, poems recently written which show that the writer has emotionally experienced a political situation and assimilated it through his specific function into the substance of poetry. It is of this kind of poetry that Wilfred Owen is the real ancestor. It is animated by the same unsentimental pity and sacred indignation. It does not wish to make poetic capital out of the suffering of others. As Spender says in a poem about the unemployed:

> No, I shall weave no tracery of pen-ornament
> To make them birds upon my singing tree.

It is simple and emphatic. It gets probably as near to communist poetry as bourgeois writers under a bourgeois régime can hope to get. And it suggests the lines on which such writers must work for the present. . . .

SOURCE: extracts from ch. VIII of *A Hope for Poetry* (Oxford, 1934), pp. 47–50, 54–6.

Stephen Spender   (1937)

'From Poetry to Politics'

The best of the contemporary poets who write of political themes have been led from poetry to politics, not to politics from poetry. The poet is essentially sensitive to the life of his time. We happen to be living in a political age: that is to say, an age in which the future not only of individuals but also of our whole civilisation is being fought out by political parties both in parliaments, and now on the battlefield in Spain. The starting-off point of the political theme in contemporary poetry is the realisation of the historic situation in which we are living:—

> Seekers after happiness, all who follow
> The convolutions of your simple wish,
> It is later than you think; nearer that day
> Far other than that distant afternoon
> Amid rustle of frocks and stamping feet
> They gave the prizes to the ruined boys.
>
> (W. H. Auden)

Why should poetry be concerned with public affairs rather than with the private interests of the individual? The answer is that it is precisely within the consciousness of many separate individuals that the political struggle is taking place. So far is this true that the critics of the modern school of poetry own it themselves when they say that poetry should be beautiful in the sense that beauty, like gardens, provides a quiet escape from the noise and traffic of our time. But poetry claims the right to go to the very centre of the problems with which the mind of man is most passionately concerned. It is not that the themes of love, landscape and the beautiful have no place in contemporary life, but that they are not the central drama of our time, which is the historic struggle as it effects the mind of the individual. . . .

But the poet is still primarily poet and not politician. The fact that poets happen to choose political subjects for their poems to-day is a comment on the life of our time, in which political issues have become so important, rather than on a change in the attitude of the poets themselves, who are certainly more inclined to be the critics of reality than the hidden legislators of mankind. It is true that occasionally a poet may decide that 'writing is no use to-day, what we want is action' etc. This attitude is, of course to misunderstand the nature of poetry altogether, and he who adopts it is more likely to be a politician for whom poetry is only the growing pains of a protracted adolescence, than a true poet. For poetry is concerned not with action but with the vital sources from which the necessity of action springs. When I say that modern poetry is political, I am not thinking of John Cornford giving up poetry in order to fight the fascists in Spain, but of the fact that the best poetry of our time, the outstanding poems of Thomas Hardy, the war poems of Wilfred Owen, Eliot's *Waste Land*, much of Auden's poetry, is concerned with the individual faced by an unprecedented crisis in the history of civilisation, and with far-reaching public calamities such as the Great War, the prospect of a greater war, and the crisis in the capitalist system.

Poetry which is not written in order to advance any particular set of political opinions may yet be profoundly political. Thus although Marxists would not agree with the consciously expressed beliefs of some of the poets whom I have mentioned, yet they would accept their interpretation in imaginative terms of the crisis taking place in the mind and soul of man. Only the poets, the Marxists and some psychologists have acted or written in a way which reveals a realistic understanding of the significance of the period of history through which we are living.

However much we admire the actions of a John Cornford or a Rupert Brooke, poetry is not the same as action and a poem is not the same as a political thesis. Political action is a short-cut by which the individual conforms to the particular shape which the political will assumes at a given moment – a strike, a war to save democracy. To be a poet is not to give out the propagandist word of order, nor even to re-state in an imaginative idiom the materialist philosophy from which actions, seeming at times contradictory and opportunist, spring; it is to understand and interpret the need for justice and civilised values, from which the materialist philosophy and all the actions resulting from it are themselves a projection.

The political thesis translated into terms of poetry is, like the life of action, also a short cut if it enables the poet to accept at second hand what he can only know by his understanding and experience of life. By 'experience' I do not mean only action and participation I mean the ability of the artist to imagine and recreate life in an idiom which is unique to him and for that very reason entirely convincing to the audience which enters into his mind. . . .

I do not agree that the right function of poetry in the revolution is propaganda, least of all propaganda of so crude a nature. The function of a political poetry is vividly to bring into our consciousness the origins in life from which political theory and action spring, and at the same time to face, on another plane of reality, the significance and implications of that which is being done. Now although propaganda may spring from a real necessity, that does not mean that it is realistic, any more than a lie becomes true because it is necessary.

It may be argued that the Marxist poet who had a complete grasp of all the issues involved would always be able to follow the 'party line', and even interpret party propaganda from day to day, because his valuable function would be to relate the necessity of the day and moment to the fundamental purpose of the political movement. Now even supposing that the party line of action were in fact always consistent with that Marxist interpretation of life which is indeed of great value to the poet, this still would not be true. For the poet is bound to condition what he feels, relating it to a whole view of life, he is not bound to feel all the implications of a whole view of life at any given moment. I repeat that he is not dealing with absolute truth or a dialectic, he is dealing with reality and establishing the significance of his emotional reactions to reality, by stating what are the conditions within which he experiences these emotions.

It is best to illustrate my argument with concrete examples of the poet's attitude towards reality, and no example could be better than war, where one sees political action in its most expressive form.

Now the poet may believe, as Wilfred Owen and Siegfried Sassoon believed during the Great War, that his side is in the right, so far in the right even that he feels bound to fight for it. The attitude of the propagandist to the war which the poet supports is, of course, that everything should be done – by heroic propaganda for Our side, atrocity propaganda against the Other side, even by the pretence of 'not shirking realities' – to make war seem, in the last analysis, desirable: and perhaps necessity does indeed justify the lying propagandist, since he is entitled to feel that, by whatever means, the war must be won. The poet, however, is under an entirely different obligation to truth: he is bound to condition his direct responses towards his experience of war.

Wilfred Owen was the greatest English war poet and he wrote some poems creating with great intensity the horror of war, and attacking all the lies of war propaganda. This does not mean that Owen stated the final truth about the Great War. He did not even pretend to see the War as a whole or from the viewpoint of a future historian. He had certain experiences and he did not lie about them. He stated the mood and mental environment within which they will go down to future ages as true. One of the lies which he opposed most resolutely was propaganda about War heroes. This does not mean that he denied there was heroism in war: on the contrary he writes in the Preface of his Poems that his book is 'not about heroes. English poetry is not yet fit to speak about them.' He adds 'All a poet can do to-day is to warn. That is why the true poets must be truthful.' Truthful to their own experience.

What Owen did oppose is the propagandist lie which makes the dead into heroes in order that others may imagine that death is really quite pleasant. If there is a heroism in war, it is not beautiful. It is too terrible for the propagandists to describe. And the poet who would attain the paradiso of the War heroes, must first of all pass through an inferno far worse even than that of Owen's fragmentary poems. . . .

I have said earlier in this essay that poetry is the conditioning of emotional truth, a way of relating the poet's feelings to objective reality. In the single poem the poet explores the limitations of a single subject: in his life-work he explores the limitations of his own soul. 'Greatness' in poetry is universality: the conditioning of that which is true in the widest possible context and which contains the greatest possible amount of what Henry James called 'felt life'.

Universality in poetry cannot be attained by a 'correct' attitude of mind. A comprehensive philosophy of life cannot be translated into poetry. The poet's greatness must spring from that which he has felt in life: knowledge is only an implement with which he approaches life, it is no substitute for life itself. . . .

SOURCE: extracts from 'Poetry', in *Fact*, no. 4 (July 1937), pp. 18–19, 20–2, 25–7, 29–30.

2. THE POETS ON EACH OTHER

Stephen Spender   (1951)

On Auden

The ordering, intellectualising and tidying of Auden's own experiences and his acute psychological observation of other people, is developed a stage further towards a classical precision and detachment in *Nones*.[1] The Island of Ischia, near Naples, enters a good deal into these poems; and perhaps living for some months of each year there has given Auden a shot of Latin and the Latin viewpoint. The alternating long and slightly shorter lines of one of the best poems in the book, 'In Praise of Limestone', reminds one of the alternation of hexametre and pentametre, and the manner is that of the civilised conversational monologue, enlivened by shock phrases from the slang of a group who correspond in Auden's mind to a campy Roman smart set:

> That is why, I suppose,
> The best and worst never stayed here long but sought
> Immoderate soils where the beauty was not so external,
> The light less public and the meaning of life
> Something more than a mad camp.

'A mad camp' must be an imprecise, if not offensive phrase, in the minds of many readers, but in Auden's poem it has the effect of identifying the tone of the monologue with a certain stratum of conversation in real life. Auden is serious within the convention of an idiom which is thought of as being essentially unserious. This is another link with the later Latin poets. Ideas of Rome, the fall of the Roman empire, and so on predominate in this book (one of the best poems is 'The Fall of Rome'). Another link with such a poet as Propertius is the defiant way in which this serious insistence on unseriousness – on reducing the cosmos to the personal and the gossipy even – sets private experience up in opposition to a) the public calamity threatening at every moment to destroy us and b) the managerial view of society. Of course, in doing this, Auden is not just making a gesture of self-assertion, he is fighting for the whole position of poetry; because if we live in a world entirely dominated by external happenings or by governmental and centralised reasonings and generalisings, poetry is no longer possible. For poetry assumes that the particular image in which a particular experience descends to a particular person is significant – significant potentially to all, since all living is particularisation of experiences among the separate consciousnesses which make up all humanity. But the catastrophic viewpoint which so many people share today is that particularisation is impossible, either because there is not time for it (since we all may be wiped off the face of the earth within the next ten minutes), or because the idea of catastrophe is a public one which overwhelms and wipes out in the minds of individuals the significance they attach to a private imagery. The atom bomb is no one's private symbol: but it makes *Symbolisme* seem merely chichi. The managerial view of society, which may be presented to us as the only possible answer to the catastrophic one, tells us that – for the time being at any rate – only generalised concepts based on officially provided statistics matter. Managerial action may save our society by turning everyone into a Lowest Common Multiple of the Common Good. But poetry, although it may be tolerated, is on the whole subversive, because it indicates a tendency to refuse to consider oneself as a common denominator.

So that Auden who is often regarded on the Left as a Lost Leader, is in our time very much the leader who is fighting for the position of poetry still to say something. He has realised that it is useless for the present generation of poets to attempt *Ulysses* or *Finnegans Wake*: works into which a whole lifetime was poured and which demand a whole lifetime of attention from their readers. He accepts the context of a situation which tells us that in a world of the Atom Bomb, the Unamerican Activities Committee and the Welfare State, literature can no longer be thought of, as it was by Henry James, as the most serious activity, in the sense of its really mattering. The fiction that politics exist to bolster up the values of a civilisation no longer exists: still less does the one that poetry can affect policy. So the Conversation Piece becomes Auden's idiom; and he fights a battle out of outposts of footnotes and trenches between parentheses. . . .

The two first poems in the volume, 'Prime' and 'In Praise of

Limestone' are examples of the beautiful construction of Auden's thought, experience and writing, at the very best. 'Construction' is indeed the word I mean, because it is the relationship of other situations around a central experience in a pattern as light and solid as the wing of an aeroplane, which produces the perfect fusion between Auden's personality and the power of acute moral observation of a more generalised psychological situation, which is his great gift. In 'Prime', the experience he chooses is that of waking in the morning before he has attained complete self-consciousness.

> 'I know that I am, here, not alone
> But with a world, and rejoice
> Unvexed, for the will has still to claim
> This adjacent arm as my own.
> The memory to name me, resume
> Its routine of praise and blame,
> And smiling to me is this instant while
> Still the day is intact and I
> The Adam sinless in our beginning,
> Adam still previous to any act.'

This is almost the perfect situation for an Auden poem: one of great solitude, and yet of wide and general awareness: a solitude which enters into others and which belongs to all. Not only the lines I have quoted but the whole poem, shows an exquisite delicacy.

'In Praise of Limestone' is a didactic poem which reaches far beyond the didactic. Instead of being a personal poem with a moral, it is a morality which reveals a person. The poem is a discussion of the kind of landscape which appears above limestone:

> If it form the one landscape that we the inconstant ones
>   Are consistently homesick for, this is chiefly
> Because it dissolves in water. Mark these rounded shapes
>   With their surface fragrance of thyme, and beneath
> A secret system of caves and conduits; hear these springs
>   That spurt out everywhere with a chuckle
> Each filling a private pool for its fish and carving
>   Its own little ravine whose cliffs entertain
> The butterfly and the lizard.

The landscape here is a construction made to illustrate the thesis about limestone: but, as often with Auden, what is used to illustrate becomes far more than illustration, it becomes nature poetry of a high order. The poem goes on to examine the lack of ambition of those who remain in the limestone landscape: 'the best and the worst', it explains, go to other landscapes.

> 'Come!' cried the granite wastes,
> 'How evasive is your humour, how accidental
> Your kindest kiss, how permanent is death.' (Saints-to-be
> Slipped away, sighing.)

The limestone landscape, then, becomes part of an interrelated pattern of landscape-behaviour: becomes, as it were, a limb of a complete geographical personality with separate landscape parts. The only other writer I can think of who is thus convincing in personalising geography is Joyce: and I suppose that some recent poems of Auden are provinces conquered by *Finnegans Wake*. But in its own right, 'In Praise of Limestone' is, I think, one of the great poems of this century.

SOURCE: extracts from 'Seriously Unserious', in *Poetry* (Chicago), 78 (1951), pp. 352–3, 355–6.

NOTE

1. [Ed.] Spender's essay constitutes a review of Auden's volume *Nones*, published in 1951.

Stephen Spender   (1967)

On MacNeice

'Brilliant' was, I suppose, the epithet inevitably applied to Louis MacNeice by his contemporaries at Marlborough School and Oxford University. In his case it is especially suitable because it suggests a somewhat opaque surface shining, but also concealing. The question which one asked oneself with MacNeice was what went on fathoms below and perhaps also many miles above this surface. It is a question which perhaps haunted him too, for one of his metaphors is of the iceberg, a third above and two-thirds below the surface. A surface, let me emphasise, does not necessarily have to be superficial. It has texture, radiates light, but all the same provokes questions.

In his personal relations, the opacity of surface resulted in many people finding MacNeice aloof, disdainful, detached and cold. He had a way of leaning back and gazing at one through half-closed eyes which scarcely covered a mocking glance. Secrets he surmised about oneself he did not intend to share, the glance said. They were for his notebook, which might be a long poem kept from day to day – *Autumn Journal* – or an autobiographical sketch written long after the event, but sharply remembered – *The Strings are False* [1965].[1] In his reminiscences even of a friend as close to him as Auden, there are patches of reserve which read like ice that has not melted in the surrounding pool of quite genuine admiration and affection. . . .

The brilliant opaque surface which he exhibited in his behaviour remains . . . a problem for the reader in his work. It is not only that one tries vainly much of the time to penetrate the centre of MacNeice's own sensibility; one also finds oneself trying vainly to get at the centre of people and experiences he describes. In the autobiography he tends to see people as bundles of qualities of which they are made, as mirror-like and brittle as his own brilliance. He excels at describing stretches of behaviour of friends, acquaintances, landscapes, cities. But everything seems as though painted on a moving band. He observes people through those unflickering half-closed eyes which never blink, but he never seems to ask what it is that makes them tick.

The result of this is a peculiar kind of negativism. In portraying his own attitudes – his liking for the Heraclitean philosophy, his irreligion, his distrust of politics, his personal relationships – he presents us with paintings on the moving band as brilliant as those of his wife or of a mistress. But while he is painting them he seems conscious that the attitudes will soon be replaced by others.

More than anything else he is aware of flux, and his two longest poems – *Autumn Journal* [1939] and *Autumn Sequel* [1954] – are both journals written from day to day, without his knowing, when he wrote one section, what would come after it. It seems very extraordinary that he should have chosen to write *Autumn Sequel* in *terza rima*: the form which, ever since Dante, poets have used when they wished to draw conclusions, and the one perhaps least suited to poetic journalising. The earlier poem, *Autumn Journal*, consists of brilliant technical improvisations, with much variety to suit changes of mood –

and for that reason alone seems the greater success. Perhaps MacNeice chose the form of *Autumn Sequel* as an act of defiance, throwing down the gauntlet at Dante. In a way, for mastery of rhyme and metrics it is a dazzling technical success, if you can – as poets did in the nineteenth century – separate technical achievement from the suitability of the form to the material.

But in the twentieth century poets have made a mystique almost of thinking that the material should create the form, rather than the form be a frame into which the material is put. And in his strengths as well as his weaknesses, MacNeice belongs more to the nineteenth than to the twentieth century. His attitude to writing poetry – which is to put skill before everything, to be inclusive in his attitude to technique and to material, and never to ask himself the question of a poem, 'Is this too long?' – is Victorian, and still more so the general spectacle he presents of the mind trained in Christianity, the classics and philosophy, using this training as a sceptical discipline for questioning the religion, the learning and the philosophy, without ever expecting to find the answer.

It is difficult, then, to fit MacNeice into a modern poetry course. Modern poets have made form inseparable from content, and above all they seek conclusions, some structure of philosophy or belief on which to base their poetry. Yet MacNeice cannot be relegated to the nineteenth century either. He had qualities of temperament, and he had the mastery, to carry forward into the twentieth century some of the attitudes of the nineteenth. If his content does not always justify the expansiveness of the form, the buoyancy and gaiety of his temperament does. To be convinced that MacNeice has something to say which his medium carries, one has to read section XXIII of *Autumn Journal*, which is about the end of the Spanish Republic, or the parts of *Autumn Sequel* about Gwilym (Dylan Thomas). Ultimately he is a poet of temperament, of gaiety and melancholy cultivated by wit, taste and learning, and held together by courage: the virtue he most admired. One of his most ambitious, not altogether successful, poems is 'The Kingdom': an attempt to chart, with many examples

> an underground movement,
> Under the crust of bureaucracy, quite behind the posters,
> Unconsciously but palpably there – the Kingdom of individuals.

It is about people who recognise in one another, behind the mask, the real person, and as such it is moving, encouraging, coming from this very lonely man: the poetry of shared life, but not of terrible solitude. Terrible solitude when it does occur is death, and perhaps Mac-Neice's best poems are the ones he wrote at the end of his life when he had an intuition of this approaching conclusion.

SOURCE: extracts from 'The Brilliant Mr MacNeice', in *New Republic*, 156, no. 4 (28 Jan. 1967), pp. 32–4.

NOTE

1. [Ed.] Spender's essay is in the form of a review of MacNeice's *The Strings are False: An Unfinished Autobiography*, edited by Elton R. Dodds, published in 1965.

Stephen Spender (1970)

On Thirties Poets

. . . Interviewer: During the Thirties someone called you the 'Rupert Brooke of the Depression'. Did you feel then, or do you feel now, that fame came too quickly and too easily? You wrote at the time that you felt yourself to be alarmed by your success.

SPENDER: Well, you see, I come from a journalist's family and I obviously have a secret craving for very vulgar publicity. At the same time I despise this. I think it is repellent and odious. I've never really been able to separate the journalistic side of myself from the side of myself which is something else. All that I find extremely embarrassing. I think what really happened, if I was called the Rupert Brooke of the Depression by Geoffrey Grigson in *New Verse*, when I was young – and I think this has had an effect on my whole career, my whole writing – was that it was something I simply couldn't deal with. I find that everything that anyone says about me or writes about me – and this is another reason why I have not published a book of poems for so long – is just something I can't deal with. I feel extremely embarrassed. After all, one writes poems to give a little pleasure, fundamentally, and you find yourself being treated as if it is a crime or an offence to do so, and this is a situation I simply can't deal with at all. I just tend to withdraw and not want to publish things. It is an unresolved problem, I think.

. . .

When you are called upon to review books by your contemporaries, do considerations of this kind weigh with you? Do you worry about hurting them?

Well, I do much more now. When I was young I was a very unkind reviewer. I think I was very spiteful often. If one thought one had an insight through one's own writing, into why someone was very bad, one didn't hesitate to say so. Perhaps one didn't notice enough the better side of his writing. If you are very nasty to someone in a review, even though there are good critical reasons for being nasty, a certain psychological animus goes into it all the same. People like Leavis and Grigson, who have written consistently harsh reviews of young writers, are to be defended on the grounds that, after all, they are saying what they think and they are observing high standards. It is important that some critics should be severe. On the other hand, as a person reviewing unkindly himself, I became aware that severity may be justified objectively yet subjectively be malicious. Again, when one is young, one doesn't think – especially if one is vulnerable oneself – that one is going to hurt anyone else. You gradually realise, though, that you do hurt other people. Perhaps there are a few people who ought to be put down, but ——

Do you in any way resent being categorised as a Thirties poet?

I don't resent it. In a way it amuses me. And of course going over all that material is interesting. If you meet young writers who think of you as belonging to the Thirties, they start asking you about it and you start trying to explain. I always find this quite amusing and quite interesting, so I don't resent it.

Do you think you would have written very differently had you come to your, so to speak, maturity in a different decade? Say the 40s or the 20s?

If I had never met Auden – I was at Oxford with Auden, and then I was writing extremely romantic poetry – then I would be much closer to those neo-Romantic poets of the 40s. Whether this would have been a good thing or not I don't know. Before meeting Auden I was writing extremely bad poetry. Terribly romantic outpourings, and enormous quantities of them. I wrote three or four poems a day sometimes. Therefore it was possible, it seemed of great benefit, to completely change my attitude, and to write poetry much more consciously and in a much more workmanly kind of way. On the other hand, I sometimes think that perhaps I suppressed some kind of romantic urge that might have had an interesting development. I don't know.

. . .

What do you think of New Verse,[1] *looking back?*

Well, when it started I didn't like *New Verse* very much. I remember getting a letter either from Michael Roberts or from Geoffrey Grigson in which whoever it was, starting his anthology or starting his *New Verse*, said that the other has begun laying down mines and we are going to start a creeping fire. You suddenly realised that one was supposed to be part of some gigantic literary war and that this literary war was being dramatised by, really, high-class literary journalists. Notably Geoffrey Grigson and Michael Roberts – and, later, John Lehmann with *New Signatures*. They were the people who invented the 1930s. It really wasn't us. And, after all, during all this time I wasn't at the centre. I was in Germany most of the time.

Of the poets of the 1930s, are there any whose subsequent careers have surprised you? A number of them have disappeared from view.

I think that when one is young one has a very distinct illusion that one knows exactly the worth of everyone's talent. One or two people have turned out to be better than I thought. For instance, Bernard Spencer.[2] I knew Bernard Spencer. I was an undergraduate with him, and we edited *Oxford Poetry* together. He was an extremely charming man, but I didn't really think he was talented. I thought he was rather hard-working and sensitive and a bit ineffective. I'm afraid I slightly despised him in the way that one does despise one's contemporaries. And Louis MacNeice. I don't think I ever realised how good Louis MacNeice was. He was a very intelligent, scholarly person, but I always thought he was a minor, whimsical talent. I now think he was much better than that.

. . .

What about Auden? Do you see him as a central figure now in the way that you did then?

As a matter of fact, I think the whole talent, the whole genius of Auden, has been never to be exactly a central figure. That may be precisely why he's maintained so well his importance. He's a central figure on the margin, as it were. Gerald Heard made a brilliant remark about Auden, when Auden was about 22. He said, he's really like a monk who writes notes in the margin of a text. If you think, say, of Auden's attitude to the history of his time, he's always making brilliant comments on what is going on in his time – which he is always slightly outside. But of course you can be such a brilliant commentator that you become more important than anyone else. Or you can make comments that are remembered long after everyone has forgotten the things commented on. So today the attitude of the young to him is that in a way he means nothing to them, but on the other hand they are also conscious somehow of this marginal figure. And occasionally this marginal figure moves into the centre of the text. A poem like *The Shield of Achilles* is much more than a marginal comment like, say, the note to 'New Year Letter'. It is something which moves absolutely into the centre and I think one or two poems he wrote do that.

Do you think what some critics have called a nervous blankness at the centre of his poetry where personal things are concerned, do you think this weakens his achievement as a whole?

Yes, I've thought a lot about that. I used to think that there are some poets who, when you read their lines, you feel you have finger on the pulse. Keats above all. Reading a line by Keats is like having a drop of his quintessential blood in a phial, isn't it? Keats is always Keats, rather than Keatsian. Auden is always Audenish. He produces an atmosphere, a climate. You hardly ever feel that this is the essential life blood. I don't know whether this is a strength or a weakness. It's just a fact of life. The worst you could say is that Kipling is like this. He's always Kiplingish, without one ever feeling immediately in the presence of the living, breathing Kipling. With Auden it's partly a very conscious attitude towards the word 'I'. Auden is an egotist in a way, but it's a very concealed kind of egotism. It's something he hardly ever presents the reader with. He's very adroit at handling his own egotism, keeping it offstage. You were asking me before about his influence on me, or about my awareness of him: I'm aware of him as a critical force, but not as a direct influence. For better or worse – probably for *my* worse – we are absolutely different kinds of writer. We really have very little in common.   ...

SOURCE: extracts from 'A Conversation with Stephen Spender', in *The Review*, 23 (1970), pp. 21, 22–3, 25–6, 26–7.

NOTES

1. [Ed.] There are several extracts from *New Verse* in this Casebook. The journal was founded in 1933 and edited (1933–39) by Geoffrey Grigson; it was devoted to new poets and to criticism of 'contemporary relevance'.

2. [Ed.] Extracts from an essay by Martin Dodsworth on Bernard Spencer's poetry are presented in section 3 of Part Three, below.

C. Day Lewis   (1937)

On Auden

It is a good thing when writers can express in public their affection and respect for a distinguished colleague. I met Auden first at Oxford eleven years ago: I knew very soon that he was and would be the best poet of my generation, and I have never had any reason to change my mind. Other contributors will no doubt be calling attention to his unusual powers of assimilation, to the vigour of his personal idiom and its revolutionising effect upon the verse of our day, to the extraordinarily consistent development of his own work – a true imaginative growth emerging at each stage without precociousness or hesitation from the previous stage. I would like to add this note on the revolutionary content of his writing. His satire has been criticised at times as irresponsible: this is to misunderstand its motive and aim: in so far as it proceeds from the life of one social class, a class which has lost its responsibility and civilising impetus, the terms of this satire are bound to be superficially irresponsible. But no contemporary writing shows so clearly the revulsion of the artist from a society which can no longer support him, his need to identify himself with a class that can provide for his imagination.

SOURCE: contribution to *New Verse*, 'Auden Double Number', nos 26–27 (November 1937), p. 26.

W. H. Auden   (1964)

On MacNeice

The only selection from a poet's whole production which can or should have any authority with the public is the one made by himself. He alone can see the poems from the inside and evaluate them in terms of the kind of poetry he is trying to write. In his foreword to a selection he made in 1959, Louis MacNeice wrote:

These are not, I assume, my eighty-five best poems – nor, even though I like them, the eighty-five which I like best. I have excluded some which, *of their kind*, seem better than some I have let in. . . . My main object has been to illustrate different phases *and* different kinds of my work.[1]

The other kind of selection which, though without authority, is legitimate, is the one which each reader, once he is familiar with the whole range of the poet's work, makes for himself solely on the basis of his own personal taste, and that is all this selection is. As a fellow poet of the same generation and a personal friend, it would be both dishonest and impudent of me to play the schoolmaster-critic and select poems, not because I like them, but because of their possible significance to a literary historian. I have, for instance, included nothing from *Autumn Sequel* or *Ten Burnt Offerings*. Posterity may judge me a fool, but it seems to me that, in the early nineteen-fifties, Louis MacNeice struck a bad patch – a misfortune which can befall any poet and often does. I would not call the poems from this period bad – like everything he wrote, they are beautifully carpentered – but I do find them a bit dull. Luckily for him and for me, this period did not last long, and his last three volumes contain, in my opinion, his finest work. Needless to say, the omission of a poem from this selection does not necessarily imply that I do not like it. A selection has no right to compete on the market with the Collected Poems, as mine certainly would, were I to include everything I admire.

Again, it is not for me, as a contemporary and a friend, to attempt a serious critical evaluation of Louis MacNeice's poetry. That task I must leave to a younger generation, confident that a just judgement will be a favourable one, and that his reputation will steadily increase with the years.

SOURCE: Introduction to *Selected Poems of Louis MacNeice*, edited by W. H. Auden (London, 1964).

NOTE

1. [Ed.] *Eighty-Five Poems: Selected by the Author* (London, 1959). An earlier selection of his verse by MacNeice – *Selected Poems* – had been published in 1940.

Louis MacNeice   (1937)

To W. H. Auden (21 October 1937)

Dear Wystan
I have to write you a letter in a great hurry and so it would be out of the question to try to assess your importance. I take it that you are important and, before that, that poetry itself is important. Poets are not legislators (what is an 'unacknowledged legislator' anyway?), but they put facts and feelings in italics, which makes people think about them and such thinking may in the end have an outcome in action.

Poets have different methods of italicisation. What are yours? What is it in your poetry which shakes people up?

It is, I take it, a freshness – sometimes of form, sometimes of content, usually of both. You are very fertile in pregnant and unusual phrases and have an aptitude for stark and compelling texture. With regard to content, the subject-matter of your poems is always

interesting and it is a blessing to our generation, though one in the eye
for Bloomsbury, that you discharged into poetry the subject-matters
of psycho-analysis, politics and economics. Mr Eliot brought back
ideas into poetry but he uses the ideas, say, of anthropology more
academically and less humanly than you use Marx or Groddeck.[1]
This is because you are always taking sides.

It may be bad taste to take sides but it is a more vital habit than the
detachment of the pure æsthete. The taunt of being a schoolboy
(which, when in the mood, I should certainly apply myself) is itself a
compliment because it implies that you expect the world and yourself
to develop. This expectation inevitably seems vulgar to that bevy of
second-rate sensitive minds who write in our cultured weeklies.

'Other philosophies have described the world; our business is to
change it.' Add that if we are not interested in changing it, there is
really very little to describe. There is just an. assortment of
heterogeneous objects to make Pure Form out of.

You go to extremes, of course, but that is all to the good. There is
still a place in the sun for the novels of Virginia Woolf, for still-life
painting and for the nature-lover. But these would probably not
survive if you and your like, who have no use for them, did not plump
entirely for something different.

Like most poets you are limited. Your poems are strongly physical
but not fastidiously physical. This is what I should expect from
someone who does not like flowers in his room.

Your return to a versification in more regular stanzas and rhymes
is, I think, a very good thing. The simple poem, however, does not
always wear too well. At first sight we are very pleased to get the swing
of it so easily and understand it so quickly, but after first acquaintance
it sometimes grows stale. A. E. Housman, whom I join you in
admiring, was a virtuoso who could get away with cliché images and
hymn-tune metres, but, as you would, I think, admit, his methods are
not suitable to anyone who has a creed which is either profound or
elaborate.

I am therefore a little doubtful about your present use of the ballad
form. It is very good fun but it does not seem to me to be your *natural*
form as I doubt if you can put over what you want to say in it. Of
course if you can put over half of what you want to say to a thousand
people, that may well be better than putting over two thirds of it to a
hundred people. But I hope that you will not start writing down to the
crowd for, if you write down far enough, you will have to be careful to

give them nothing that they don't know already and then your own end will be defeated. Compromise is necessary here, as always, in poetry.

I think you have shown great sense in not writing 'proletarian' stuff (though some reviewers, who presumably did not read your poems, have accused you of it). You realise that one must write about what one knows. One may not hold the bourgeois creed, but if one knows only bourgeois one must write about them. They all after all contain the germ of their opposite. It is an excellent thing (lie quiet Ezra, Cambridge, Gordon Square, with your pure images, pure cerebration, pure pattern, your scrap-albums of ornament torn eclectically from history) that you should have written poems about preparatory schools. Some of the Pure Poets maintained that one could make poems out of anything, but on the ground, not that subject was important, but that it didn't matter. You also would admit that anything can go into poetry, but the poet must first be interested in the thing in itself.

As for poetic drama, you are now swinging away from the Queer Play. This, like the formal change in your lyrics, is also a good thing and also has its danger. But the danger is not so great for you as it would be for some. Whatever the shape of your work, it will always have ideas in it. Still, when authors like Denis Johnston, who can write excellent straight plays, feel impelled to go over to crooked plays and 'poetic writing', there must be some good reason for it and it may appear perverse in you to forget your birthright and pass them in the opposite direction to a realism which may not be much more natural to you than poetry is to them.

These are the criticisms which occur to me at the moment. I have no time to expand on your virtues, but I must say that what I especially admire in you is your unflagging curiosity about people and events. Poetry is related to the sermon and you have your penchant for preaching, but it is more closely related to conversation and you, my dear, if any, are a born gossip.

Yours ever,   Louis MacNeice

Source: 'Letter to W. H. Auden', *New Verse*, 'Auden Double Number', nos 26–27 (November 1937), pp. 11–13.

NOTE

1. [Ed.] Georg Walther Gröddeck: German psychologist and social theorist. His works include *Book of the It*, *Exploring the Unconscious*, *The Unknown Self*, and *The World of Man*.

Louis MacNeice   (1938)

On Thirties Poets

. . . The younger poets whom I most admire, Auden and Spender, write differently from all these poets [previously discussed – Ed.] – Pound and Eliot, Dylan Thomas, William Empson (who so much differ from each other) – because they are more interested in the world of concrete people. Empson is interested in formulas for objects but not in anything he can handle. He studies science from an arm-chair. He is no participant. Auden and Spender are participants; their 'spiritual forms' – to use a conception of Blake's – have hands as well as eyes.

So Auden and Spender, who live in a concrete world, tend to use their images neither as merely algebra nor purely aesthetically for the sake of the image itself. They approach, therefore, the parataxis of the early Chinese poets. They verge sometimes on allegory but, as they are primarily interested in what idealist philosophers used to call the concrete universal, they do not often use particular images merely as counters for generalities.

In Auden the imagery is often dramatic, the meaning being absorbed in the image as an actor is absorbed in his part (or, conversely, as the part, as set down on paper, finds its body in the actor). Auden is a very concrete poet who, consciously or unconsciously (probably consciously because he has read much psychology), often uses a dream technique:

> The horns of the dark squadron
> Converging to attack;
> The sound behind our back
> Of glaciers calving.

In dreams the hierarchies of life break down. Distances in time and place, distinctions between things merely thought of and things perceived, are overruled. If I dream I am in England thinking of Australia, I may suddenly see Australia itself either in diagram form as a map or realistically – the blue gums spurting up beyond my garden. If I dream I am reading a book I may suddenly find I am also living the book. If I dream that I hear a word mentioned – say 'porpoise' – I may suddenly see the porpoise itself materialise. When I say that Auden uses a dream technique, I mean for instance that he is very fond of that figure which Aristotle classes as a species of metaphor – the particular standing for the general. As in the dream, if porpoises are mentioned, I do not think of porpoises in general or of 'porpoiseness', but may even see a particular porpoise crystallise out of nothing. Hence Auden's notorious catalogues. His generalities always crystallise into instances and to keep them clear-cut he often leaves out the links – the 'as ifs', the 'for examples'; he does not explain how the porpoise got into the garden.

But Auden is versatile. He often uses the rhetorical or classical image as practised by A. E. Housman:

> The flag of morn in conqueror's state
> Enters at the English gate:
> The vanquished eve, as night prevails,
> Bleeds upon the road to Wales.

For Auden admires Housman and Housman's turns. Housman sometimes overdid his turns as in

> The goal stands up, the keeper
> Stands up to keep the goal—

or his conceits as in

> Fall, winter, fall; for he,
>   Prompt hand and headpiece clever,
>   Has woven a winter robe,
>   And made of earth and sea
>   His overcoat for ever,
>   And wears the turning globe.

But such writing, while running the risk of vulgarity, is crisp and alive, and Auden is willing to take anything alive for his model and lump the vulgarity. Thus his later poems show the influence of popular wit as exemplified in Cole Porter's songs or in American folk-ballads; witness 'Cocaine Lil', one of Auden's favourite ballads:

> Early in the morning, at half past three,
> They were all lit up like a Christmas tree.

As well as using his dream parataxis and his popular rhetoric, Auden uses the cerebral-epigram:

> Touching is shaking hands
> On mortgaged lands—

or the traditional method of allegory:

> That later we, though parted then
> May still recall those evenings when
> Fear gave his watch no look;
> The lion griefs loped from the shade
> And on our knees their muzzles laid
> And Death put down his book.

The allegory here is still fairly concrete, once more reminding us of a dream.

Sometimes his metaphors are mere rhetoric and do not ring true:

> Noble emotions organized and massed
> Line the straight flood-lit tracks of memory
> To cheer your image as it passes by. . . .

but it is rarely that Auden's analogies are ill digested, fail to become concrete. Often, like Eliot, he achieves the condensed, significant phrase:

> The rigid promise fractured in the garden.

Sometimes he succeeds with a mixed metaphor:

> And all sway forward on the dangerous flood
> Of history, that never sleeps or dies,
> And, held one moment, burns the hand.

Often a quick comparison is so pregnant that it implies a whole attitude – an attitude to contemporary religion:

> cathedrals,
> Luxury liners laden with souls,
> Holding to the east their hulls of stone,
> The high thin rare continuous worship
> Of the self-absorbed.

or to British nationalism, as in his poem on Dover:

> the lighthouses
> That guard for ever the made privacy of this bay
> Like twin stone dogs opposed on a gentleman's gate.

Spender's images are not so sharp or self contained as Auden's. He tends to fuse metaphor and subject:

> That programme of the antique Satan
> Bristling with guns on the indented page
> With battleship towering from hilly waves. . . .

But he also achieves the pregnant phrase, as of the 'prisoners' who

> lean their solid eyes against the night

or

> The watching of cripples pass
> With limbs shaped like questions

where the comparison does two things at once.

But Spender's most effective use of imagery is when one image pervades and controls a whole poem, as in the poem beginning 'After they have tired of the brilliance of cities. . . .' This poem is dominated by the word 'snow' with its associations of hunger, universality and clarity:

> it is death stalks through life
> Grinning white through all faces
> Clean and equal like the shine from snow.
>
> And our strength is now the strength of our bones
> Clean and equal like the shine from snow. . . .
>
> We have come at last to a country
> Where light equal, like the shine from snow, strikes all faces. . . .
>
> But through torn-down portions of old fabric let their eyes
> Watch the admiring dawn explode like a shell
> Around us, dazing us with its light like snow.

. . . I have been discussing here the ways in which images can be used rather than the spheres from which they are taken, for this latter belongs still more properly to the study of subject-matter. I have already maintained that images approximate to properties; from this it follows that images frequently have more in common with their theme than is given by a mere analogy or mathematical parallel. Thus while a poet like Day Lewis, whose theme is the modern industrial world, its economics and its politics, takes his images especially from such things as pylons, power-houses, spies, frontiers, aeroplanes, steam-engines, a poet like Spender, whose approach to the same world, and therefore that world itself, are more mystical, is still very free with the stock mystical symbols – roses, crystal, snow, stars, gold. And a poet like Charles Madge, who is obsessed by curious coincidences, uses images from astrology.

I find that I use images myself (*a*) to clarify a picture, (*b*) to express an idea with more concentration and more shock to the reader than it would have if stated baldly or explicitly. I allow myself the use of many different types of image, for example, the sensuous type:

> The murderous grin of toothy flowers

or (of the sea):

> With Thor's thunder or taking his ease akimbo
> Lumbering torso, but finger-tips a marvel
> Of surgeon's accuracy.

– though here the sensuous effect is largely due to onomatopoeic writing.

I also use the cerebral image:

> The minnow-twistings of the latinist who alone
> Nibbles and darts through the shallows of the lexicon.

and the blend of cerebral and sensuous as (of aeroplanes):

> When these tiny flies like nibs will calmly draw our death
> A dipping gradient on the graph of Europe.

This last is almost a metaphysical image, but the picture of the moving aeroplanes is intended to persist.

Sometimes, more fantastically, I take several images and ring the changes on them. Thus in a philosophical poem, 'Homage to Clichés', I think of the brute Other, the fate which we cannot influence: (*a*) as an Egyptian Rameses, (*b*) as a tenor bell (which we cannot peal but can only play chimes upon), (*c*) as a black panther (black because unknown and because the black panther is popularly said to be untamable). The movement of each of these three will be the movement of Fate:

> The ringers are taking off their coats, the panther crouches,
> The granite sceptre is very slightly inclining. . . .

The present trend, however, is to reduce images in proportion to properties. This is because, as I have said, poets are now more interested in subject, and that a subject from the concrete objective world. The few poets to-day who, like Laura Riding, Robert Graves and Norman Cameron, philosophise in their poetry, *have* to use images because bare philosophy belongs to science rather than to poetry. Witness Norman Cameron's excellent poem on the principle of Love:

> He bloomed in our bodies to the finger-tips
> And rose like barley-sugar round the lips.

But most of the other poets 'philosophise', if they do philosophise, more in the manner of Wordsworth. For Wordsworth the objective world of nature is an embodiment, not a concealment, of something like the Platonic Forms. He does not therefore require many images because his properties carry their own message.

☆

. . . Pound, as the one-time leader of the Imagists, believes in making the part do duty for the whole, whether in description or syntax. The rapidity of movement thus attainable, the 'quick shots', to use a film term, of things in particular aspects, have been much prized by many of the younger poets, whose obscurity . . . is often merely due to their 'cutting'.

Thus Auden's poems, in the volume published in 1930, were written in a sort of telegraphese, the less important words such as articles and conjunctions, even demonstrative and relative pronouns, being often omitted. He was aiming thereby at an economy difficult to attain in English, which is an uninflected language. His most regular trick is asyndeton, which is still much practised by most of these poets in their eagerness not to be diffuse:

> Past victory is honour, to accept
> An island governorship, back to estates
> Explored as child; coming at last to love
> Lost publicly, found secretly again
> In private flats, admitted to a sign.

This modern verse syntax sometimes appears stilted, as when Spender writes:

> Supposing then you change
> Gestures, clamp your mind in irons,

> By boxed degrees transform into past history;
> Stand on the astringent self-created promontory,
> A Greek as simple as a water-clock,
> And let the traffic creak beneath.
> You'd live then in the tricks of dreams, you'd be
> Not living, but a walking wish, private and malicious
> As my cracked aunt, or, if blown, like a banker.

Much of Spender's writing indeed has the pedantic quality of lecture-notes; this can be a virtue when the notes do not fall apart but are held together by a strong lyrical sentiment.

As described in chapter VI [see previous section of this excerpt – Ed.], Auden, Spender and their fellow poets, especially Day Lewis, draw many images from the modern industrial world, its trappings and machinery. Day Lewis seems to me sometimes to force this modern imagery, applying it according to too ready-made a formula:

> Go not this road, for arc-lamps cramp
> The dawn; sense fears to take
> A mortal step, and body obeys
> An automatic brake.

But the catholic principle is right which allows him in the same sequence of poems to use a traditional or 'poetic' image:

> Or as a poplar, ceaselessly
> Gives a soft answer to the wind:
> Cool on the light her leaves lie sleeping
> Folding a column of sweet sound.

The catholic principle is good as long as it does not become dilettante eclecticism; everything the poet uses must be first *felt* as appropriate.

In the same way modern poets often use terms borrowed from various spheres of technical writing – psychological, scientific or sociological. Such language is valid provided the poet is himself in a position to use it naturally and provided the ideal normal reader can be expected to understand it. Coleridge maintained that the philosopher comes nearer to 'the real language of men' than the peasant. Modifying this we may say that any language which is pruned, concentrated and meticulously used, tends to become technical and that therefore it is only natural that the poet, when looking for his 'real language', should borrow the technical terms of other thinkers who have already used a process of distillation similar to the poetic one. But he must not, in tapping these new sources, let them go to his head. Thus Auden in his undergraduate poems overdid what he called his 'clinical' vocabulary.

Poets are always in danger of writing to a cut-and-dried recipe. As a child . . . I believed that rhyme and the use of the second person singular were enough to make a poem. When I was at Oxford I felt almost the same about grammatical inversion – 'Came the Dawn' – or the use of 'strange words' such as 'colubrine' or of stock poetic words, vaguely evocative, such as 'dolorous' and 'languorous'. So the undergraduate imitators of Eliot felt that a poem's success was guaranteed by broken syntax or tags of foreign languages or the mention of rats and bones. And many young poets now feel that you can make a poem with a pylon. . . .

SOURCE: extracts from the chapters VI and VIII, on 'Imagery' and 'Diction', in *Modern Poetry* (Oxford, 1938; 2nd edn 1968), pp. 105–10, 111–13, 146–9.

PART TWO

Some Contemporary Critics

Michael Roberts (1932)

'New Poetic Possibilities'

. . . The writers in this book [*New Signatures*][1] have learned to accept the fact that progress is illusory, and yet to believe that the game is worth playing; to believe that the alleviation of suffering is good even though it merely makes possible new sensitiveness and therefore new suffering; to believe that their own standards are no more absolute than those of other people, and yet to be prepared to defend and to suffer for their own standards; to think of the world, for scientific purposes, in terms which make it appear deterministic, and yet to know that a human action may be unpredictable from scientific laws, a new creation.

These are not really logical problems at all; they are aspects of an emotional discord which can be resolved neither by reasoning nor by action, but only by a new harmonisation such as that which may be brought about by a work of art. The fact that each of the writers in this book has solved this problem in his own way without recourse to any external system of religious belief therefore opens up new poetic possibilities.

SOURCE: extract from the Introduction to *New Signatures* (London, 1932), pp. 12–13.

NOTE

1. [Ed.] Among the poets published in the volume were W. H. Auden, C. Day Lewis, Stephen Spender, Richard Eberhart, William Empson, John Lehmann and A. S. T. Tessemond.

Michael Roberts   (1937)

On Contemporary Poetry

Five years ago, in some 'Notes on English Poets' which appeared in *Poetry*'s 'English Number' of February 1932, I spoke of three groups of English writers. First, those whose work is 'predominantly metaphysical and, in the widest sense, religious'. Second, those whose poetry 'deliberately leaves a discord in experience, which is to be removed only by action, not by an inner balancing of impulses'. Third, those who 'have made a careful study of the French *surréalistes*'. Roughly speaking, the classification will still serve, and the three groups correspond more or less to three age groups. In the first, there is T. S. Eliot, Edwin Muir and Herbert Read. In the second, W. H. Auden, Cecil Day Lewis, Charles Madge and Stephen Spender (Mr Auden in his new book of poems speaks of the writer's duty to 'make action urgent and its nature clear'). The third group now includes several writers, George Barker, Dylan Thomas, David Gascoyne and Roger Roughton, who were unknown five years ago. William Empson, now as then, stands by himself, nearer perhaps to the first group than to any of the others. Since 1930, his ingenious, closely reasoned metaphysical poetry has received in England some of the recognition it deserves. . . .

The provisional classification which I have been using obviously focuses attention on the *content* of poetry, and especially the explicit content. In so doing, I am representing a general tendency to demand that poetry shall talk sense and express moods which can be part of our ordinary life. Poetry of this kind is the verbal equivalent of some experience which may happen to us independently of the poem: the strictly poetic value of the poem lies in the fact that it makes us articulate; the aesthetic, moral or intellectual value depends on the quality of the perception, mood and thought. Some of the poems of Louis MacNeice, Ronald Bottrall, and still more those of James Reeves, seem at first sight to depend entirely on a photographic accuracy, very little on sensibility, and not at all on the value of their ideas and sentiments. In this sense their poetry is 'pure'; they set out to describe what they see; they do not try to arouse sympathy or indignation (which is easily done by falsely simplifying the vision).

But absolute detachment is impossible; observation is itself an activity, the expression of desires; and really 'pure' poetry would be unreadable. In the poets I have mentioned, a closer acquaintance with the poems shows a more or less coherent intellectual and moral attitude.

All poetry is more or less propagandist, though in poetry which shows a wide and clear understanding, the explicit propagandist intention is the consequence, rather than the cause, of the vision. Poetry becomes effective as propaganda only when, by its strict poetic quality, it first awakens in us a mood which we recognise as the exact equivalent of the poem, and which then, by repetition, makes the mood take its place among our habitual responses to the world. The person who is already familiar with the inarticulate mood or thought which the poet is attempting to express, will find it hard to judge the poetic quality of the writing.

One trouble with most of the socialist poetry that is being written (more is being written in America than in England) is that it has no poetic merit at all: it sets out to repeat thoughts and moods which are already articulately known. It has no value apart from that of the ideas and sentiments which it expresses. Good poetry necessarily deals with that which has not already found exact expression: the poet is never a good party man. He may say things clearly which were vaguely in many people's minds already, or he may tell them things which they need to know and do not, but he cannot be judged by his ideological orthodoxy; for what he is saying is sometimes other than a mere repetition or logical extension of existing doctrine. Auden, Spender and Madge are sometimes called communist poets, and Eliot a Christian poet, but their importance depends on the fact that they see more and speak more clearly than the ordinary communist or ordinary Christian. They aim at clear and exact speech in the interests of understanding, and the gulf which separates them from the ordinary politician is greater than that which separates the poets themselves. Thus the mood of Charles Madge's poem on Vienna (which is one of the best sonnets of our time) is one with which, I imagine, Mr Eliot would deeply sympathise; but it would be wholly foreign to some members of the communist party. Anger and bitterness and fear may have their own poets, and no doubt they would be popular, but I see no sign of the emergence of such poets in England today. The prevailing mood of Spender and Auden, as of Eliot, is one of grief and sympathy rather than anger or denunciation.

It is in this sense that their poetry is political: they have a clear idea of the kind of life which they wish to see in Europe, and they express the temper in which more and more Englishmen wish those changes to be made. To many people it seems that a combination of gentleness and knowledge, with firm convictions of right and wrong and readiness to act, is the alternative to doctrinaire ruthlessness. . . .

Two qualities seem to me rare in English poetry today. The first is a sense of personality: the poets mostly speak in their own characters and very little dramatic poetry is being written, though Mr MacNeice has attempted it in his eclogues. The characters in the poetic dramas which have appeared seem to me to be thin and incompletely human: they are humours rather than personalities. It may be argued that they are intended to be symbols, rather than pictures of people, but I would maintain that the most adequate and necessary symbols are complete and human characters.

The second lack is the power of writing narrative. I can see no reason why imaginatively convincing narrative should be more difficult to produce today than it ever has been. It is sometimes argued that, owing to the development of the novel, character and narrative are no longer the concern of poetry; and that poetry must restrict itself more and more to the exploitation of the music-making and image-building power of words. Science and philosophy, it is argued, were once expounded in verse, but the versification was a frippery and was therefore discarded by the writers. Similarly versification is said to be an impediment to the development of narrative or character.

This argument, I think, starts from the wrong end. Science and philosophy and prose fiction are limited precisely because they refrain from using the characteristic devices of poetry. They do not say all that the properties of language make possible. If the versification is an arbitrary brutality imposed on the narrative, by all means let it be abolished: but if we look at the question from the other side we see that the sense of personality, and the interest of narrative, are among the instruments which the writer can use to produce his total effect. One of the striking things about Auden and Eliot is that they have not forsworn these instruments and that they have purposes large enough to demand their use.

SOURCE: extracts from 'Aspects of English Poetry, 1932–1937', in *Poetry* (Chicago), 49 (January 1937), pp. 210, 211–14, 216–17.

Christopher Isherwood   (1937)

On Auden's Early Poetry

If I were told to introduce a reader to the poetry of W. H. Auden, I should begin by asking him to remember three things.

First, that Auden is essentially a scientist: perhaps I should add, 'a schoolboy scientist'. He has, that is to say, the scientific training and the scientific interests of a very intelligent schoolboy. He has covered the groundwork, but doesn't propose to go any further: he has no intention of specialising. Nevertheless, he has acquired the scientific outlook and technique of approach; and this is really all he needs for his writing.

Second, that Auden is a musician and a ritualist. As a child, he enjoyed a high Anglican upbringing, coupled with a sound musical education. The Anglicanism has evaporated, leaving only the height: he is still much preoccupied with ritual, in all its forms. When we collaborate, I have to keep a sharp eye on him – or down flop the characters on their knees (see 'F.6' passim); another constant danger is that of choral interruptions by angel-voices. If Auden had his way, he would turn every play into a cross between grand opera and high mass.

Third, that Auden is a Scandinavian. The Auden family came originally from Iceland. Auden himself was brought up on the sagas, and their influence upon his work has been profound.

Auden began writing poetry comparatively late; when he had already been several terms at his public school. At our prep-school, he showed no literary interests whatever: his ambition was to become a mining-engineer. His first poems, unlike Stephen Spender's, were competent but entirely imitative: Hardy, [Edward] Thomas and Frost were his models:

The Carter's Funeral

Sixty odd years of poaching and drink
And rain-sodden waggons with scarcely a friend,
Chained to this life; rust fractures a link,
   So the end.

Sexton at last has pressed down the loam,
He blows on his fingers and prays for the sun,
Parson unvests and turns to his home,
    Duty done.

Little enough stays musing upon
The passing of one of the masters of things,
Only a bird looks peak-faced on,
    Looks and sings.

Allendale

The smelting-mill stack is crumbling, no smoke is alive there,
Down in the valley the furnace no lead ore of worth burns;
Now tombs of decaying industries, not to strive there
    Many more earth-turns.

The chimney still stands at the top of the hill like a finger
Skywardly pointing as if it were asking: 'What lies there?'
And thither we stray to dream of those things as we linger,
    Nature denies here.

Dark looming around the fell-folds stretch desolate, crag-scarred,
Seeming to murmur: 'Why beat you the bars of your prison?'
What matter? To us the world-face is glowing and flag-starred,
    Lit by a vision.

So under it stand we, all swept by the rain and the wind there,
Muttering: 'What look you for, creatures that die in a season?'
We care not, but turn to our dreams and the comfort we find there,
    Asking no reason.

The saga-world is a schoolboy world, with its feuds, its practical jokes, its dark threats conveyed in puns and riddles and understatements: 'I think this day will end unluckily for some; but chiefly for those who least expect harm.' I once remarked to Auden that the atmosphere of *Gisli the Outlaw* very much reminded me of our schooldays. He was pleased with the idea: and, soon after this, he produced his first play: *Paid on Both Sides*, in which the two worlds are so inextricably confused that it is impossible to say whether the characters are really epic heroes or only members of a school OTC.

Auden is, and always has been, a most prolific writer. Problems of form and technique seem to bother him very little. You could say to him: 'Please write me a double ballade on the virtues of a certain brand of toothpaste, which also contains at least ten anagrams on the names of well-known politicians, and of which the refrain is as follows. . . .' Within twenty-four hours, your ballade would be ready – and it would be good.

When Auden was younger, he was very lazy. He hated polishing and making corrections. If I didn't like a poem, he threw it away and wrote another. If I liked one line, he would keep it and work it into a new poem. In this way, whole poems were constructed which were simply anthologies of my favourite lines, entirely regardless of grammar or sense. This is the simple explanation of much of Auden's celebrated obscurity.

While Auden was up at Oxford, he read T. S. Eliot. The discovery of *The Waste Land* marked a turning-point in his work – for the better, certainly; though the earliest symptoms of Eliot-influence were most alarming. Like a patient who has received an over-powerful inoculation, Auden developed a severe attack of allusions, jargonitis and private jokes. He began to write lines like: 'Inexorable Rembrandt rays that stab . . .' or 'Love mutual has reached its first eutectic . . .' Nearly all the poems of that early Eliot period are now scrapped.

In 1928, Spender, who had a private press, printed a little orange paper volume of Auden's poems. (This booklet, limited to 'about 45 copies,' is now a bibliophile's prize: the mis-prints alone are worth about ten shillings each.) Most of the poems were reprinted two years later, when Messrs Faber and Faber published the first edition of their Auden volume: here is one of the few which were not:

> Consider if you will how lovers stand
> In brief adherence, straining to preserve
> Too long the suction of good-bye: others,
> Less clinically minded, will admire
> An evening like a coloured photograph,
> A music stultified across the water.
> The desert opens here, and if, though we
> Have ligatured the ends of a farewell,
> Sporadic heartburn show in evidence
> Of love uneconomically slain,
> It is for the last time, the last look back,
> The heel upon the finishing blade of grass,
> To dazzling cities of the plain where lust
> Threatened a sinister rod, and we shall turn
> To our study of stones, to split Eve's apple,
> Absorbed, content if we can say 'because';
> Unanswerable like any other pedant,
> Like Solomon and Sheba, wrong for years.

I think this poem illustrates very clearly Auden's state of mind at that period: in this respect, its weakness is its virtue. Auden was very busy trying to regard things 'clinically,' as he called it. Poetry, he said, must concern itself with shapes and volumes. Colours and smells were condemned as romantic: Form alone was significant. Auden loathed (and still rather dislikes) the Sea – for the Sea, besides being deplorably wet and sloppy, is formless. (Note 'ligatured' – a typical specimen of the 'clinical' vocabulary.)

Another, and even more powerful influence upon Auden's early work was non-literary in its origin – in 1929, during a visit to Berlin, he came into contact with the doctrines of the American psychologist, Homer Lane. (Cf. Auden's own account of this, in his 'Letter to Lord Byron', Part Four.) Auden was particularly interested in Lane's theories of the psychological causes of disease – if you refuse to make use of your creative powers, you grow a cancer instead, etc. References to these theories can be found in many of the early poems, and, more generally, in *The Orators*. Lane's teachings provide a key to most of the obscurities in the 'Journal of an Airman' (Mr John Layard, one of Lane's most brilliant followers, has pointed out the psychological relationship between epilepsy and the idea of flight.)

The first collaboration between Auden and myself was in a play called *The Enemies of a Bishop*. The Bishop is the hero of the play: he represents sanity, and is an idealised portrait of Lane himself. His enemies are the pseudo-healers, the wilfully ill and the mad. The final curtain goes down on his complete victory. The play was no more than a charade, very loosely put together and full of private jokes. We revised the best parts of it and used them again, five years later, in *The Dog Beneath the Skin*.

It is typical of Auden's astonishing adaptability that, after two or three months in Berlin, he began to write poems in German. Their style can be best imagined by supposing that a German writer should attempt a sonnet-sequence in a mixture of Cockney and Tennysonian English, without being able to command either idiom. A German critic of great sensibility to whom I afterwards showed these sonnets was much intrigued. He assured me that their writer was a poet of the first rank, despite his absurd grammatical howlers. The critic himself had never heard of Auden and was certainly quite unaware of his English reputation.

The scenery of Auden's early poetry is, almost invariably, mountainous. As a boy, he visited Westmorland, the Peak District of

Derbyshire, and Wales. For urban scenery, he preferred the industrial Midlands; particularly in districts where an industry is decaying.
His romantic travel-wish was always towards the North. He could
never understand how anybody could long for the sun, the blue sky,
the palm-trees of the South. His favourite weather was autumnal;
high wind and driving rain. He loved industrial ruins, a disused
factory or an abandoned mill: a ruined abbey would leave him quite
cold. He has always had a special feeling for caves and mines. At
school, one of his favourite books was Jules Verne's *Journey to the Centre
of the Earth*.

A final word about Influences – or perhaps I should say, crazes. For
Auden is deeply rooted in the English tradition, and his debt to most
of the great writers of the past is too obvious to need comment here.
The crazes were all short lived: they left plenty of temporary damage
but few lasting traces. The earliest I remember was for Edwin
Arlington Robinson. It found expression in about half a dozen poems
(all scrapped) and notably in some lines about 'a Shape' in an Irish
mackintosh which malice urges but friendship forbids me to quote.
Then came Emily Dickinson. You will find her footprints here and
there among the earlier poems: for example,

> Nor sorrow take
> His endless look.

Then Bridges published *The Testament of Beauty*, and Auden wrote the
poem beginning: 'Which of you waking early and watching day-
break . . .' which appeared in the first Faber edition, but was
removed from later impressions. Finally, there was Hopkins: but, by
this time, Auden's literary digestive powers were stronger: he made a
virtue of imitation, and produced the brilliant parody-ode to a rugger
fifteen which appears at the end of *The Orators*.

SOURCE: 'Some Notes on Auden's Early Poetry', *New Verse*, 'Auden Double
Number', nos 26–27 (November 1937), pp. 4–9.

Francis Scarfe   (1941)

On Day Lewis

Like Auden, Day Lewis is a deceptive poet, with a great deal of irrelevance in his work, but beneath it some solid virtues. He has sometimes been described as a Georgian gone wrong, and it is certain that in spirit he does not quite belong to the Auden group with which he has been associated. But he is a Georgian with a difference, a Georgian who has read Eliot, Hopkins and Marx – and that means a great deal.

Lewis has been a slow developer as a poet, and it is hard, at the present time, when comparing his later with his earlier work, to understand why his *Transitional Poem* and *From Feathers to Iron* were so wildly acclaimed ten years ago. It was, I think, because he came forward at the right time with a concrete enthusiasm, with an overwhelming desire to create and defend something constructive. This was a new note after the decade of despondency which had followed on *The Waste Land*.

Transitional Poem (1929) was anything but a flying start. At that time all the young poets were modelling themselves on Eliot, and Lewis was among them, but only in a mild way. This mild way was in imitating the new fashion of adding pedantic notes to his otherwise inoffensive poems. These notes were stuffed with Spinoza, Dante and Donne, with a little Wyndham Lewis and Sophie Tucker thrown in as light refreshment. The name of Wyndham Lewis is significant. This explains a great deal of the 'toughness' and the air of positiveness which have been maintained by Day Lewis ever since his earliest works. The main Note is important: 'The central theme of this poem is the single mind. The poem is divided into four parts, which essentially represent four phases of single-mindedness: it will be seen that a transition is intended from one part to the next such as implies a certain spiritual progress and a constant shifting of aspect. As far as any definitions can be attached to these aspects, they may be termed (1) metaphysical, (2) ethical, (3) psychological, while (4) is an attempt to relate the poetic impulse with the experience as a whole. Formally, the parts fall with fair accuracy into the divisions of a

theorem in geometry, i.e. general enunciation, particular enunciation, proof, corollaries . . . etc.'

It is to be regretted that, with all these intentions, the poem is far
from being as logical or as compactly built as the note suggests:
anyone reading it without this note might regard it only as the usual
type of miscellaneous collection of poems. In any case, if there is a
main subject, it is rather different from, and more important than, the
note suggests. In the first poem he writes:

> It is certain we shall attain
> No life until we stamp on all
> Life the tetragonal
> Pure symmetry of brain.

In the second part, Lewis does not particularise this general theme.
Instead, a tense struggle seems to develop, when the poet considers in
many of its aspects, not the problem of 'single-mindedness' so much
as the problem of sensuality. Though some of this is presented in
rather a silly way –

> The man who nuzzles
> In a woman's lap
> Burrows towards a night
> Too deep for puzzles

– there is a characteristic honesty, and a hint of Lewis's later power,
in

> It seems that we must call
> Anything truth whose well
> Is deep enough;
> For the essential
> Philosopher-stone, desire,
> Needs no other proof
> Than its own fire.

This is admirably written, and the clipped effect of these short lines,
the directness of the statement itself, shows clearly that Lewis was
striving after a concise style with no frills. The main point here is that,
after fourteen poems, the poet has contradicted his first premiss. After
two more he goes even farther, writing:

> Let logic analyse the hive,
> Wisdom's content to have the honey.

The first quality of Day Lewis is his good sense.

The Third Part of the *Transitional Poem* is a chaos of personal experiences, many of them too recondite to be of immediate interest. This part is an assertion of individualism, and as such does not seem to emerge logically from the previous poems:

> Mine is the heron's flight
> Which makes a solitude of any sky.

This, again, is excellent: it is also, in conjunction with the kestrel image used in later poems, another indication of Lewis's point of contact with the Auden–Spender group, the conflict between individual- and mass-salvation.

The Fourth Part, which aims at so much, with its supposed presentation of corollaries, is also very chaotic, but tense in spite of occasional rhetoric. One of the most important points made, since it defines and characterizes all Lewis's subsequent work, is to be found, however inadequately expressed, in Poem 33:

> I stretched a line from pole to pole
> To hang my paper lanterns on. Poor soul,
> By such a metaphysical conceit
> Thinking to make ends meet!
> This line, spun from the blind heart –
> What could it do but prove the poles apart?
> More expert now, I twist the dials, catch
> Electric hints, curt omens such
> As may be heard by one tapping the air
> That belts an ambiguous sphere.
> Put down the tripod here.

It is evident that Lewis saw the weakness of all intellectual attempts to solve anything by abstract logic alone: this amounts to a refutal of his Euclidian conception of his first long poem, and decides a new direction for his work: that of basing all his judgements of life and human nature on the study of concrete instances and living men. And in fact there is as much difference between his conception of poetry in 1929 and that which he arrived at by 1935 as there is between telepathy and wireless.

The *Transitional Poem* is one of the strangest poems of the thirties, since it is the product of one of the strangest minds. This Poem 33 especially is an image in miniature of his future work. Consider, for a moment, his characteristic titles: *Transitional Poem* [1929]; *From Feathers to Iron* [1931]; *The Magnetic Mountain* [1933]; *A Time to Dance* [1935]; *Overtures to Death* [1938]; 'Starting Point'.[1] They show Lewis as having a sort of Kafka uneasiness, an urgent desire always to be going somewhere else or beginning something new. This is typical of the English romantic conception of space, that thought 'If anything goes wrong I'll go to America', or 'Perhaps I would be better off in Australia'. (This is what led, says one of my friends, to the British Empire, where people went not so as to make something better, but merely to escape from Britain.) Secondly, this desire for movement is paralleled by a constant preoccupation with the hardness, the resistance of matter. We find in the *Transitional Poem* dozens of instances of this: for example – 'Strata undiagnosed'; 'love's geology'; 'basalt peace'; 'authority of ice'; 'where is the true the central stone'; 'jag of sense'; 'hammered out on lead'; 'Himalayas of the mind'; 'muscular stream'; 'digest an adamant'. There are dozens more, which are completed in the obsession with mountains and hills, which later gave its title to *The Magnetic Mountain*. Beside this idea of solidness, there is another constant image in Lewis which is of great interest. In his earlier poems especially he is obsessed by the image of flying sparks (a psycho-analyst would call it an obsession with sperm), and this flying spark later crystallises in the numerous electricity images, the 'electric hints' quoted above becoming a full conception of electricity with all its attendant metaphors – 'When the charged batteries of desire', etc. These basic images, the one type of solidity and immobility, the other type of instability and movement, reunite very well in the later poems with their imagery of turbines, girders, cantilever bridges, wires, pylons and wheels. This mechanical imagery can sometimes be overdone, but it is a mistake to believe, as some critics have believed, that this is in any way superficial or affected. Lewis, to my mind, is not merely being schoolboyish or trying to be 'tough', but this type of imagery is fundamental to his conception of the modern world. And that this was all latent in the *Transitional Poem* is a fact which refutes those critics who have said that Lewis owes all his 'modern dress' to Auden. Such signs as there are of Auden in this poem are very slight indeed. His basic imagery is indicative of his own, and no other poet's, neurosis. When he developed it later, he gave it a more positive value by using it in a social context.

Having said so much, there is little need for a detailed analysis of Lewis's later work. His development has been logical, and not disappointing. Although he has occasionally written nonsense such as

'Grecians awake, salute the happy norm' and the poem 'Take a whole holiday in honour of this', by the time he reached the *Overtures to Death* he had practically subdued this weakness, save for an occasional reference to death in an Audenesque or Wyndham Lewis manner as 'bailiff' and 'Mister'.

The theme of *From Feathers to Iron* was the approaching birth of a child, and within its limits the subject was better treated than in the *Transitional Poem*, as well as allowing a wider range of reference. Here the most permanent side of Lewis's work makes its appearance: those excellent lyrics about love and nature.

In these lyrics, Lewis is a far more sympathetic person than in those other poems in which he is a boyish Hemingway with an unnatural veneer of toughness: he can write:

> Now she is like the white rose-tree
> That takes a blessing from the sun;
> Summer has filled her veins with light,
> And her warm blood is washed with noon;

or:

> Now the full-throated daffodils,
> Our trumpeters in gold,
> Call resurrection from the ground
> And bid the year be bold.

The only defect in some of the lyrics is their sudden and ill-judged change of tone, as in the poem which begins 'Come as the wind is whirling our summer away' and ends with a catalogue of insulators, turbines and freight.

The Magnetic Mountain shows a further development in both tone and idiom. By this time Lewis had fallen more under Auden's influence and had re-read Hopkins. There was also a change of direction. Lewis, as the above quotations show, is primarily an exultant poet with an immense gusto. In *The Magnetic Mountain* this gusto, fully realised in his images of kestrel, bridges, furnaces and pistons, is now deadened by a gloomy note which seems less natural and less spontaneous. It is the gloom of an optimist at a funeral, feeling it his duty to pull a long face. This is found in certain ominous poems and threatening lines like

> Positively, this is the end of the track.
> It's rather late and there's no way back.

This was a rather distressing way of imitating Auden. Most of the poems in *The Magnetic Mountain* show Lewis continually whipping up an immense hustle and bustle of departure to the Mountain –

> Then I'll hit the trail for that promising land,
> May catch up with Wystan and Rex, my friend

– which gave the impression of a Sunday School treat and the Salvation Army let loose. This excitement was inevitably followed by fits of depression, gloomy tags of mass-observation which only ended in another fit of bustle. Someone has said the Magnetic Mountain was Auden. It might also have been a father-complex similar to Wordsworth's, who was also obsessed by mountains. On the immediate surface, the Mountain is more obviously Communism and the Communist State; and, whether by coincidence or design, the Mountain recalls the image of La Montagne, which was the first name of the great revolutionary mass of Jacobins in the early years of the French Revolution. *The Magnetic Mountain*, with all its exuberant faults, was certainly the heartiest piece of Left propaganda written in the thirties. It is more exhilarating on a first reading than on the second. But its lyrical parts had great moving power, and have so still.

Since *The Magnetic Mountain*, two important things have happened to Day Lewis as a poet. First of all, he has established himself as a narrative poet. Both his long poem about Airmen and 'The Loss of The Nabara' are overlaid with description, but the latter can compete with the best naval narratives in our language. This poem is not sufficiently well known. Of all the poems produced about the Spanish war, many of them, like Auden's and Barker's, on a high emotional level, this is the only solid narrative, and written with sustained feeling;

> Canarias, though easily she out-paced and out-gunned her,
> Finding this midge could sting,
> Edged off, and beneath a wedge of smoke steamed in a ring
> On the rim of the trawler's range, a circular storm of thunder.
>   But always Nabara turned her broadside, manœuvring
> To keep both guns on the target, scorning safety devices.
> Slow now the battle's tempo, irregular the beat
> Of gunfire in the heart
> Of the afternoon, the distempered sky sank to the crisis,
> Shell-shocked the sea tossed and hissed in delirious heat. . . .

The poem is so much an organic whole, and heroic in the best sense, that no isolated quotation can adequately convey its power. This is a line which Lewis will probably develop increasingly, and for which his translation of *The Georgics* (though his style as a translator is heavier than his own style) has more fully prepared him.

The second important development is that, without losing his rather Priestley-like solidness and common sense, Lewis is becoming less aggressive and can present an argument more concisely than ever before. This is to be seen especially in the half-dozen lyrics he has contributed to numbers of *The Penguin New Writing* during the war. The Communist of yesterday, now rather chastened and a member of the Home Guard, has summed up his outlook on the situation perfectly well in his short poem 'Where are the War Poets?':

> It is the logic of our times,
> No subject for immortal verse,
> That we who lived by honest dreams
> Defend the bad against the worse.

This power of epigrammatic writing completes that richer descriptive power he attained in 'The Nabara', and the spirit of the poem quoted above is fairly representative of the younger poets' spontaneous reaction to the war. For they are determined that things will have to be better after the war than they were before. I must confess that until I wrote this essay, in rather a hurry in the few days remaining to me, I was more indifferent to Lewis's work than I am now. I find in it, reading it for perhaps the last time, a deep integrity and a firm attachment to the best human aspirations, as well as a growing and now mature ability to express them.

SOURCE: essay on 'The Development of Day Lewis' in Scarfe's *Auden and After: The Liberation of Poetry, 1930–1941* (London, 1941), pp. 1–9.

NOTE

1. [Ed.] Here and elsewhere poem-titles are italicised when identical to individual volumes of verse published by Day Lewis. This convention has, where practicable, been followed in material on other poets in this volume.

Francis Scarfe   (1941)

On MacNeice

. . . MacNeice showed himself at once in his first book a pitiless critic of modern society, and it is on this aspect of his work that we shall dwell for the moment. He brought an almost exclusively destructive attitude to modern life, which he set out to analyse in a variety of ways:

> It is better we should go quickly, go into Asia
> Or any other tunnel where the world recedes,
> Or turn blind wantons like the gulls who scream
> And rip the edge off any ideal or dream.
>
> (from *Poems*, 1935)

'And rip the edge off any ideal or dream': that is the function of the analyst, and of the common-sense school. It is this Stendhalian 'horror of being a dupe' which dictates all MacNeice's subsequent writings on politics, literature, nature and love. Writing at that time of Communism, he said:

> But before you proclaim the millenium, my dear,
> Consult the barometer –
> This poise is perfect, but maintained
> For one day only.

In this respect he differs from the Auden group with which he has long been associated; he refuses, like poets younger than himself such as Allott, Symons, Dylan Thomas and Barker, to take any definite stand. But that did not affect his deep awareness of the oncoming destruction of many precious things:

> Our freedom as free lances
> Advances towards the end;
> The Earth compels, upon it
> Sonnets and birds descend;
> And soon, my friend,
> We shall have no time for dances.

This ominous note, 'no time for dances', is one which occurs frequently in MacNeice's books, especially in *Autumn Journal* [1939]. The third section of *Autumn Journal* – in which book, by the way,

MacNeice broke away from his Gauterian purity of form – is well worth some attention if an analysis of his social attitude (though this is not the best way of approaching a poet) is to be complete.

In this section, MacNeice ventures into the social problem of work, and with a certain superior contempt, mingled with pity, contemplates the working man:

> Now the till and the typewriter call the fingers,
>   The workman gathers his tools
> For the eight-hour day, but after that the solace
>   Of films or football pools
> Or of the gossip or cuddle, the moments of self-glory
>   Or self-indulgence. . . .

This contemplation then gives rise to a more positive declaration which shows where MacNeice's true sympathies lie:

> Most are accepters, born and bred to harness,
>   And take things as they come,
> But some refusing harness and more who are refused it
>   Would pray that another and a better Kingdom come,
> Which now is sketched in the air or travestied in slogans
>   Written in chalk or tar on stucco or plaster-board
> But in time may find its body in men's bodies,
>   Its law and order in their heart's accord,
> Where skill will no longer languish nor energy be trammelled
>   To competition and graft. . . .

But it is characteristic of MacNeice – who thereby reveals a delicate sensitiveness under his occasionally devil-may-care exterior – that as soon as he approaches something positive he recoils. He suddenly suspects that he, also, has 'the slave-owners's mind', that he also wants 'the skimmings of the cream', and replies that habit has largely made him so:

>   for habit makes me
>   Think victory for one implies another's defeat,
> That freedom means the power to order, and that in order
>   To preserve the values dear to the élite
> The élite must remain a few.

This is the common objection of the intellectual and the refined to problems of universal education and universal equality and justice, but MacNeice finally refuses this attitude, though not so definitely that he can avoid concluding with no more than a hope that he will have courage to pursue his instinctive belief in the equalities of man:

> but the worst of all
> Deceits is to murmur 'Lord, I am not worthy',
> And, lying easy, turn your face to the wall.
> But may I cure that habit, look up and outwards,
> And may my feet follow my wider glance,
> First no doubt to stumble, then to walk with the others,
> And in the end – with time and luck – to dance.

It is, then, his intellectual honesty which has kept this poet apart from the impetuous stream of Left poets.

But this hesitation to adopt any preconceived ideology does not rob MacNeice of one of his greatest charms, his outspokenness on current affairs, though it gives an unusual colour to his interpretation of them. A good instance of this is his treatment of the Munich affair in 1938 in his *Autumn Journal*. Already, like George Barker, he foreshadowed the abdication of some of his group from the present war. He saw the Munich crisis, with no surprise, as something for which we had long been waiting and working:

> And at this hour of the day it is no good saying
>   'Take away this cup';
> Having helped to fill it ourselves, it is only logic
>   That now we should drink it up.

But he goes much farther than this. The irony of this entire section of the poem is subtle, cutting many ways: against the statesmen responsible, against the people, and against himself also, for many of the reactions he satirises appear to be not far from his own:

> And we who have been brought up to think 'Gallant Belgium'
>   As so much blague
> Are now preparing again to essay good through evil
>   For the sake of Prague.

And after the Munich agreement between Hitler and Chamberlain:

> The crisis is put off and things look better
> And we feel negotiation is not in vain –
>   Save my skin and damn my conscience. . . .
>
> . . . And stocks go up and wrecks
> Are salved and politicians' reputations
>   Go up like Jack on the Beanstalk; only the Czechs
>   Go down without fighting.

The disgust in this ironic 'we', and the ambiguous last line are fairly balanced by the unmistakable relief which penetrates the passage.

But it looks very odd in face of his previous sneering comparison of
Czecho-Slovakia with 'Gallant Belgium'. . . .

There is no need to pursue this enquiry farther, having once
ascertained that the 'common sense' poet, in such an age as ours, has
a very thin time when compared with the Augustans, who lived in a
world of more ordered ideas, more calculable politics, and who,
because of the stable background to which they could refer, could
write with a sureness which is now no longer possible. For theirs was
the Age of Reason, and ours the Age of Unreason; and our 'common
sense' is very different from theirs.

But the sense of frustration seen in these topical passages goes deeper,
for it is almost the centre of MacNeice's work. MacNeice is as
disillusioned as an Oscar Wilde character, and perhaps the reason is
not far to seek, since he is an Irishman. England, Ireland, classical life
and literature, Christmas, almost everything is touched, in Mac-
Neice's poems, with these belated rays of the Celtic Twilight, in spite
of that equally powerful Celtic exuberance which overjoys the reader
of such poems as 'Bagpipe Music'. In that finely written 'Eclogue
from Iceland' even the inimitable Ghost grouses freely. In the
'Eclogue for Christmas' he gives full rein to his scorn for all the things
he dislikes in the modern Americanised Britain; it begins:

> The jaded calendar revolves,
> Its nuts need oil, carbon chokes the valves,
> The excess sugar of a diabetic culture
> Rotting the nerve of life and literature;
> Therefore when we bring out the old tinsel and frills
> To announce that Christ is born among the barbarous hills
> I turn to you whom a morose routine
> Saves from the mad vertigo of being what has been.

MacNeice has returned several times to this theme, the paganisation
of Christ and Christmas, both in 'The Earth Compels' and the *Autumn
Journal*, and in almost identical terms. The cheap baubles, the coveted
trifles, are symbolic of the uneducated desires, the thwarted longings
of the people.

But, on the other hand, MacNeice's conception of certain elements
of culture is equally negative. In an energetic passage on the Greek
world he admits that even there he does not feel at home:

These dead are dead,
And when I should remember the paragons of Hellas
   I think instead
Of the crooks, the adventurers, the opportunists,
The careless athletes and the healthy boys
. . .
And the trimmers at Delphi and the dummies at Sparta, and lastly
   I think of the slaves.
And how one can imagine oneself among them
   I do not know;
It was all so unimaginably different
   And all so long ago.

And elsewhere, true to his Aristotelian rationalism, he makes short work of Plato, or reaches the limits of matter-of-factness when he writes:

Not but what I am glad to have my comforts;
   Better authentic Mammon than a bogus God;
If it were not for Lit. Hum. I might be climbing
   A ladder with a hod.

This is not so far removed from the attitude of some of the younger poets who secretly cherished 'culture' but who were so angered at being consistently called 'Left Intellectuals' that they affected to despise their education: Gavin Ewart, for instance, wrote a poem about 'the scurfy, doddering Dons' of Cambridge which reflects such a state of mind.

MacNeice lacks one of Auden's stabilising qualities, his understanding and love of England, but he has written some of his finest poems about remote islands, about Iceland, the Hebrides, in whose mists and grey solitudes he feels most at home. It is evident by this, and his Irish habit of beating his nurse when he writes of his home country:

Why should I want to go back
   To you, Ireland, my Ireland?
The blots on the page are so black
That they can't be covered with shamrock.
. . .
And she gives her children neither sense nor money
Who slouch round the world with a gesture and a brogue
   And a faggot of useless memories.

– it is evident from such things that MacNeice is a fundamentally Romantic poet, struggling vainly to repress his feelings, trying to give a casual air to his most sincere opinions, trying, perhaps, to write in a way which is alien to him: in a word, he is damnably Irish. . . .

The above observations are, admittedly, incomplete. So far, the best of MacNeice's talent has gone into his shorter poems, some in a metaphysical style, some descriptive poems, one or two classical themes or translations. His group of 'Eclogues' show a definite dramatic sense and a power for verse dialogue which should fit him for the verse drama. It is in the shorter poems that a fine sense of form is most clearly shown, with a clear-cut neatness and little of the facetiousness which spoils his more ambitious efforts. For obvious reasons I refrain from commenting on these shorter poems such as 'Stylite', 'Chess', 'Show', 'Circe', 'Cuckoo'. As the bulk of his work has been topical, common sense and light, I have approached him chiefly from that angle, only to find that his qualities of form and style do not yet show to their best advantage outside the short lyric. His common-sense attitude to life and poetry has led to a series of negations: there is no centre, as yet, to his work. But if he can bring the same qualities to his didactic work as he does to the lyric, or develop his aptitude for drama, he may well prove himself a poet of major importance.

SOURCE: extracts from the essay, 'Louis MacNeice: Poetry and Common Sense', in Scarfe's *Auden and After: The Liberation of Poetry, 1930–1941* (London, 1941), pp. 56–62, 67.

PART THREE

Modern Views

1. INDIVIDUAL ASSESSMENTS

Richard Hoggart   On Auden: The Preacher and
the Uncertainty of Tone   (1951)

... Auden ... is vigorous and constructive; he aims at a synthesis; he
looks towards 'the directed calm, the actual glory'. But he has never
thought social ambulance work sufficient. He is, finally, a moralist,
concerned with the problem of human guilt. Of that his own guilt, the
guilt of the comfortably reared Englishman, is only one form:

> Nor ask what doubtful act allows
> Our freedom in this English house,
> Our picnics in the sun.
>
> [Poem 2, *Look, Stranger!* (1936)]

The fact that Auden largely fails as a satirist, though not as an ironist,
may be attributed to this insistent practical sense. He is so anxious to
effect an improvement that he is disabled for the more violent kinds of
satire.

He sees society as sick; not only as sick politically, so that she
throws up such monstrous growths as Fascism, but as revealing, by
these outward symptoms, an inner ailing. He insists on the need for
both political and psychological healing; he addresses himself to sick
creatures of a sick society (he, too, is a sick creature). This special
quality of the relationship between artist and audience determines the
manner of most of his work.

Politically and economically, Auden might have said in the thirties,
we move from slump to strike to war to slump and so on;
psychologically we are assailed, with the help of scientifically applied
mass-suggestion, by the creeping secret diseases of civilisation. We
are a society of out-of-work and frustrated persons. More, we are
without belief, without organic unity; we are 'depressed in the vale of
no faith'. Our world is cold, inhibited, out of balance, all brain and no
heart:[1]

Never before was the intelligence so fertile;
The heart more stunted; the human field become
Hostile to brotherhood and feeling like a forest.

[Commentary at end of *Journey to a War* (1939)]

We should distinguish between Auden's concern for society and that of the writers usually associated with him. Like them, he is concerned at the disintegration of modern life; he lays more stress than they on the fact that that disintegration comes from an inner sickness which starts with the individual. As a result, he is on the whole less susceptible than his colleagues to vague idealised hopes.

It follows that Auden's field of action as a preacher is a two-fold one: political reform, through exposition and action – in common with some others he joined movements, attended committees and wrote an occasional 'ephemeral pamphlet'; and psychotherapy, through the spreading of the findings of psychology and the awakening of a sense of its importance. For Auden the psychological reformer, as Louis MacNeice said, almost anything will become (*a*) an example or symbol of a neurosis demanding cure, or (*b*) an example or symbol of how a neurosis produces good (since Auden believed, in the middle thirties, that all progress is due to neurotic restlessness). For Auden, the political reformer, almost anything will be (*a*) a product of the enemy, of reaction, and therefore bad; or (*b*) a relic of the obsolete past, perhaps once good but now to be deplored; or (*c*) an earnest of better things, a pioneer of the future. This view is most crudely and, in parts, most brilliantly expressed in *The Orators* [1932; 1934]. It derives partly from Blake's idea of the tension of contraries:

Without contraries is no progression. Attraction and Repulsion, Reason and Energy, Love and Hate, are Necessary to Human Existence. From these contraries spring what the religious call Good and Evil.[2] [Blake, *The Marriage of Heaven and Hell*]

It probably derives also from Prinzhorn, a psychotherapist whose work Auden much admired.[3]

If all progress is due to neurotic restlessness, the artist himself is a self-cured neurotic. His neurosis has been of the second type; it has produced good. (Readers of Freud will recognise a debt to the *New Introductory Lectures on Psycho-Analysis*.) Auden adds: 'There must always be two kinds of art, escape art, for man needs escape as he needs food and deep sleep, and parable art, that art which shall teach men to unlearn hatred and learn love.'[4] That sentence is particularly interesting: it expresses both Auden's sense of responsibility and his urge to amuse; it uses the word 'love' in a special way; it suggests one reason for Auden's attempt to write popular verse.

Auden has subscribed to Wilfred Owen's statement: 'All the poet can do today is to warn': he understands by 'warn' something very wide. His constant comment, analysis and assessment are informed by a sense of urgency, of crisis and of responsibility, by an anxiety to improve society:

> We pray the power* to take upon themselves the guilt
> Of human action, though still as ready to confess
> The imperfections of what can and must be built,
> The wish and power to act, forgive, and bless.

> ['Their Last Will and Testament', *Letters from Ireland* (1937)]

So, deliberate and widespread preaching is essential. To realise that 'kindness to ten persons' is not enough may cause us great 'metaphysical distress', but is necessary. A mind of this sort is never likely to regard art as an end in itself.

But in talking of the moral ends of art, one presupposes the existence of an audience able to appreciate the manner in which art works. Each generation has to rediscover the nature and value of the artistic process. In literature, to be still axiomatic but more precise, each generation must think back to first principles if meaning and content are to be kept fresh and significant, and language to be revivified by being brought into fresh contact with meaning. In a period when art is widely disregarded, the artist's audience will be small, since it can consist, in the main, only of those who are out of sympathy with their society's prevailing attitudes. Auden may on occasion hopefully address himself to 'writers and shopgirls'; but in the nature of the case, his shopgirl readers can be no more the average shopgirls than he can be Ethel M. Dell. And even to those who might have listened, nothing came over, in most cases. The gap hindering communication was not often bridged, and never on a large scale.

For here is a primary problem. The phenomena of modern life – the super-cinemas, the barnyard press and all the rest – are known to everyone. To the writer who is also a moralist they have a significance – as the symptoms of a profound disease – which he must strive to make clear to his audience, an audience which is itself implicated in

* Sc. for men of goodwill – R.H.

the cancerous state of affairs. But most people have lost the habit of listening, indeed the ability to listen, to their parable writers. And too often the writer's convenient technical shorthand (e.g. political and psychological phraseology) will dismay even the best-intentioned amateur. So somehow the writer, spread-eagled between the two worlds, has to evolve understandable signals, has at the least to communicate with that small proportion from all grades of society which feels in some way as he does.

This state of affairs, Auden seems to have decided in the thirties, demands all kinds of adjustments from the writer who sets out to bridge the gap; it demands, for instance, that he learn something of sociology and psychology, the better to analyse with their tools; it demands that he be allusive, trying all the time to relate his knowledge to the dilemma which he is considering; it demands many adjustments in form and technique. I leave aside for the moment the question of the high cost to the writer of thus applying his gifts.

In all this we may find reasons for the varied and surprising tones of voice used in Auden's early verse. He wants to find and speak positively to an audience (all the more because he is reacting from the disillusionment common among writers in the twenties). But he is far from clear as to whom he is addressing himself: there may be several possible audiences, though they can scarcely be addressed all at once. This dubious relationship to his audience – and the technical decisions which were taken in an attempt to resolve these doubts – largely account for the inconsistency of his attack. One need only compare the confidence in the voice of, say, Jane Austen when she discusses her characters – the assurance with which she lays down her counters of communication, knowing that a large number of meanings are shared with her readers, that there is firm ground between them – to appreciate the case of the writer in this century. So Auden often wobbles from the ironic to the portentous –

> In the hour of the Blue-Bird and the Bristol Bomber,
> His thoughts are appropriate to the years of the penny-farthing:
> He tosses at night who at noonday found no truth.

– from the pally to the patronising, from the intellectual to the over-obvious, from the consciously rhetorical to the flatly idiomatic:

> Creatures of air and darkness, from this hour
> Put and keep our friend in power.

> Let not the reckless heavenly riders
> Treat him and us as rank outsiders.

[Opening chorus, *The Dog Beneath the Skin* (1935)]

Sometimes it seems as though he cannot sustain an attitude to his audience for long; he is not sure how they are thinking: perhaps they have ceased to listen.

This kind of uncertainty can prevent a poet from singing freely about the things he finds worth praise: we affect cynicism towards those with whom our relationship is insecure; we enthuse with friends. It is true that Auden's irony is partly inspired by his perverse wit, by a wish to attack pomposity and pretension, and to debunk the grandeur raised on false assumptions, and the 'face' which hides a disinclination to examine one's own shortcomings. But he is ironic primarily because that manner is one of the most suitable, under present conditions, for verse of the kind he felt impelled to write. He learned something from Langland about the use of irony for commenting on a wise area of public and private life; he learned something from T. S. Eliot about the special uses of irony for the modern urban poet.

But irony is too oblique in its manner to satisfy Auden for long at a time; he usually has to change to a more direct approach, to find an outlet for his strong sense of purpose. Hence the assertiveness, alternately pleasing and annoying, the frequent exhortation and invocation, the talking at the reader (again, after the style of Langland), the rashes of imperatives and vocatives. Sometimes the attack may be sharp and invigorating:

> What do you think of England,
> This country of ours where no one is well?

[*The Orators*, i, i (2nd edn, 1934)]

At other times it is the voice of doom – 'The game is up for you and for the others'; 'Know then, cousin, the major cause of our collapse'; or a magisterial laying-down of the law – 'It is time for the destruction of error'; or a warning finger – 'The dancers do not listen; but they will'. At its worst it becomes drum-beating, button-holing, cheer-leading; it has something of the 'I'm saved, are you?' air, the manner of the muscular moralist and ethical bruiser, the bright gusto of the gymnast of the psyche:

Drop those priggish ways for ever, stop behaving like a stone;
Throw the bath-chairs right away and learn to leave yourselves alone.
If we really want to live, we'd better start at once to try;
If we don't, it doesn't matter, but we'd better start to die.

[Poem 22, *Poems* (1930)]

Certainly Auden does not allow himself to be carried away by such enthusiasm as swept some of his friends into dynamo-and-allotment imagery. But, though he may not hail new dawns quite as frequently as most, much of his political verse – in particular the earliest, and that contained in *New Signatures* (1932) and *New Country* (1933) – already has a strong period flavour. Both those anthologies, looked back at from across the war years, seem as dated as *The Yellow Book*,[5] and the nostalgia which the reading of them can produce is probably similar to that which the earlier collection induced in our uncles. Part of the regret is for adolescence in a period when enemies seemed conveniently well-defined, and which had, behind all its excited denunciations, a sense of 'history on the move', a sense still of progress, and that through a fairly clear-cut struggle. The strangely complete confidence in some matters, the lack of further doubts about some areas of our life, the slogan-bandying and naïve red-flag-wagging seem comparatively prosperous in these more doubtful times. That all the best-known poets of the thirties feel this today is clear from their recent verse.

Auden could make play on occasion with the familiar properties of the progressive afflatus, e.g. with dawns and poets, both exploding; with frontiers, spies, airmen, power-stations; with floods, upthrusts, and any other abstract or concrete noun for a 'forward movement'. Often, after commending the force of his analysis, one is discouraged, as Mr R. G. Leinhardt has pointed out, by an over-easy optimism.[6] After the force of:

> The old gang to be forgotten in the spring
> The hard bitch and the riding master. . . .

he drops to: 'the lolling bridegroom, beautiful there'; after the acute detail of the poem 'Sir, no man's enemy', he ends on a plea for: 'New styles of architecture, a change of heart'. Similarly, in the Prologue to *Look Stranger*, he rounds off some competent analysis with a vision of the future, driving: 'For the virgin roadsteads of our hearts an unwavering keel.'

Many factors have led Auden to the soap-box and pulpit; the sum of them may reduce, but does not entirely remove the force of the assertion that he often, and particularly in his first volume, hectors and nags, that the reader is too often given strong propaganda in verse which is competent but careless. But through it all, and driving him to these expedients, there runs a deep concern and humility. That humility may be seen – after all the various attitudes have been discarded – in the whole manner of 'Sept. 1st, 1939'. Today the drumbeating has almost disappeared; the irony remains, along with the more direct verse whose object is to examine the nature of the truths to which Auden now subscribes. And the concern will never be lost, for:

> We are created from and with the world
> To suffer with and from it day by day.

['Canzone' (1946)]

SOURCE: section 3, 'The Preacher and the Uncertainty of Tone' of ch. II in Hoggart's *Auden: An Introductory Essay* (London, 1951), pp. 34–41.

NOTES

[Reorganised and renumbered from the original – Ed.]

1. In all this there are debts by Auden to Eliot, Lawrence and others.

2. Blake is demanding here what Bernard Blackstone – *English Blake* (Cambridge, 1949) – calls 'the acceptance of the human totality'.

3. Relevant here are pp. 159 and 177 of Prinzhorn's *Psychotherapy*.

4. W. H. Auden, 'Psychology and Art', in G. Grigson (ed.), *The Arts Today* (London, 1935). [This essay is excerpted in section 1 of Part One, above – Ed.]

5. *The Yellow Book*: a quarterly which appeared in the 1890s and was predominantly associated with the work of the 'aesthetes' and 'decadents'.

6. In a review in *Scrutiny*.

Barbara Hardy   The Reticence of W. H. Auden   (1964)

I

Auden is always talking about the feeling behind poems and in poems, whether he is classifying poetic kinds, or defining sources of poetic power, or recoiling – with some sympathy – from the unrestrained outpourings of Lawrence, or responding in warm fellow-feeling to the austerity of Frost. His interest in the relation between the feeling behind the poem and the feeling in the poem is there in the disingenuous banter of 'The Truest Poetry is the Most Feigning' (*The Shield of Achilles*) and in the careful unpeeling of the reasons why a certain poem cannot be written in 'Dichtung Und Wahrheit' (*Homage to Clio*). But even his more sympathetic critics talk about him as a poet writing just from the head. G. S. Fraser, for instance, would either like to like Auden better than he does or else likes him more than he thinks he should, and the three essays in *Vision and Rhetoric* sound a 'Vorrei e non vorrei' of goodwill and disapproval. Actually, if everything Fraser says about Auden were true, then he ought to be really ferocious: Auden lacks 'personal immediacy' and 'has never been interested either in his own experience, or the experience of other people, for its own sake; he has been interested in it as an instance of a general case, of the sort of thing that happens'. It is not surprising that Fraser does not think that Auden is 'fundamentally' a religious poet, finds no evidence in the volume *For the Time Being* of 'any profound *personal* spiritual experience' and feels sure that the religious thinking is not new but to be found in 'Sir, no man's enemy'.[1]

My contention is that Auden *is* interested in personal experience and that he writes the kind of poetry which engages us, in every sense of the word, by the recognisable voice of personal feeling. It is sad to find feeling left out of Monroe Spears's list of Auden's poetic attractions: 'entertainment, instruction, intellectual excitement, and a prodigal variety of aesthetic pleasures'. I suppose feeling might be tucked away among those prodigal pleasures, though it certainly gets scant attention in the scholarly exegesis of *The Poetry of W. H. Auden*.[2] Spears cannot be entirely forgiven for this neglect on the grounds that his concern is purely conceptual. His observations on Auden's technique are fascinatingly and consistently reminiscent of the sort of thing Auden himself says we tend to say about emotionless aesthetic Ariel-poems (like Peele's beautiful 'Bathsabe's Song'): 'If one tries to explain why one likes the song, or any poem of this kind, one finds oneself talking about language, the handling of the rhythm, the pattern of vowels and consonants, the placing of caesuras, epanorthosis, etc.' I think this list should bring a faint blush to Professor Spears's cheek. Of course he knows that Auden is not an Ariel-poet, because Ariel-poets are not interested in serious matters, but he does not share Auden's proper assumption that an interest in serious matters ought to involve the heart as well as the head. Or if he does, it does not show.

It might have shown to advantage, for instance, when Spears calls 'The Prophets' a religious poem in which Auden is entertaining Christianity rather than fully believing in it, but says the 'Epilogue' (to *New Year Letter*) seems fully committed. Like Fraser, Spears talks about religious poetry without looking closely at questions of feeling and he seems to be excessively interested in finding 'evidence' for belief *in* the poetry.

More important and less misleading than this talk about entertaining beliefs without actually holding them is Auden's observation that Speech, as an artistic language, has the 'serious defect' of lacking the Indicative Mood: 'all its statements are in the subjunctive and only possibly true until verified (which is not always possible) by non-verbal evidence' ('Dichtung Und Wahrheit'). The difference between 'The Prophets' and the 'Epilogue' seems to me to lie in the decorous presence in the one and decorous absence in the other of transitive feeling and its personal voice. I would call 'The Prophets' a poem which had religious feeling (never mind about 'evidence' for profound spiritual experiences) and the 'Epilogue' a poem which discussed religion and the context for belief without needing to express feeling about God in a transitive form. The difference between 'The Prophets' and 'Sir, no man's enemy' seems to me to lie in the decorous feeling in the first and the indecorous lack of feeling in the second. 'Sir, no man's enemy' is cast coldly and arbitrarily in the form of prayer (or strikes us as cold and arbitrary) because it shows none of the feeling prayer ought to have for the God it prays to, no trust or affection or doubt or fear or anguish, and none of the feeling of wanting and sorely needing the things being prayed for. Compare it with Herbert or Donne or with the Hopkins prayer-sonnet, 'Thou art indeed just, Lord, if I contend/With thee; but, sir, so what I plead is just', to which it may perhaps owe the idea of God not being an enemy as well as the feudal-religious Sir.

But it is best compared with a poem by Auden. 'The Prophets' has the authentic-sounding voice of love, and even shows Auden using the 'natural style' he snipes at as unnatural in 'The Truest Poetry'. It was written, by the way, in 1939 and so had the advantage of getting into *Another Time*, whereas Auden's other religious poems of the Forties ('Kairos and Logos', 'In Sickness and Health' and others) may have been neglected because they never appeared in a small separate volume but got lost in the random arrangement and reprinted poems of *Collected Shorter Poems*. 'The Prophets' begins with a compressed and oblique account of those prophetic relationships of love and reverence which prepared the poet for belief, and moves into a climax of joyful and trusting recognition. God is never actually named and some readers on the way to understanding the poem are – just about – able to read it as a poem about human love:

> For now I have the answer from the face
> That never will go back into a book
> But asks for all my life, and is the Place
> Where all I touch is moved to an embrace,
> And there is no such thing as a vain look.

The Eureka-feeling at the end has a finality and faith and identification that some poets include in the range of human love, but not Auden. The point I want to emphasise is that the poem depends on expressing this feeling of relationship. The possibility that Auden never actually experienced this feeling outside the poem – he may have been trying out a fantasy about discovering God, or imitating someone else's experience or transferring the romantic 'You at last' feeling to a religious context which it could realistically inhabit, or recording a dream (Eureka-feelings can be most impressive in dreams) – seems beside the point.

II

'The Prophets' is rare in its direct and simple unbaring of feeling. At the end of 'The Truest Poetry' Auden says '. . . love, or truth in any serious sense,/Like orthodoxy, is a reticence'. In the Prologue to *The Dyer's Hand* he says ' "Orthodoxy", said a real Alice of a bishop, "is reticence." ' (I do not know the reference.) 'The Prophets' is a discreet and quiet poem, but many of Auden's expressions of relationship are much more reticent. The reticence takes many forms, not all of them quiet. Strident imperatives, casual sloppiness of word and phrase, exaggeratedly rigid doggerel, extravagant hyperbole, exaggerated coldness, many forms of anti-climax, all can be forms for his reticence. The anti-rhetoric of such devices often gives a serious appearance of urgency or passion or desperation or mission which has no time to concern itself overmuch with art. Prospero can deliberately try to do without Ariel. But Auden seldom, if ever, slips into purely imitative maladroit form: he will give the appearance of mechanical regularity or contemptuous speed or facile casualness or cheap wit, but when one comes to analyse (best of all, especially in the case of verse-form, to imitate) these racy reticences it soon becomes apparent that much art has gone into their artlessness. A good example is 'Heavy Date', a 'light' love poem which sounds as if it was dashed off spontaneously like the random thinking which is its ostensible subject but which is metrically most carefully regularised, like the subject-matter which takes us to a skilfully contrived conclusion.

It would of course be quite wrong to suggest that all Auden's styles are styles for reticence. Almost every volume from 1930 onwards has one poem or more written in a grand or, let us say, 'ceremonious' style, using dignified vocabulary, formal syntax, and solemn intricate harmonies. There are the sober meditations of '1929', the sonorous villanelles of 'Kairos and Logos' and the very disturbing 'Memorial for the City' with its moving and dignified conclusion in plain speech: 'I was the missing entry in Don Giovanni's list: for which he could never account'. Auden has used 'the wry, the sotto-voce,/Ironic and monochrome' throughout his writing, but never as an exclusive style. His reticence often takes an oblique or teasing form for feeling, but there are many poems, like these, which use a simply appropriate form, a conventional decorum.

III

But there is one style of reticence which runs through all his work, beginning in the 1928 volume.[3] This whole volume (*pace* Monroe Spears, who says that its 'most obvious characteristic is the detached, clinical, objective attitude, with modern and scientific imagery') has the appearance of being deeply rooted – perhaps too deeply rooted – in personal experience. (The one obvious exception is a poem in the manner of Hardy, No. XII. 'The four sat on in the bare room'.) Some of the most obscure poems, such as No. 1, which appears to be a seven-part poem about a love-affair, traced through moments of crisis, only some of which seem to rise into moving definition, are probably obscure because half-embedded in private experience, meaningful to a particular reader who could read between the lines, localise the images, and recognise the feeling. But this is just a guess, made not in the interests of speculation but because Auden's successful reticence seems to be the minimal public emergence of this kind of private experience. Auden has often been accused of vagueness, but it might be more appropriate to call it over-specification. Nothing is so vague in its effect as the highly particularised reference which we do not happen to understand, and it is this, rather than emotional swimminess, which is characteristic of Auden's very early verse. But when he does achieve the minimal lucidity there is a very compelling effect of being let in on a real feeling which we can feel without knowing its history and causality. This is, I suggest, the effect of Poem xi, probably the most familiar of the 1928 Poems because reprinted in *Collected Shorter Poems* as 'The Love Letter' and in the Penguin Selection as 'The Letter'. This is the unrevised version:

> From the very first coming down
> Into a new valley with a frown
> Because of the sun and a lost way
> You certainly remain. Today
> I, crouching behind a sheep-pen, heard
> Travel across a sudden bird,
> Cry out against the storm, and found
> The year's arc a completed round
> And love's worn circuit rebegun
> Endless with no dissenting turn.
> Shall see, shall pass, as we have seen
> The swallow on the tiles, Spring's green
> Preliminary shiver, passed
> A solitary truck, the last
> Of shunting in the Autumn; but now,
> To interrupt the homely brow,
> Thought warmed to evening through and through,
> Your letter comes, speaking as you
> Speaking of much but not to come.
> Nor speech is close, nor fingers numb
> If love not seldom has received
> An unjust answer, was deceived;
> I, decent with the seasons, move
> Different or with a different love,

Nor question overmuch the nod,
The stone smile of this country god,
That never was more reticent,
Always afraid to say more than it meant.

It seems to be a poem about two letters, the one received and the reply, which is the poem itself. At least the poem is transitive, addressed to You. It begins with a brief and understated comment on the beginning and the duration of the love: 'You certainly remain' expresses its feeling very quietly. There are two times in the poem: the ignorant past when he was alone in the storm, remembering and still believing in a future: 'love's worn circuit rebegun / Endless with no dissenting turn', and the time after he got the letter, which casts its shadow on the reported past so that 'frown', 'lost way', 'worn circuit', and 'shiver' all belong to both times and can be read as both innocently appropriate to the past and ominously appropriate to the future. The exposure, storm, crying out of the bird, and the solitude are all sources of compression, and say in a laconic enactment what the situation was and is. The letter which breaks the news is also described laconically, 'Speaking of much but not to come'. The feeling of love, hope, and the loss of hope are not enlarged on. Feeling is not described at all, but implied by the reticent form and language, which decorously convey the pressure of the feeling which is controlled in decent silence. The knotted negatives of 'Nor speech is close', the impersonal form of 'If love not seldom has received', the compression of the movement to 'was deceived', the ellipsis and shift of tense which seems to blurt out this particular instance, all contribute to the reticence. The double time and its emotional duplicity, the clipped style, and the refusal to express direct feeling, all quietly weigh feeling and evaluate as they define. Thus the poem is not merely one which sets up a tension between austere form and strong unexpressed feeling, but is, or becomes, a poem about reticence. 'I, decent with the seasons' uses decency in the sense of propriety, passing on properly as the seasons pass on (they are all stated or implied in the poem) and also suggests the decency of taking things quietly, without fuss, with a stiff upper lip. And the final significant appearance of the landscape is to create a climactic image of reticence: the reticence which withholds the explanation one may desperately ask of gods and nature, the reticence which is at least not deceitful – someone may have said more than they meant in the submerged history of this love and the reticence which is that of the poem itself, which is perhaps not about breaking your heart in decent silence but about not breaking it. The loss is endurable, and an extravagant grief would be out of place and perhaps dishonest. The austerity and compression of the poem is a perfect form for the austerity and restraint which it discusses, and the form is dynamic, taking us on in time, taking us through a moving process of feeling. We may at one stage think that the reticence means stoicism, but at the end it seems to mean honesty. The lack of history and character and causality throws the full weight upon the feeling, which is neither cold nor vague, though it is just possible to see that its austerity might be misread as detachment without passion and that its vagueness about the unnecessary elements might be found obscure by readers who wanted fuller and more obviously exciting 'treatment'.

IV

This minimal anecdote which suppresses almost everything but feeling, which has a reticence of concentrated passion, and which asserts the privacy of the relationship as an essential part of love for individuals and God, seems to me to be Auden's most original and characteristic achievement as a love poet. It is of course not his only manner in love-poetry and is clearly less popular than the fuller anecdote in 'Lay your sleeping head, my love', much anthologised and in my view much less interesting. It dramatises fairly fully a situation and a locale (time, place, position), has characters with some characteristics, and gives us a compressed but fairly elaborate reflection on love in general, its likeness and unlikeness to religious ecstasy, its powers and limitations, its social vulnerability. It attempts to place the future of the relationship and the beloved both realistically and affectionately. It has the have-your-cake-and-eat-it sophistication of Byron (and is indeed rather like the description of Juan asleep in Haidée's arms. 'There lies the thing we love with all its errors'), but its interest seems to me to be chiefly the interest of a story rather than a dynamic evaluation or definition of feeling of the kind to be found in 'The Letter'. The two first published volumes, *Poems* (1930) and *Look, Stranger!*, have their share of austere and reticent love poems. In 'Upon this line between adventure' and 'To lie on the back, the knees flexed' compression and suppression are used for more erotic subjects, where the concentration of feeling and the privacy have their special effects of tension and intimacy. 'The chimneys are smoking' from *Look, Stranger!* strikes me as a fine poem where social concern is subordinated to the emotional discussion, acting as a metaphor in the definition of personal relationship. It opaquely defines a very private feeling whose very privacy is brought out into the open and discussed:

> Then lightly, my darling, leave me and slip away
> Playful, betraying him nothing, allaying suspicion:
> His eye is on all these people about us, leading
> Their quiet horrified lives. . . .

Many of these poems of the thirties have a personal subject which is often overlooked in their political context, just as the feeling in some of the religious poetry is unnoticed – at least by the critics – perhaps because of the sheer conceptual difficulty and interest. At times, of course, the personal emotion is subordinated to the political subject, as in '1929'. At times the two are held in dramatic tension, as in 'A Summer Night, 1933', where the personal relationship stands as representative of a community, stands for the sheltered, expensive, cultivated, pleasurable, furtive, insecure, loving privileges of a certain class, which must go but which can perhaps bequeath at least the powers of love. The tone is modulated to give the necessary movement to a large subject. It includes the tenderly light and allusive echoes of 'Au près de ma blonde' and the death-wish:

> Though we would gladly give
> The Oxford colleges, Big Ben,
> And all the birds in Wicken Fen,
> It has no wish to live.

And the private loving knowingness of

> And when the birds and rising sun
> Waken me, I shall speak with one
> Who has not gone away.

And the generalisation of Auden at its very best, in a simile which has as much feeling in the invented second term as in the situation it describes:

> As through a child's rash happy cries
> The drowned voice of his parents rise
> In unlamenting song.

One of my reasons for drawing attention to Auden's love poetry is that it indicates the importance of the personal voice elsewhere, in the religious and political verse, which both depend on the transitive expression of love as Eros and Agape mutate. But the personal voice addressed to the special reader can come in almost gratuitously, to give not an appropriate feeling to a poem about God or society but an unexpected influx of personal feeling in a fairly impersonal poem. In *Nones*, for instance, we find several instances of the way personal feeling can flood a poem with immediacy and warmth and can give the impression that it is steadily available. In 'In Praise of Limestone' there is a point towards the end – at the beginning of the last stanza – when into a meditative line is suddenly inserted 'My Dear', though with as yet no change in the tone or feeling. It is a tiny pre-echo, a faint heralding of the most moving turn to address a particular person at the very end of the poem:

> . . . Dear, I know nothing of
> Either, but when I try to imagine a faultless love
> Or the life to come, what I hear is the murmur
> Of underground streams, what I see is a limestone landscape.

It comes as the kind of surprise which, once taken in, seems natural and inevitable. The poem has no transitive appearance until the first 'my dear', and even then it is only preparatory. This is a reticence, too, transforming the poem's form and giving the impression of a love which is in the background not because removed from other considerations but because it can always move easily into the forefront of any subject, being the most important feeling, the most important person. The poem alludes with the ease of confident (but not over-confident) love to this particular reader, but its warmth extends also to the 'life to come' and the limestone landscape. There is a beautiful decorum in the way the subject of love brings in the loving tone, especially since the question of imagining faultless love has come up, and the human lover might require to be confronted and not excluded. But the personal feeling also acts as a medium for the feeling for God and nature . . . . Auden's withholding of the personal tone until the end permits him to make a climax beyond the capacity of the earlier intransitive meditation. . . .

SOURCE: extract from 'The Reticence of W. H. Auden', *The Review*, 11–12 (1964), pp. 54–62; reprinted in Professor Hardy's *The Advantage of Lyric: Essays on Feeling in Poetry* (London, 1977), pp. 84–92.

NOTES

1. [Ed.] G. S. Fraser, *Vision and Rhetoric* (London, 1957). His essay on MacNeice from the same book is included in this Casebook.

'Sir, no man's enemy' was not included by Auden in his *Collected Shorter Poems* (1966) but is contained in such anthologies as R. Skelton's *Poetry of the Thirties* (1964). It may also be found, along with other poems not included in later editions of Auden's poetry, in E. Mendelson (ed.), *The English Auden: Poems, Essays and Dramatic Writings* (London, 1977). In this collection 'Sir, no man's enemy' is Poem XXIII on p. 36.

2. [Ed.] Monroe K. Spears, *The Disenchanted Island: The Poetry of W. H. Auden* (London, 1963).

3. [Ed.] Auden's first volume, *Poems*, was privately published by Stephen Spender in 1928. Those poems in that volume which remained unpublished during Auden's lifetime have been included in Mendelson's collection, *The English Auden*, op. cit., Appendix IV, pp. 436–42. Mendelson also reprints those poems in the 1928 volume which Auden included in the successor-volume, *Poems* (1930) but did not reproduce thereafter.

Justin Replogle On Auden: The Pattern of Personae (1969)

. . . Auden's early poetry can be very confusing for even the most skilful readers. Even internally consistent poems can be puzzling enough, with their variety of speakers, allegorical landscapes and private allusions. When inconsistent, they almost defy description. But since much of the complexity, and nearly all the inconsistency, is caused by the hostility of what I have called Poet and Antipoet, these terms now make it possible to describe more fully . . . the enormously complicated situation in these early poems. Schematic description will best simplify the complexities. If individual poems, though internally coherent, can contradict each other, let us consider the numerous possibilities for confusion in Auden's early work. His temperament is split into two forces or personae, Poet and Antipoet, each with its own style, beliefs, inclinations, predispositions and habits. Within the allegorical landscape of these early poems are three classes of people who speak: the sick, the well, and the neutral observers. How may these five elements be combined?

First, a sick speaker may appropriately use:
1. the Poet's voice
    - straightforwardly to confess and analyse his own sickness;
    - pompously to indicate indirectly his sick foolishness.
2. the Antipoet's voice
    - to reveal his own clownish sickness or banality.
3. awkward and contradictory combinations of the Poet's and the Antipoet's voices
    - to reveal his own confused sickness.

Second, a healthy speaker may appropriately use
1. the Poet's voice
    - to analyse or denounce sickness and suggest a cure (but he must avoid the dangers of pomp and pretentiousness).
2. the Antipoet's voice
    - to denounce and abuse the sick and show by his manner the healthy vigor of life (but he must avoid appearing foolish or banal himself, and he must avoid making what he attacks appear trivial by his comedy – or seem a complete spoof).
3. awkward or contradictory combinations of the Poet's and Antipoet's voice
    - never (except to mock the Poet by mimicry. In this case the Poet must be clearly identified as one of the sick. If the Poet speaks as one of the healthy, accurately analysing sickness, and is then mocked or parodied, the poem collapses).

Third, a neutral speaker may appropriately use
1. the Poet's voice
    - to analyse, describe conditions, and suggest cures (but he must avoid the danger of pretentiousness and unintentional self-parody).
2. the Antipoet's voice
    - only at its mildest (though he may be permitted enough wit and verbal dexterity to indicate his intelligence and rhetorical skill).
3. awkward combinations of the voices
    - never (except when mimicking the frivolous or banal sick, and even this is dangerous).

Charts and lists may be unattractive substitutes for exposition, but I believe this one provides an outline of the major complexities of personae in Auden's poetry from about 1928 to about 1935, though it comes nowhere near exhausting all of them. Given his own temperamental fluctuations and this involuted web of subtleties in his personae, it is hardly surprising that time after time Auden sails along the edge of disaster and often falls over. I do not imply, of course, that he purposely, or even consciously, fashioned the tangle of dramatic alternatives outlined above. Many things (some perhaps inadvertent) contributed to its growth: his almost compulsive habit of allegorising nearly everything he touched, from nouns to entire volumes; his continual use of speakers separate from himself; his uncertainty about the role of poetry itself. All these and other temperamental inclinations and gifts produced this almost fantastically complex poetic situation, filled with the possibility of suddenly dropping into an abyss of self-contradiction.

Poems examined so far, though they may contradict one another, have been internally consistent. Many others are not. I will not attempt to examine a failure for each type on my list, but the whole subject deserves some detailed attention. Poems that explode and collapse under pressure from the incompatible parts of Auden's temperament are among the most striking features of his early work and the seed ground for later growth.

Inconsistent and contradictory poems are appropriate if their speaker is sick, and therefore purposely made to look awkward and incoherent. In all other cases such poems are simply flawed. The *author* is disorganised and contradictory. Distinguishing between the two is not always easy. The most notoriously unclear case is the ode that begins 'Though aware of our rank and alert to obey orders. . . .' Joseph Warren Beach, a perceptive reader, spent eight pages of his book mulling over the puzzle of this poem before he tentatively advanced a conclusion.[1] He decided reluctantly (but rightly I think) that the speaker is not Auden, but one of the sick. Auden is outside the monologue, more knowing than the speaker, healthier, showing some contempt for him. Yet Beach's problem – and everyone's – is that Auden's partisanship is too faint (indicated almost entirely by private myth details described in Chapter One). Since the speaker alternates awkwardly between the Poet's solemnity and the Antipoet's foolishness, no one who assumed Auden to be the speaker could decide for certain whether the speech or the mockery of it is the message. But if we assume the speaker to be sick, then the poem's contradictions are appropriate. This will explain why the speaker's pompous solemnity contrasts ludicrously with his clownish slips:

> Your childish moments of awareness were all of our world,
> . . .
> At night your mother taught you to pray for our Daddy.
> . . .
>
> [*Collected Poetry* (1945), p. 137]
>
> To stand with the wine-dark conquerors in the roped-off pews,
>   Shout ourselves hoarse:
> 'They ran like hares; we have broken them up like firewood.'
> . . .
>
> [*CP*, p. 138]

Interpreted this way the poem shows Auden standing outside the poem laughing at the speaker's performance. But this is certainly not clear. Even a careful reader could think Auden agrees with the speaker and thereby reverse the poem's message. Apparently we are expected to discover, without external comment, that the speaker is unreliable, that the truth (or most of it) is the opposite of what he says. Yet his unreliability is so faint as to be scarcely discernible. Maybe Auden simply miscalculated (which is easy enough to do in such a case). Or he may have written the poem for his friends, for whom faint clues were enough. Or he himself may have wavered, unable to decide how foolish the speaker was.

If we decide that 'Though aware of our rank and alert to obey orders . . .' is a consistent poem whose consistency fails to be clear, what are we to think of poems where the speaker's reliability is never established, even by ultrasubtle clues? 'Not, father, further do prolong / Our necessary defeat. . . .' is an interesting case of this. The poem seems to contain a sick speaker solemnly requesting the quick destruction of his illness. But how is the poet related to this speaker? If the poet stands apart (neutral or one of the healthy) all flaws in the poetry – bad lines, pompous diction, exaggerated hysteria, farcical behavior – reflect appropriately on the sick speaker. But if the poet approves of the speaker, or if speaker and poet are identical, all such lapses are either breaches of decorum or failure of craft. I think this particular poem begins with Auden speaking as Poet, soberly petitioning for health. But in trying to maneuver his grave formal speech through some extremely involuted Anglo-Saxon syntax he stumbles into unintentional comedy:

>   These nissen huts if hiding could
>   Your eye inseeing from
>   Firm fenders were.
>   . . .

[*The Orators* (1932, 1934), p. 110]

With some minute changes indicating that this comedy was intentional, Auden could, without changing a word of the quoted lines, make this utterance appropriate. The speaker could be made into one of the comic sick, or into a healthy Antipoet parodying the pompus Poet. But without such indications the speaker's flaws are the author's flaws. Auden makes a mistake. The poem flounders. His Poet steps across the border between high dignity and comic pomposity, and decorum is broken.

'Consider this and in our time . . .' is a slightly clearer case. The speaker here is the Poet, neither sick nor healthy, but a neutral observer. Exalted and omniscient, he looks down on a sick culture. His language, extremely formal and rigorously abstract, borders on the pedantic. Describing a hotel dining room, he uses an idiom even Cowper might have blushed at. Through the window he sees

>   . . . insufficient units
>   . . .
>   . . . constellated at reserved tables
>   Supplied with feelings by an efficient band

[*CP*, p. 27]

that is, while people eat, musicians play. Elsewhere the diction, though still stiffly formidable, may be accepted as proper for this very learned and correct Poet, who never calls a mountain a mountain if its proper classification is 'massif', who says that clouds 'rift', and speaks in phrases such as 'life's limiting defect' and 'derelict works'. All these the tolerant reader might swallow, forgiving the Poet for being a bit of a stuffed shirt, but noting in his favor that he is unbending enough for a few happily low-brow clichés: 'admire the view', 'leisurely conversation', 'within a stone's throw'. But what are tolerant readers to think later on, when the idiom suddenly becomes undeniably pompous on the one hand and hilariously undignified on the other?

>   And mobilize the powerful forces latent
>   In soils that make the farmer brutal
>   In the infected sinus, and the eyes of stoats

[*CP*, p. 28]

the speaker says at one point. Do what with the soils? we exclaim. *Mobilise* their *forces?* To infect what? Sinuses and stoats' eyes? Can we accept this as serious speech? Can Auden, who later made high comedy out of just such incongruous juxtapositions, have stumbled accidentally into this preposterous style? If we believe so our credulity will soon get a further buffeting. Juxtapositions that follow are even more fatal to solemnity. After plunging from lofty dignity to sinuses and stoats' eyes, the speaker next frightens the sick with the bogey of a destructive 'rumour . . . horrifying in its capacity to disgust', a rumor likely to become for them 'A polar peril, a prodigious alarm'. In an earlier version this mock-heroic utterance was then followed by a stanza that continually demolished the stuffy speaker's decorum. And as his Poetic mask fell away, to our great surprise we discovered underneath something of a gleeful, naughty urchin issuing slangy low-brow threats ('The game is up for you'; 'It is later than you think'). He also showed a leering fascination for queer neurotic symptoms, especially sexual, and was not above making everything comic by purposely linking together the most unlikely incongruities. For instance, among his list of doomed neurotics were those 'Who are born nurses; who live in shorts / Sleeping with people and playing fives' [*Poems* (1930), p. 88]. The speaker, who began as a Poet, turned into an Antipoet. Can Auden possibly have fallen unintentionally into such comic circumstances? I think the answer is yes – that is, at *first* the comedy was unintentional. Once it began, Auden purposely continued it. The first lapses seem clearly unplanned. And even at the end the poem struggles bravely to maintain some vestige of its formal idiom and Poetic persona, as though retention of both were part of the original plan. The disaster occurs, I think, because though Auden as Poet is forced to be solemn, elevated, and seriously concerned with large weighty matters such as the evolution of cultural collapse, he wears this mask somewhat awkwardly. While he is fully behind it when the poem opens, it is somewhat askew. The manner is not native to him and he gets it just slightly wrong. The formality is misplaced in an epithet or two, the tone is faintly too high, gravity rises into pomposity, pedantry replaces correctness, colloquial idiom slips in to mar the finish. The contrast between the too-high and the mundane inadvertently threatens to create the very incongruities at the heart of the mock-heroic. But when the Poetic speaker steps accidentally across the line separating the formal from the comically pompous, Auden begins to revel in the new possibilities. His

exuberant Antipoetic tendencies, longing to burlesque pretentious-
ness, take over. Whenever his own speech releases a great deal of
verbal energy, Auden's Poet is in danger. High spirits begin to creep
in, and Auden may begin to play with the medium. 'Watch this', he
says, in effect, as he makes the Poetic speaker perform an even more
daring locution. Another step and all will be burlesque. In the early
poetry Auden often takes that step, by mistake or by yielding to
temptation. Then the Poet, with his dull gray decorum, disappears.
The Antipoet takes command. The stage is filled with clowning,
parody, self-mockery, and verbal play of all sorts, while the Poet's
message gets reversed. . . .

Auden's failure to unify personae and maintain decorum does not
mean that each inconsistent creation is completely bad, or that his
consistent works are always good. Many readers will surely prefer
inconsistent Antipoetic poems to consistent ones featuring an overly
pompous Poet. Occasionally we may rejoice when the Poetic
speeches, growing tiresomely solemn, are shattered by the Antipoet
leaping on stage to clown around. Better a flaw in decorum than a
stuffed shirt Poet. In any case flaws are not fatal to art. Even the worst
of Auden's early work usually exhibits great verbal energy, and verbal
energy is the *sine qua non* of poetry. He may sometimes lose control, but
at least there is an energy that needs controlling, and its mere
presence is the most promising omen in the work of a beginning poet.
Nevertheless Auden's incompatible swoops from Poet to Antipoet
raise important doubts about his early philosophical themes. Much
can be made of Auden the penetrating social analyst, who shows a
profound understanding of both the sick and the healthy, and who
surveys all from an omniscient hawk's-view perspective. But most
generalisations made about this 'Auden' are not quite right. The early
Auden scarcely fits the image of that disapproving, sober cultural
analyst built up by journalists and public. One part of his temperament seemed profoundly content with life as he found it, and when he
spoke as a grave cultural diagnostician and activist leader, he
sometimes had to invent personae whose earnest disapprovals were so
alien to some of his own inclinations that he could scarcely keep from
burlesquing them. Auden the social critic is only part of the total
Auden. There is also an Auden who mocks social criticism. The
messages in the early poetry are not merely inconsistent, then, but
sometimes the complete reverse of each other. And these contradic-

tions, since they clearly do not all occur accidentally, show something else about the early Auden. He often cared more about the liveliness of the total verbal performance than about philosophy, ideas, social themes, or his role of cultural critic. (In the long run, of course, this must be true for any good poet. Auden ruined some early poems by wrecking his speakers in order to play with their speech. But the skills learned from this made him a much greater poet later on.) His contradictions also raise interesting questions about the status of all his early themes. Subtle parody never deviates far from a straight-forward treatment of the thing parodied. Without changing a single word, in fact, a sober speech can be parodied merely by placing it in a spoofing atmosphere. Such an atmosphere can be created by the simple knowledge that a given writer is a parodist, a leg-puller, a wit. When we know this we always have to look twice at everything he says, to make sure the clever jokester is not laughing up his sleeve while we earnestly mistake his parody for its solemn opposite. Auden's open parody of his own themes creates this atmosphere of doubt, and the careful reader will proceed cautiously. How seriously did Auden and his friends take some of those completely solemn poems, the ones with decorum intact, where the Poet dominates throughout? Since some poems show that Auden and his friends occasionally thought of the Poet's high-serious persona as a joke, is it not possible that in some others where the tone was diligently sober, the diagnosis oracular, the Poet's authority awesome, that these made the spoof even more hilarious? How often was Auden privately laughing at his public solemnly pondering those enigmatic utterances that apparently embodied grave profundities. Sometimes, surely, he pulled the audience's innocent leg. But whatever the prevalence of this (and it is interesting to notice that self-parody appears especially in those works most openly directed to the attention of Isherwood, Upward and Warner), the Antipoet's appearance, briefly or in full performance, throughout the early years, shows Auden's wavering inability to take seriously either his Poet's messages or style. . . .

[Replogle proceeds to substantiate his case further (pp. 114ff.) by analysing the changes Auden made to titles of his poems at different stages in his career. He notes that in a large number of cases titles are retrospective 'comments made by the Antipoet on rereading the old utterances of the Poet'. Good examples are Poem III ('Since you are going to begin to-day') from *Poems* (1930), which in *Collected Shorter*

Poems (1966) is titled 'Venus Will Now Say a Few Words'; and Poem I ('Will you turn a deaf ear') from *Poems* (1930), which in *CSP* (1968) is titled 'The Questioner Who Sits So Sly'. Poem II 'Doom is dark and deeper than any sea-dingle', which becomes 'Something is Bound to Happen' in *Collected Poems, 1930–1944* (1945), is changed again, to 'The Wanderer', in *CSP* (1966) – Ed.]

SOURCE: extracts from ch. 2, 'The Pattern of Personae', in Replogle's *Auden's Poetry* (Seattle, 1969; London, 1970), pp. 130–9, 112–14.

NOTE

1. J. Warren Beach, *The Making of the Auden Canon* (Minneapolis, 1957), pp. 84–92.

Graham Hough   MacNeice and Auden
(1967)

A new collected Auden and the final collected MacNeice: no one of my age and condition can pretend to write of these with complete detachment.[1] Any English bourgeois intellectual, born in the first decade of this century, moderately well read, moderately travelled, moderately academic and not too happy about it – anyone like this, even without their talent, has shared too much of their experience ever to see their poetry from the outside. That is why so much that has been written about them is of the 'I knew him well, we were at school together' kind. Well, I didn't and we weren't; and the fragmentary glimpses and overlappings are distracting blurs on the screen. So one must try to look at the poetry as poetry, to speak only of styles and attitudes revealed by the poetry, forgetting persons and biographies, affections and dissents, as though one were much older, or much younger, or had come from another country.

What one cannot forget is the time; and a very bad time it was. Auden and MacNeice had much in common, and the chief thing they had in common was their age. So much in their work seems an almost automatic reaction to a history in which we all share. Not quite unavoidable; there are poets who stand outside it, or respond in a way that was unique and wholly different. For Auden and MacNeice the groove worn by English social history since 1930, shallow though it may look, has been too compelling. Both were formed irrevocably by the thirties. The tone of their writing is the tone of the day, a tone shared by others who were not poets. It is a tone which claims complicity with other BBC feature writers, other cultural functionaries, other Anglo-American dons. This may be a bad thing – it may be a good thing; it was at least a little world to speak from, a group to address. But it brings them very close to an essentially unpoetical, even anti-poetical, culture: a culture from which it is hard to imagine that the best kind of poetry could ever spring. It was a culture of scepticism, or attenuated faith; not *croyant*, but not quite infidel either; not quite left but not quite right, and certainly not comfortable in the middle; shocked, distressed, in a way engaged by the wars and revolutions; but not really in any of them; a culture of non-participants. This is said without malice, and as a simple matter of fact. Unlike most of Europe we were not occupied, only bombed; we did not have a revolution, only an Education Act; and in the background there was always that false Shangri-la, the United States.

The other thing they had in common was their class, and their odd relation to it. O hellish public schools, O awful Oxford, O the complacencies of inherited culture, too weak to nourish its participants, too strong to leave them unmarked. There was no country like England in the thirties, where so many intellectuals were apologising for their own youth, and then apologising for the apologies by relapsing into little in-group jokes. It is a kind of uneasy honesty: I am what I am, but I'm not very proud of it; my friends stand for something decent, even if it's not much; the great world has turned so bestial that it is better to fall back on the little values that one shares with old companions rather than to rely on the great ones that have been so vilely corrupted. The moral law within can be trusted, slightly moth-eaten as it is; as for the starry heaven above, no one can claim much kinship with that. For both these poets are more concerned with telling the truth than with poetry; telling the truth, I mean, on some simple correspondence theory of truth; not claiming to feel more than the historical situation warrants, or differently from what one actually feels at the given moment, never writing cheques for more than there is in the bank. This is a very unpoetical state of mind. Greater poets expect the cheque to be honoured by the poem, not by their feeling or the historical situation. A poem, if it achieves its own rightness and completeness, is a valid draft of the whole world's stock of nobility and splendour, whatever the meanness of the actual situation, or the historical impotence of the author. Auden and MacNeice are rarely willing to make this claim; and it is this more than any change of rhetoric or period style that puts them in a different sphere from Yeats.

So much for what their culture gave them: the more important question is what they made of it. Here the answers begin to diverge: for Auden has done far more with this unpromising situation, has disposed his material in a far more masterful fashion.

McNeice's collected volume is really a sad one. It can hardly fail to command liking and sympathy, but it is pervaded by a conscious sense of fulfilment unachieved. The great imagists Eliot and Pound had made it their aim to purify the dialect of the tribe; the later generation to which Auden and MacNeice belonged tried rather to take it over bodily. Slick talk, triviality, the argot of a group, are used with irony; often the irony is effective; sometimes it manages to suggest by their very absence the values that it cannot state. But this is the weapon of the writer at bay, not of the writer in full possession of his powers. *Méfiez-vous de l'ironie surtout en moments d'impuissance.* Moments of impotence are common enough nowadays, and language chosen with irony in view tends to a self-defeating automatism. The poet's own voice, if he has one, is taken over by the voice he intends to parody. This happens often with Auden, and far too often with MacNeice. The tone of the time suits Auden well enough – he was able both to use it and to transcend it; but it is hard to feel that MacNeice was at ease with the language that was available. He was a poet who could have added his individual note to an established tradition – the Caroline lyric or the Augustan couplet. But in his years there was nothing of assurance and dignity to attach himself to, and he was all at sea.

So often he settles for the second-best. Poetry is made with words, and all his words will allow him is a rather shallow goodfellowship; vague conviviality; moderate attachments and quirky velleities; bodings of doom that go off with a damply emphatic fizzle; and all these undercut and criticised by the style, as though even while the words were forming themselves their inadequacy was realised – inadequacy to something better that is really there but never manages to find its way out. The shorter poems often begin with a lyrical tenderness that is immediately checked by the fashionable jolts and mumbles. The long poems often degenerate into a low-toned obsessive muttering, like that of a man talking dully to himself after a hard day at the office and a couple of drinks. The fact is MacNeice was neither a man of ideas nor a creator of form. Faced in the war years with the collapse of a world, he responds with sincerity and feeling but also, it must be said, with banality. And a slight reflection, a real but small impression, will be cobbled up into a verse so ramshackle, so rough-and-ready, that one has to read it several times to make sure that there is not some unsuspected principle of organisation. Alas, as a rule, there is not. Too straight-forward, too unassuming, to raid the past in the wholesale manner of Eliot and Pound, he lacks a model: or the models that really suit him, the classical ones on which his taste was formed, did not often suit what had to be said.

One is unhappy to say this; but it seems to be so, for most of these five hundred pages. Indeed he almost says it himself. Luckily this is not all. A selection, not very large, could be made (I hope it will) of achieved and beautiful poems which reveal with great clarity the talent that misdirected itself or was buried in miscellaneous flotsam and irrelevant circumstance. It would not, I think, show MacNeice in the light in which he is usually thought of; the more genial pieces with their real appreciation of the pleasures and variety of the world would not be much represented. They are often undistinguished in phrasing and rhythm. When he achieves a finer control it is almost always in darker moods. 'An Eclogue for Christmas' (1933) is not only one of the best-known but also one of the best of his early poems. The dialogue form suited him; no need to reconcile contradictions intellectually, the poet can be equally present in both speakers; on the one hand the modernist worldling:

> I who was Harlequin in the childhood of the century
> Posed by Picasso beside an endless opaque sea;

On the other hand the grumpy acceptor of something obstinate, earthy, and unchanging:

> It is better to die in situ as I shall, one place is as bad as another
> Go back where your instincts call.

This grasps a moment in the modern English consciousness, the same moment as was grasped by Cyril Connolly in *The Unquiet Grave*. Where we go next nobody knows, for we are still in it. . . .

. . . Much later, in fact in the year before his death, he wrote a sequence of five poems, *Memorandum to Horace*, which applies the same note to his own condition, and in which he greets a kindred spirit across the centuries. He plays delicately between the Horatian reminiscences and the modern instances; and the formal satisfaction of the achievement offers a consolation, if no hope. Indeed, he did not see much to hope for, and a sad late poem, 'Goodbye to London', tells us why −

> Then came the head-shrinking war, the city
> Closed in too, the people were fewer
> But closer too, we were back in the womb.
> Nevertheless let the petals fall
> Fast from the flower of cities all.
>
> From which reborn into anticlimax
> We endured much litter and apathy hoping
> The phoenix would rise, for so they had promised.
> Nevertheless let the petals fall
> Fast from the flower of cities all.
>
> And nobody rose, only some meaningless
> Buildings and the people once more were strangers
> At home with no one, sibling or friend.
> Which is why now the petals fall
> Fast from the flower of cities all.

If times had been different, MacNeice might have been a sort of English Horace with the same alternation between the stoic and the epicurean. But the years between 1925, the date of his first volume, and 1963, the date of his last, were not much of a time for myrtles and roses, and it is an unindulgent realism that is his most authentic note.

The new Auden volume extends to 1957 − to the end, that is, of *Homage to Clio*. For the most part it repeats collections already existing, with the usual omissions, alterations and reappearances. We have had so many complaints of Auden's editorial habits that I don't want to repeat them. It is maddening to get hold of a new edition and find old familiars missing, others altered and mutilated, but clearly the poet has the right to revise his own verses. I do wonder, all the same, just what is going on. Auden stoutly denies in the Preface that he has ever attempted to revise his former thoughts and feelings; and we can think, if we like, that all the changes are what some of them obviously are, made on stylistic grounds. Some poems, he says, have been thrown out because they were dishonest or bad-mannered or boring. 'Sir No Man's Enemy' has disappeared and 'September 1939' – on which of these grounds does not appear. All the same, to omit them does look like a revision of former feelings; and I do not know what is achieved beyond a useless disavowal. These poems are so well known, so often anthologised, so uniformly present in earlier editions that no obliteration now will unwrite them or delete them from the poetic canon that has been built up. One song from 'The Sea and the Mirror' is given; why not more, or none? Three stanzas are lost from the poem in memory of Yeats – the stanzas that no one forgets, about Time who worships language and pardons all things to those who write well. The section to which they belong is hopelessly mutilated without them. On the other hand, the cruel but clever poem about A. E. Housman reappears after many years' absence. And there are numerous tinkerings of a lesser significance. I can see no rhyme or reason in them; and indeed, not much for the whole edition.

But to give up bibliographical nagging: what sort of a poet does the volume as a whole reveal? Not by any means the whole of Auden; for without *The Orators*, without 'The Sea and the Mirror', without the brilliant prose passages in that work, and in *For the Time Being*, much that is most characteristic is absent. If most modern poets were represented simply by their shorter poems they would not suffer much. With Auden this is not so. Not very many of his poems achieve perfect detachment and completeness, the quality of floating away entire, independent of their author or their surroundings. He is an occasional writer, and a copious one; the enormous impact he has made has been various and diffused. He himself hates the idea of pure poetry, as he never tires of telling us; it is the whole mass of warning, exhortation, preaching, journalism in both prose and verse, that has moved us; not its perfection but its intelligence, relevance and honesty. We really need a fat volume comprising all the poetry, warts and all, including *The Orators*, and *The Dog Beneath the Skin*, which Auden himself considered a failure. We could do our own skipping. And if a selection is to mean much it should be on a broader base than this.

The poems in this edition are arranged in a chronological order, and it is now much easier to trace a line of development. The work of the late twenties and thirties retains its power. Most of the things it warned against have happened, most of the things it looked forward to haven't; but the poetry has stood up to the flux. The prevailing imagery – the ruined land, the spy, the conspirator, the threat of catastrophe, now that we no longer tie it up to a particular situation, remains as a vivid fiction. Not quite serious; there are too many echoes of *The Boys' Own Paper* and the scoutmaster's talk, and used in a curiously double-edged way: partly to assail the enemy – bourgeois society; and partly to undercut the pretensions of the assailants. It is the honest but uncomfortable attitude of the left-wing schoolmaster, personally pledged to destroy the system, but emotionally and institutionally tied to many of its values. The divided allegiance is perilous, its results sometimes confusing; and I can imagine a future time in which the whole thing will become totally unintelligible. But I suspect it will retain its strength for a good many years yet.

These poems are full of private references and hermetic language. These remain as impenetrable as ever, but curiously they are not damaging. Where the surface meaning contains so much preaching and threatening, the gaps in logic and intelligibility serve a positive purpose; they are windows letting in a rich, uncertain radiance. The language of conflict is omnipresent, to choose the right side is of supreme importance; yet it is never a matter of simple black and white. The very failures and neuroses can be beneficent for they bring crisis and psychic revolution nearer.

The unseriousness of Auden is a serious subject for discussion. Apart from a few early pieces strongly influenced by Anglo-Saxon verse, almost all his poems until the war are in a sense parodies – parody folk songs, parody ballads, parody sermons. It is a trickily literary art, working always by a visible gap between the style and the message. Armageddon is announced in a boys' adventure story, the twilight of the gods in a prize-day address. In the middle and later poetry, fairy tales and myths are used in the same fashion. There is no other poet who raids the bric-à-brac of legend with such irreverence and such unconcern. At times he draws on a very wide range of learning, but large areas of his poetry seem to prefer what could be found in a very well-stocked nursery:

> Just as his dream foretold, he met them all:
> The smiling grimy boy at the garage
> Ran out before he blew his horn; the tall
> Professor in the mountains with his large
> Tweed pockets full of plants addressed him hours
> Before he would have dared; the deaf girl too
> Seemed to expect him at her green chateau;
> A meal was laid, the guest-room full of flowers.

This is brilliant and charming; but the attitude towards the myths, adventures and dilemmas is always quizzical. What was simply *believed* in childhood or in earlier ages is now taken as a fanciful indulgence. And this is sometimes seen by Auden's critics as frivolity. But Auden is like Byron in that he is always at his most serious when his manner is most uncommitted. Slapdash, parody, self-parody, are his weapons in a real engagement; and the fanciful indulgences always have a moral in attendance. He is unlike Byron in that he never attempts to present us with real love stories, real battles, real shipwrecks – only their reflections in a shifting and distorting mirror. This is, perhaps, the consequence of a certain tenuousness in his relation with the physical and sensuous world. His early poems are intensely English in their atmosphere, not because they offer us a window on the visible English scene, but because they present English legends, English stereotypes, English tics and obsessions. After he left for America there is hardly a sign that he derived any nourishment whatever from the world around him. His liveliest response is to ideas, and the response is to mythologise them. Marx, Freud, Gröddeck, Kierkegaard, a miscellany of anthropologists and historians, have provided the ideas; Auden has re-combined them into a kaleidoscopic series of images, glimpses, miniature narratives, none of them firmly grappled with or seriously taken up, yet each serving as a moral flashlight, a momentarily-illuminated metaphysical signpost.

The energy and the illumination are in these flashes. Sometimes it is a moment of wit, of ballad-like poignancy or surrealist astonishment:

> Fleeing from short-haired mad executives,
> The sad and useless faces round my home –
>   *   *   *

> 'O where are you going?' said reader to rider,
> 'That valley is fatal when furnaces burn,
>   *   *   *

> Far from his illness
> The wolves ran on through the evergreen forests,
> The peasant river was untempted by the fashionable quays.

The demon that haunted his early verse was merely Drivel – relatively harmless, because though tiresome when present, he had no long-range effects. In the post-emigration period the twin demons are

Snuffle and Gabble, more sinister and more pervasive in their influence. Drivel produced 'Uncle Henry' and 'Halfway'; and it doesn't matter much – we needn't read them. Snuffle produced those terrible pieces 'In Sickness and in Health' and 'Many Happy Returns' – the unconventional radio parson offering his cheery non-sectarian admonitions. Gabble produced the 'Bucolics', and (outside the limits of this volume) most of *About the House* – and they cannot be so easily dismissed, for they are apt to leave nasty smells behind in otherwise satisfactory places. Auden's religious and quasi-religious poems are not acts of devotion, they are homilies, and homilies require more authority than he can command. His light verse and occasional pieces require form, both social and metrical, that now seems to be lacking: what we get is clever, and sometimes agreeable, party chatter that nevertheless offends because it is always pretending to be poetry and falls so far short of it. Delight, affection and resentment are the sentiments that Auden evokes at this period. Delight at the verbal sparkle, the fertility of ideas, the wide and unpompous erudition. Affection; who could fail to feel affection for a poet who can turn out all the miscellaneous lumber of myth, history, and childhood memories that we all have lying around the house, and before our eyes transmute it into something shining and precious. Resentment – perhaps unworthy, but we feel it because the real wisdom, the authentic good will, are not quite pure, contaminated with platitude, self indulgence and smugness.

Then, out of the middle of this varied and uncertain material, arise objects of such gravity and beauty that we forget all the rest. There is 'Lay Your Sleeping Head, My Love', that rare thing, a modern love poem. There is 'The Sea and the Mirror', not included in this volume; the verse sure and serene in its movement, the variations on the themes of *The Tempest* not clever but profound; the prose passages, the only Shakespearian criticism in the world that anyone reads for pure pleasure. Later, there is 'The Shield of Achilles', a poem in which the myth is used with perfect simplicity and seriousness to contrast the dream vision of the classical heroic age with the modern reality of war, oppression and consequent moral vacuity:

> A crowd of ordinary decent folk
> Watched from without and neither moved nor spoke
> As three pale figures were led forth and bound
> To three posts driven upright in the ground.

> The mass and majesty of this world, all
>   That carries weight and always weighs the same
> Lay in the hands of others; they were small
>   And could not hope for help and no help came:
>   What their foes liked to do was done, their shame
> Was all the worst could wish; they lost their pride
> And died as men before their bodies died.

Contrary to popular belief Auden is not generally a political poet; here is one of the few political poems of our time that can stand up to comparison with Yeats's 'Nineteen Hundred and Nineteen', though it is very different in its sombre unrhetorical realism.

Auden is too close to us not to leave us at times dazzled, enchanted – at times irritated and repelled; but in the end, beyond the sentiments I have confessed, the prevailing one must be gratitude.

SOURCE: 'MacNeice and Auden', *Critical Quarterly*, IX, 1 (Spring 1967), pp. 9–12, 12–17.

NOTE

1. [Ed.] Graham Hough's article constitutes a review of W. H. Auden, *Collected Shorter Poems, 1927–1957* (London, 1966) and *The Collected Poems of Louis MacNeice*, edited by E. R. Dodds (London, 1966).

G. S. Fraser   Evasive Honesty: The Poetry of Louis MacNeice   (1959)

. . . Nothing could be more vivid, more frank, more candid, even in a sense more indiscreet than some of [MacNeice's] best poetry. All the cards seem to be, even casually, on the table. At the same time, reading his poems one has the feeling sometimes that one has been subjected to an intelligence test; or that his hands, as he deals the cards on the table, move with disquieting speed. To use another metaphor, he is both in life and in poetry a man whose manner, at once sardonic and gay, suggests that he is going, perhaps, to let one in on a disquieting secret about something; one finds that he hasn't. The quality that one is left remembering, the poetic as well as the personal quality, is a kind of evasive honesty. Both the strength and the weakness of his best poems, like the strength and the weakness of the personal impression he makes, rest on the sense that a good deal is held in reserve. What it is, I have only a faint idea; but I have a feeling that he would be a more important poet, if it were less fully held in reserve, yet that the strength even of his slighter poems depends on one's intuition that there is so much of it.

He is a poet, I think, whom it is sensible to discuss in terms of his conscious attitude to life, his moral tastes and preferences, what he feels about the problematical world we are living in, since that mainly, and only occasionally deep personal feelings, seems to be what his poems are about. When his *Collected Poems* came out in 1948, he was the one poet of the 1930s in whose work the years of the Second World War did not seem to have brought about a sharp break. Mr C. Day Lewis, for instance, in the 1930s was often writing, to my mind rather unsuccessfully, either in a manner diluted from Hopkins or in a manner taken over from Mr Auden's coarser scoutmaster vein. He was writing about the 'state of the world', rebelling against it. At some period in the 1940s, one noticed that he was writing, much more successfully, in a manner that owed something to Hardy, something to Browning and Clough, and that he was writing about the personal life. As for Mr Auden himself, he has run through styles almost as Picasso has, he has reminded one of Laura Riding, Byron, Rilke, Yeats, he has perversely forced interesting matter into what seems a strangely inappropriate mould, like the Anglo-Saxon alliterative metre of *The Age of Anxiety*; the very beautiful purely personal manner with its long lines and its florid vocabulary which he has forged for himself in recent poems like 'In Praise of Limestone' is composite, not simple; through the kaleidoscope of successive styles, we now see that he has had a more consistent attitude all along than we thought. Mr MacNeice's attitude has always been a firmly fixed one, and his style has changed only from a young man's concentration on images to an older man's care for structure. His short poems have been much more often successful than his poems of a certain length (the only two of his longer poems that I admire quite whole-heartedly are two from the middle of the 1930s, 'Eclogue for Christmas' and 'Death and Two Shepherds'). In this again, he is not exceptional; the number of poems of more than three or four pages which are completely successful in their way is, I suppose, a very small fraction indeed of the number of poems of three or four stanzas which are completely successful in theirs. There is a case, in fact, for thinking of Mr MacNeice as a poet who has sacrificed an unusual gift for concentration to a misguided ambition to deploy himself at length. But, failures or successes, Mr MacNeice's poems express from his beginnings to now an attitude to life which is admirably coherent: that of the left-of-centre Liberal, and, morally, that of the man who is out at once to enjoy life and to shoulder his social responsibilities. The typical attitude is one of a sane and humorous, and sturdily self-confident, social concern.

What may put some readers off is that this is so much (polished, learned, alarmingly witty though Mr MacNeice is) the decent plain man's attitude. Decency, measure, courage, a lack of pretence, a making of the best of good things while they last, and a facing up to bad things when they have to be faced, these are the good insider's virtues. Mr MacNeice's standpoint is the standpoint of common sense. He is subtle enough, however, to realise that the standpoint of common sense can be defended only through dialectic and paradox; he does not try to fight the plain man's battles with the plain man's weapons. It is on an acceptance of paradox that his own consistency is based (he was very interested in his youth in the paradoxes of the modern Italian idealists, not only Croce, but Gentile):

> Let all these so ephemeral things
> Be somehow permanent like the swallow's tangent wings.

Thus one of Mr MacNeice's favourite figures (as he has noted in a lively and perceptive essay on his own work) is oxymoron: the noun and epithet that appear to contradict each other. He might himself be described in that figure as an intolerant liberal or a large-hearted nagger. He wants a world in which all sorts and conditions of men can have their say; but when their say, as so often, proves slack, or insincere, the say of

> The self-deceiving realist, the self-seeking
> Altruist, the self-indulgent penitent,

he loses his patience. It takes all sorts to make a world, certainly, but making is an activity, and the sorts he approves of must really put their shoulders to the wheel, must really creatively work to *make* it. More broadly, to underline yet again this paradoxical consistency, one might say that it is Mr MacNeice's taste for variety, contrast, obstinate individuality – combined with his feeling that all these

things, all 'the drunkenness of things being various', must somehow
join in the 'general dance' – that unifies his vision of the world. (The
problem of the One and the Many, like the problem of Essence and
Existence, crops up again and again in Mr MacNeice's poetry. The
swallows are ephemeral existents but the pattern their tangent wings
make seems to claim to be an eternal essence. Perhaps the submerged
nine-tenths, both of his poetry and his personality, is a speculative
metaphysician, of an unfashionably ambitious sort.)

The danger of Mr MacNeice's liberal, humanistic attitude, so
admirable in so many ways in itself, is that it is too often, especially in
his longer poems, liable to slacken down into mere moralising. Take
such a passage as this:

> . . . it is our privilege –
> Our paradox – to recognize the insoluble
> And going up with an outstretched hand salute it.

One agrees, of course, at some though not at all levels, with what is
being said (one does not agree, but this is certainly not an application
Mr MacNeice will have had in mind, that one should greet the
apparently insoluble political divisions of our time, as Browning
greeted the Unseen, with a cheer). One is unhappy about the way of
saying. Is not the tone of voice, too flat in one sense, and too stretched
in another, the orator's tone rather than the poet's? When, in a long,
ambitious poem, full of such moralistic passages, I come for instance
on this,

> The paradox of the sentimentalist
> Insisting on clinging to what he insists is gone,

I do feel, I confess, a sense of relief. The tone is right, there, these two
lines are tight, witty, hit straight home. The moral *fact* is presented,
the moral judgment is left (as I think it should be) to the reader.

Readers of that collected volume of 1948 often found themselves, I
imagine, like myself, lingering a little wistfully over the dash,
vividness, and gaiety of the earlier poems. But the later poems also
deserved careful reading. Mr MacNeice was tired, as he explained in
a prose piece written about that time, of 'journalism', and tired of
'tourism', tired of the poem as a mere footnote to experience; he aimed
now at making all the parts of a poem fit coherently together, even if
that involved the sacrifice of the brilliant inorganic image and the
witty irrelevant sally. 'Thus the lines', he wrote, 'that I am especially

proud of in my last book are such lines as these (of the aftermath of war in England):

> The joker that could have been at any moment death
> Has been withdrawn, the cards are what they say
> And none is wild . . .

or (of a tart):

> Mascara scrawls a gloss on a torn leaf

(a line which it took me a long time to find).' Both passages are essentially exploitations of the poetic pun. A card in a gambling game that can become any other card is called 'wild'; the joker, which is not really a proper member of the pack, is often used in this way as a 'wild' card. But the wider connotations of death as a cruel practical joker, or as a wild beast in the jungle waiting to spring on one, emotionally reinforce what might have been a mere piece of knowingness. The second pun, I think, is even subtler. Mascara scrawls either a sheen on a torn piece of foliage (the tart's sad eyelid shaped like a leaf) or a commentary on a torn page (from a diary say, a record of illicit self-indulgence to be destroyed). And the tart herself is like a leaf torn from the living tree of life, and the false gloss of the mascara on her eyelid is a commentary on her fate. Such Empsonian economies certainly demanded harder work from Mr MacNeice's readers than his old pieces of 'tourism',

> . . . impending thunder
> With an indigo sky and the garden hushed except for
> The treetops moving,

or his old pieces of 'journalism', his shrewd remarks in passing,

> . . . that a monologue
> Is the death of language and that a single lion
> Is less himself, or alive, than a dog and another dog.

The danger, however, that Mr MacNeice at the end of the 1940s seemed to be facing was that of sometimes relapsing – as a relaxation from the strain of much close writing and as a sop to his sense of moral urgency – into the very 'monologue' which in these lines he deplores. How far, in the last ten years, has he surmounted that danger?

Perhaps he did not wholly surmount it. In 1952, he brought out *Ten Burnt Offerings*, a set of fairly longish poems which had been originally conceived for radio (they took about fifteen minutes each to broadcast). In that book, one had a sense of an inner flagging battling with an obstinate ambition. The relevance of the themes of these ten poems, both to common problems of our day and to what one took to be Mr MacNeice's personal predicaments, seemed real but oddly oblique. The themes of the poems were themes that might have suited a prose essay: the paradox of Elizabethan culture, the dung and the flower: the harsh roots of modern ethics in Greek and Hebrew guilt and sacrifice: Ulysses and Jacob as twin competing symbols of searching and driven man: Byron as the romantic for whom the conscious pursuit of liberty becomes the subconscious pursuit of death. Such a range of topics was impressive; but it had a touch about it, also, of the Third Programme Producer with his fatigued fertility in 'new approaches'. The language showed, sometimes, that fatigue. When Mr MacNeice wrote about the Elizabethans,

> Courtier with the knife behind the smile, ecclesiastic
> With faggots in his eyes,

it was impossible to forget how much more freshly they said the same sort of thing about themselves:

> Say to the Court it glows
>   And shines like rotten wood;
> Say to the Church it shows
>   What's good and doth no good.

A wider reach can imply a shallower local penetration.

As if aware of the dangers of a stretched thinness, Mr MacNeice was fecund in metaphor:

>   because your laugh
> Is Catherine wheels and dolphins, because Rejoice
> Is etched upon your eyes, because the chaff
> Of dead wit flies before you, and the froth
> Of false convention with it. . . .

Nothing could be gayer than the 'Catherine wheels and dolphins'. But were the more painful connotations of 'etched' (a needle on the iris?) intended or relevant. Are 'chaff' and 'froth', themselves examples of conventional dead metaphor, appropriate because 'dead wit' and 'false convention' are what they refer to – but, even if so, is there not still an unpleasant though faint clash between the 'froth of false convention' and the real and beautiful sea-froth churned up, three lines back, by 'dolphins'? The ornamentation, in fact, in this book had often the air not of emerging spontaneously from the theme, but of being trailed over it, like roses over a trellis. A trellis, to be sure, would be nothing without roses, but the gaunter outlines of Mr MacNeice's thought, often half-hidden here, were interesting in themselves. His language was best where it was barest: as in the section on Byron in Lowland Scots,

> I maun gang my lane to wed my hurt,
> I maun gang my lane to Hades,

or the aside about history,

> . . . the port so loved
> By Themistocles, great patriot and statesman,
> Great traitor five years on,

or the statement of the poet's own predicament:

> This middle stretch
> Of life is bad for poets; a sombre view
> Where neither works nor days look innocent
> And both seem now too many, now too few.

Even in these fine lines, there was something to question about the texture. 'A sombre view of the situation' is a worn politician's phrase; was it being accepted with a sort of fatigue, or alluded to with a sort of irony? Bareness, at least, seemed in the early 1950s to be Mr MacNeice's growing-point: his danger, that facility of the practised writer which is so very different from spontaneity – the temptation to write because one can, not because one must. . . .

Both *Ten Burnt Offerings* and *Autumn Sequel* gave me . . . the sense that a fine talent was forcing itself. I read with far more genuine pleasure Mr MacNeice's most recent volume, *Visitations* [1957], in which he seemed to have got back for the first time in ten years or so the bite that he had in the 1930s; and in which he got away also from the snare of the blown-up, big poem, of a length suitable for broadcasting. In these new short poems or sequences of short poems he had freed himself from the twin temptations of moralising at the drop of a hat, and of ad-libbing. His mood, from the beginning of the book, was agreeably cantankerous (it is very difficult to discuss him, except in oxymorons!):

> Why hold that poets are so sensitive?
> A thickskinned grasping lot who filch and eavesdrop. . . .

He attacked snooty reviewers (or the snooty reviewer in himself):

> Yet the cold voice chops and sniggers,
> Prosing on, maintains the thread
> Is broken and the phoenix fled,
> Youth and poetry departed.

> Acid and ignorant voice, desist.
> Against your lies the skies bear witness. . . .

It is time, perhaps, that I did stop prosing on about him, that my own acid and perhaps ignorant voice did desist. I have said already, I think, all the general things I want to say. I should say finally that one would not have registered so sharply the degree of one's dissatisfaction with some of Mr MacNeice's recent poetry unless one had a very high respect for, and therefore made very exacting demands on, the range and flexibility of his art and the integrity and scope of his mind. He has tried, with a strain of conscious effort, to make himself into the wrong sort of major poet. I think that if he had only waited a little more patiently for the pressure to gather, for the poem to force itself upon him, he might have been a major poet of the right sort. He has brought intelligence and poetry together; but the intelligence has too often seemed something superadded to the poem, rather than something used up in its proper shaping.

Source: extracts from 'Evasive Honesty: The Poetry of Louis MacNeice', in Fraser's *Vision and Rhetoric: Studies in Modern Poetry* (London, 1959), pp. 179–87, 191–2.

Terence Brown   On MacNeice: The Poet and
His Imagery   (1975)

. . . In MacNeice's essay 'Experiences with Images' there is a passage vital to the understanding of his thought and its expression:

I ought by rights to explain what as a poet I am getting at. But this is not so easy, as at different times I have been getting at different things and as at all times (like all poets?) I have been answering questions I was not fully aware of having asked. But I think that, generally speaking, my basic conception of life being dialectical (in the philosophic, not in the political sense), I have tended to swing to and fro between descriptive or physical images (which are 'correct' as far as they go) and *faute de mieux* metaphysical, mythical or mystical images (which can never go far enough). 'Eternity', wrote Blake (Yeats's favourite quotation), 'is in love with the productions of Time' and I have tried to pay homage to both. But the two being interlinked, the two sets of images approach each other.[1]

The existence of this realm of the eternal, in love with the productions of time, this realm of non-being in love with, yet threatening to destroy being, is sometimes pictured in the poetry by bell images. More often it is suggested by imagery of wind and sea. It must be pointed out, however, that the 'eternity' these images suggest is remote from any normal ideas associated with that word. This is no heaven of angels, or spiritual realm where deity resides. It is no transcendent reality, more a transcendent non-reality. It is nothing-ness without which there would be no 'isness', it is non-being which allows for being. It is the unknown without which there could be no known. It is that which would destroy what is, and paradoxically permits it to be. The one depends on the other completely. In orthodox views of transcendence the transcendent exists irrespective of the existence of the world. For example, in orthodox Christian metaphysics God is said to exist in and for himself. In MacNeice's thought the 'eternal' is dependent on the world as the world is dependent on the 'eternal'.

In an early poem 'Nocturne' (a slight but effective poem) the wind is personified as he goes 'Slouching round the landscape'. The poem is simply descriptive, but ends with a note of threatening, with a suggestion that it may be a wind from beyond time, from a possible eternity, that blows through the night. Nothing is explicit; it is left to the reader's imagination. The wind is imagined to

> Sinisterly bend and dip
> Those hulks of cloud canvas,
> Probing through the elm-trees,
> Past the houses; and then pass
> To a larger emptiness.

In 'Eclogue from Iceland' it is the wind which blows to destroy the timeless moment of

> a moment's fusion
> With friends or nature till the cynical wind
> Blew the trees pale . . .

In 'June Thunder' it is the wind which presages the destruction of the beauty of a summer's day. It destroys

> All the flare and gusto of the unenduring
>   Joys of a season . . .

At one level this poem can be read as mere description. On another there is the sense of something more disturbing.

> With an indigo sky and the garden hushed except for
>   The treetops moving.

> Then the curtains in my room blow suddenly inward,
> The shrubbery rustles, birds fly heavily homeward,
> The white flowers fade to nothing on the trees and rain comes
>   Down like a dropscene.

There is something haunted about this hushed garden with the treetops moving. This is a wind which annuls the flowers and brings rain, putting an end to the delightful show of a summer's day. The poem may be a simple description, but one senses something more. Is this merely a natural wind, or the manifestation of some unknown but terrifying force? In other poems the wind continues to suggest more than itself, to suggest an alien, unknown reality. In 'The Stygian Banks' the wind is explicitly defined as symbolic of the non-being, which in a dialectical fashion attacks and yet sustains the fecund being and becoming of the garden of reality.

> Only an incoming wind which unlike the winds of the garden
>   . . .
> Flutters no paper tag on a stick in a plot,
> Moves no leaf; the dandelion puff balls
> Ignore it and we often.

But not always for there are some

> Who when the wind which is not like any wind known
> Brings to their ears from ahead the drums of the Judgement
> Slacken their pace . . .

In 'Flowers in the Interval' the poet sees himself

>   trapped on the edge of the world
>   In the wind that troubles the galaxies . . .

which is no natural breeze, and in imagining his experience of love as the discovery of a sleeping princess in a castle where

> a gay wind plays on the wheat, the plains are pearled
> With dew and the willows are silver in wind . . .

he asks the astonished question

> Can it possibly
> Be the same wind that harries the ends of the world?

What has the wind round his princess's castle to do with the wind of cosmic negation, or with the forces of non-being – the wind which in *Autumn Sequel* 'hustles' a character

> through that revolving door in the sky
> To no known point of the compass . . .   ['Canto I']

What has this 'gay wind' to do with the whirlwind of the seventh poem of *Visitations* where, through the curtainless window the wind was

> twirling the gas-drums
> And whipping all London away into interstellar negation . . .

or with the strange wind blowing round the petrified stasis of the late poem 'Another Cold May?'

> The Tulips tug at their roots and mourn
> In inaudible frequencies, the move
> Is the wind's, not theirs . . .

The majority of the wind images in MacNeice's poetry present the wind (and the force of non-being which it symbolises) as something to be feared. It is the wind which blows the cradle out of the tree-tops (a frequent image for death in MacNeice's poetry)[2] and it rarely is live-giving.[3] Occasionally, however, the attitude to the wind revealed in the imagery is ambivalent. In *Autumn Journal* he asserts 'What the wind scatters the wind saves'; and in 'Idle Talk' he realises that

> The wind that makes the dead leaf fall
> Can also make the live leaf dance.

Another major image of eternity, of the beyond, or non-being, in MacNeice's poetry (the sea) reveals a much greater ambivalence of attitude. A passage from 'Experiences with Images' reflects this: 'It was something alien, foreboding, dangerous, and only very rarely blue. But at the same time (since until I was ten I had only once crossed it) it was a symbol of escape.'[4]

The sea has constantly entered the literature of the European imagination, but with varying symbolic value. For MacNeice it most frequently seems to represent the eternal, that area beyond normal human experience, to which he adopts an ambivalent attitude. It is both destroyer and sustainer, to be both avoided and courted. In an early poem ('Upon this Beach', 1932) he describes the 'drunken marble' of the sea and urges the holiday-tripper

> Forget those waves' monstrous fatuity
> And boarding bus be jolly.

Concentrate on this world and forget the great emptiness beyond, the poet advises. In 'Wolves' the sea is a great force which threatens to engulf life and destroy it. In 'Passage Steamer' a vision of nothingness, of the petty irrelevancy of human activity in the light of the sea's immensity, comes to the poet:

> Back from a journey I require
>   Some new desire, desire, desire
> But I find in the open sea and sun
>   None, none, none, none;
> The gulls that bank around the mast
> Insinuate that nothing we pass is past,
>   That all our beginnings were long since begun.

In 'Postscript to Iceland' the sea is again a destructive force, for

> the fog-bound sirens call
> Ruin to the long sea-wall . . .

and in 'The Death Wish' the sea is the nothingness, the oblivion, suicides long for, 'mad to possess the unpossessable sea' in their impatience with the reality of living.

The sea is not always feared however. 'Nostalgia' expresses a longing for 'That under-sea ding-donging' and the complex ambivalence of attitude that consideration of nothingness and the unknown evokes in the poet, is expressed in 'Littoral' where we are

> Luxuriously afraid
> To plump the Unknown in a bucket with a spade –
> Each child his own seashore.

'Carrick Revisited' presents clearly the dialectic between the vastness of eternity (non-being, nothingness) and the particular, using imagery of sea and hard tangible reality in opposition.

> Time and place – our bridgeheads into reality
> But also its concealment! Out of the sea
> We land on the Particular . . .

In 'The Strand' the sea washes away the footsteps of visitors from the
sand leaving nothing behind, while in 'No More Sea'

> Dove-melting mountains, ridges gashed with water,
> Itinerant clouds whose rubrics never alter,
> Give, without oath, their testimony of silence
> To islanders . . .

where the word 'silence' suggests the vast nothingness sea symbolises
for MacNeice. We human beings dwell on islands in a vast empty sea
of eternity, of nothingness; we 'live embroiled with ocean'. We are
aware of the solidity of being, but also of the vast emptiness and
silence of the sea, of non-being.

In 'Mahabalipuram' the sea is a nothingness, against which the
living rock of being is defiantly existent. But here the sea is also
acknowledged as creator. Non-being is necessary for being in the
dialectical conception of life:

> The creator who is destroyer stands at the last point of land
> Featureless . . .
>   . . . the waves assault the temple,
> Living granite against dead water . . .

But the temple survives the attacks of 'squadrons of water, the dark
grim chargers launched from Australia'. *Autumn Sequel* also suggests
the fear of negation by sea imagery, and the existence of reality
against the forces of non-reality is once again affirmed by imagery of
rock against sea (as in 'Mahabalipuram'):

> this is still land, not sea,
> Still life not death . . .
>   . . . This is a room
> Of living people. Nothing perhaps avails
>
> Against the sea like rock, like doomed men against doom.

'Notes for a Biography' sees the sea, once more, as a destructive force,
because 'All seas are cruel, spendthrift, endless. . . .' while two other
later poems are evidence of the essential ambivalence, the dialectical
tension, present in the use of the sea as an image of eternal emptiness
in MacNeice's poetry. 'Nature Notes (The Sea)' sees it as

> Incorrigible, ruthless,
> . . .
> Like something or someone to whom
> We have to surrender, finding
> Through that surrender life.

The other poem 'Round the Corner' simply states (without clearly defining the attitude we should adopt towards it) that 'Round the corner is – sooner or later – the sea.' A book review written by MacNeice casts interesting light on the genesis of this poem, and helps our interpretation of it. In a review of Rex Warner's translation of *Poems by George Seferis*, he quotes one of that poet's poems:

> We knew it that the islands were beautiful
> Somewhere round about here where we are groping,
> Maybe a little lower or a little higher,
> No distance away at all

and MacNeice continues 'Which perhaps *is* an answer, on a plane just a shade above or below our own or just round the corner which after all is our own corner, so near and yet so far in fact, lies something which might make sense of both our past and future and so redeem our present.'[5] The sea in MacNeice's poem 'Round the Corner' is to be understood as a redeeming force. The great sea of nothingness, of eternity, of the unknown can be viewed positively. This conclusion is reinforced by a note MacNeice wrote to his final volume, a few days before his death. It contains a clear reference to this poem – 'I would venture the generalisation that most of these poems are two-way affairs or at least spiral ones: even in the most evil picture the good things, like the sea in one of these poems, are still there round the corner.[6] So for MacNeice the sea in 'The Casualty' was the kingdom of death as it is in 'A Handful of Snapshots', 'The Gone-Tomorrow' or in 'Jigsaws' where 'death curls over in the wave'. But in 'Western Landscape' the sea was the object of desire and longing.

Occasionally these images of bells, wind and sea are compressed into an image cluster, to form a complex new image of this aspect of MacNeice's thought. An obvious example of this is the 'under-sea ding-donging' of 'Nostalgia' or the wind in 'Round the Corner' which carried the smell of the sea:

> a wind from round the corner
> Carries the smell of wrack or the taste of salt . . .

The best example is in 'Day of Renewal' where Dick Whittington hears the sound of bells: 'Bronze tongues lost in a breaking wave'; and later in the poem

> the clappers overlap in the waves
> And the words are lost in the wind.

At quite the other end of the spectrum of images from these 'metaphysical' or 'mystical' examples (of which these last are probably the most obviously mystical) are what MacNeice in 'Experiences with Images' calls 'physical' or merely 'descriptive' images. These are images which do not suggest or embody any concepts beyond themselves. They simply attempt to realise the individual, particular, given reality of a thing, to capture what Hopkins called the 'individuation' of things. Examples of such images are legion in MacNeice's poetry and it would be impossible to do other than suggest a number of examples. The opening image of 'Under the Mountain' is of this type –

> Seen from above
> The foam in the curving bay is a goose-quill
> That feathers . . . unfeathers . . . itself

as is the image in 'Littoral', 'The sand here looks like metal, it feels there like fur'.

Yet although these images out of context seem merely descriptive, in the body of MacNeice's work they are of greater significance. The dozens of images which attempt to catch the exact, particular essence of an experience, an object or a person, begin to stand for the tangible existent world itself, which in MacNeice's thought is one pole of the dialectic of life. The sea attacks the world of being, which is a world of tangible, often beautiful entities. These images give us what the poet described in 'Train to Dublin' as

> the incidental things which pass
> Outward through space exactly as each was.

They evoke for us the ever-changing, existent, vigorous, fertile life of the world itself. It is the world he pictures in a passage in his prose work *Zoo*:

The pleasure of dappled things, the beauty of adaption to purpose, the glory of extravagance, classic elegance or romantic nonsense and grotes-querie – all of these we get from the Zoo. We react to these with the same delight as to new potatoes in April speckled with chopped parsley or the light at night on the Thames of Battersea Power House, or to cars sweeping their shadows from lamp-post to lamp-post down Haverstock Hill or to brewer's drays or to lighthouses and searchlights or to a newly-cut lawn or to a hot towel and friction at the barber's or to Moran's two classic tries at Twickenham in 1937 or to the smell of dusting-powder in a warm bathroom or to the fun of shelling peas into a china bowl or to shuffling one's feet through dead leaves when they are crisp or to the noise of rain or the crackling of a newly lit fire or the jokes of a street-hawker or the silence of snow in the moonlight or the purring of a powerful car.[7]

This is a hymn to existence itself. The same world of change, vigour and tangible reality is present in the imagery of many of the poems, flickering and flaunting its existence in the face of nothingness.

It is a world of sunlight flashing off water, of the 'Mayfly', which in a magnificent line is seen to

> Inconsequently dance above the dazzling wave . . .[8]

or the quivering of fish in a tank as in 'The Glacier' where the detailed work of the latinist is opposed to the petrification of the crawling traffic:

> And we who have always been haunted by the fear of becoming stone
> Cannot bear to watch that catafalque creep down
> And therefore turn away to seemingly slower things
> And rejoice there to have found the speed of fins and wings
> In the minnow-twisting of the latinist who alone
> Nibbles and darts through the shallows of the lexicon . . .

It is a world of 'wafers of early sunlight' and the swift fluttering movement of a viola player's hand, like a fish in a glass tank that

> Rises, remains quivering, darts away
> To nibble invisible weeds.

It is a world where

> Of night pours down on you Provençal stars . . .

and a world where

> one day catches mackerel, a thousand white

> Excitements flapping on a thousand hooks,
> And one day combs its hair with the west wind
> And takes its pinch and sneezes gulls and rooks . . .

Such imagery as this in MacNeice's poetic universe becomes more than descriptive. It comes to stand for the vigorous tangible beauty of existence itself, attacked and sustained by the cold, alien, (yet ambivalently viewed) otherness and non-being of the sea.

We have explored the main landmarks of the 'geography' created by the imagery in MacNeice's poetry, demonstrating how themes we noted in the previous chapters are pictured, given poetic clothing by certain repeated images, image complexes and motifs. The sceptic's sense that the only way to find value in experience is to create it oneself, is suggested by the quest motif and its associated imagery. The progress of man, sceptical and threatened by despair, through the continually changing flux of experience which he cannot comprehend, is embodied in images of journey and travel. But his scepticism . . . is creative for it drives him to his own kind of affirmation: of life, as a fertile, dialectical tension, between being and non-being, between everything and nothing, life and death. This conception is pictured by images and image patterns of the 'eternal' and 'physical' in dialectical opposition, of a fragile world of delightful particulars threatened by negation. The poet's sceptical dislike of any absolute systems, of any transcendence, which would freeze the flux and limitedness of experience, destroying the continually processing fertility of the dialectic between life and death, is seen in his use of images of petrification and associated motifs. His images are the embodiment of creative scepticism.

SOURCE: extract from ch. 4, 'The Poet and His Imagery', in Brown's *Louis MacNeice: Sceptical Vision* (Dublin, 1975), pp. 114–24.

NOTES

[Reorganised and renumbered from the original – Ed.]

1. Louis MacNeice, 'Experiences with Images', *Orpheus*, II (1949), p. 126.

2. For example in 'The Stygian Banks', section III:

> What when the wind blows and the bough breaks?
> Will each life seem a lullaby cut off
> And no humanity adult?

The genesis of such imagery can be seen in a detail of MacNeice's biography. He relates an incident of his childhood in *The Strings are False*: 'In the spring I committed a murder. Down in the hedge by the bottom walk in the garden, where my mother used to walk with my sister, there was a bird's nest. I could hear the little birds cheeping but the nest was too high for me to see into, so when no one was around I reached up for it and it capsized. I cannot remember seeing the nestlings fall out, but when I came past there again, there they were hanging in the hedge, little naked corpses, terrible, silent' (p. 55). This could explain the close association with death that the cradle falling from a tree has in MacNeice's poetry. It helps to explain what is a rather private image. The writer for one had never associated the nursery-rhyme incident with death.

3. This attitude may also have its genesis in MacNeice's childhood experience. He tells us in *The Strings are False* 'And Annie the cook had a riddle

which began "What is it that goes round and round the house?" And the answer was the wind but, though I knew that was the answer in the riddle, I had a clammy suspicion that in fact it might be something else. Going round and round the house, evil, waiting to get me' (p. 38). The wind is often thought of as something to be feared in MacNeice's poetry.

4. 'Experiences with Images', p. 129.

5. Louis MacNeice, 'A Modern Odyssey', *New Statesman*, LX, 1553 (17 Dec. 1960), p. 979.

6. *Poetry Book Society Selection*, 38 (Sept. 1963).

7. Louis MacNeice, *Zoo* (London, 1938), pp. 40–4.

8. The flickering flight of the mayfly occurs a number of times in MacNeice's work as an image of the ephemeral beauty of the world. Apart from this example we meet it in 'The Dark Tower' with 'The mayflies jigging above us in the delight / Of the dying instant', in 'Suite for Recorders' where the lives of the Elizabethans are 'Mayflies in a silver web which dangled over chaos', and in 'Memoranda to Horace' where the poet's monument, raised against the world is 'Weaker and less of note than a mayfly'.

D. E. S. Maxwell   On Day Lewis: Between Two Worlds   (1969)

. . . Some of the best poems in *A Time to Dance* [1935] are on the same theme [of conflicting worlds – Ed.]: 'The Conflict', 'In Me Two Worlds', 'Johnny Head-in-Air'. The first two of these Day Lewis has called 'the only two political poems of any value which I wrote' – an excessively modest verdict. Their intention is propagandist. 'The blood-red dawn', 'the red advance of life', the hosts that 'tap my nerves for power, my veins / To stain their banners red' are to obliterate 'private stars' and 'The armies of the dead'. But the emotional residue is of doubt, not triumph. Though the poet, as if from outside, rallies 'the red advance', it is he who is the object of the struggle. The 'tilting deck' of 'The Conflict', from which he 'sings / To keep men's courage up', is his own disequilibrium. In 'In Me Two Worlds' he is 'This moving point of dust / Where past and future meet, host to the 'armies of the dead' 'trenched within my bones', as well as to their antagonists, 'the men to come'. The imagery of both poems, its integrity poorly resumed by this kind of evisceration, sustains a metaphor of combat unresolved but precisely defined.

'Johnny-Head-in-Air' is an allegory, in ballad form, of the same conflict. A heterogeneous company of travellers / pilgrims struggles over a surrealistic terrain, limousines, a viaduct, telegraph poles incongruous in a folk-tale badlands. The language makes the same anachronous junctions. 'Leaden automaton', 'keen X-rays' consort with 'the frore and highest heavens', 'ferlies'; 'metaphysical' images with the stock ballad formulae: 'the crisis of the road' with

> Speak up, speak up, you skyward man,
> Speak up and tell us true.

The 'skyward man' describes two countries to which 'the cryptic way' leads. One ('to right, to right, comrades') has the eerie beauty of the Elflands which devitalise the human spirit. The other ('to left, to left, comrades') offers regeneration after toil. Asked which road to take, the 'skyward man' answers only,

> Traveller, know, I am here to show
> Your own divided heart.

Again the poem materially qualifies the implied political certainty, dramatising the emotional state of the 'divided heart'; and the ballad style, sensitively mimed and inflected, the haunting echoes of folklore, the hallucinatory settings, enlarge the relevance of the political dilemma which is their occasion.

As re-constituted in *Collected Poems*, *A Time to Dance* consists of these and other separate poems leading up to the title poem; 'A Time to Dance' is partly a narrative of the Parer-M'Intosh flight from England to Australia, partly an elegy on the death of L. P. Hedges, a fellow-schoolmaster. In the original volume it introduced a sequence setting depression England ('despair gathered together at street corners') against the airmen's spirited adventures and the 'radiant energy' of the dead friend, 'our dynamo, our warmth'. A chorus of the unemployed comments sardonically on 'flash talk of the spirit outshining death'; 'Two Songs' and 'A Carol' (given these titles in *Collected Poems*, where they precede the narrative) illuminate their plight. The poet then likens the 'radiance struck / From a deep mourning hour' of his personal loss to the strength accumulated in the martyrdoms of industrial life; and points the analogy which the pilots' technical skills and doggedness hold for the struggle of the workers. They are a metaphor of Engels's dictum, quoted in the poem, 'Freedom is the knowledge of necessity'. The remaining poems, in pseudo-jazz idiom, urge the poet's audience to love, unity, and the revolutionary spirit. The last thirty lines revert to the more formal manner, and *Collected Poems* retains these as an 'Epilogue'.

The poems preserved are no doubt those that stand best on their own. Verses like 'Yes, why do we all, seeing a Red, feel small?'[1] and 'Revolution, revolution / Is the one correct solution' flourished in a climate which we can re-construct but hardly re-inhabit naturally. In the original arrangement, however, the sequence as a whole had an uninhibited aggressiveness which it is a pity to lose. But it was inseparable from its occasion and that has gone. The sequence lived off it rather than perpetuated its life; and it has not quite the dexterity that might have produced entertaining mockeries of the popular song. The narrative and the elegy are fine poems in their own right, celebrating the heroic spirit better than the directly propagandist glosses added to them.

Noah and the Waters [1936] is open to similar criticisms. The author's foreword described it as 'something in the tradition of the medieval morality plays', dramatising in modern terms 'the choice that must be made by Noah between clinging to his old life and trusting to the Flood'. After the opening choruses three Burgesses plead with Noah to avert the Flood, then with the Waters of the Flood to undo the havoc they are causing. 'The Voices in the Flood' ('Waters of the world, unite!') reject all entreaties: appeals for moderation, offers to compromise ('No doubt there was much that needed, that cried out for, destruction'), accusations of being foreigners, threats ('My poison-gas outfit will make them froth'). Noah sides with the Flood and they 'go out in a running fight,' with the Burgesses. The Second Chorus has bidden us

> Consider Noah's fate,
> Chosen to choose between two claims irreconcilable,
> Alive on this island, old friends at his elbow, the floods at his feet.
> Whether the final sleep, fingers curled about
> The hollow comfort of a day worn smooth as holy relics;
> Or trusting to walk the waters, to see when they abate
> A future solid for his sons and for him the annealing rainbow.
> It is your fate
> Also to choose. On the one hand all that habit endears:
> The lawn is where bishops have walked; the walled garden is private. . . .

The trouble, as Julian Bell observed, is that the action fails to dramatise the choice so delicately balanced here and elsewhere in the lyric passages. It turns a critical engagement of the emotions into roustabout farce; language surrenders its functions to horseplay. More might be salvaged from *Noah and the Waters*, but it displays that weakening of concentration which Day Lewis has attributed to the demands of his political chores.

The first ten poems of *Overtures to Death and Other Poems* [1938], the last collection Day Lewis published in the thirties, exude an oppressive, despondent atmosphere. In 'Maple and Sumach', 'Regency Houses' and 'Two Landscapes' an autumn setting has the season's jaded melancholy, transferred to (or transferred from) and symbolising a debilitated human vigour. The landscapes and the Regency houses are the elegant but faded properties of a condemned society, evocative of loss, decay, not the triumph of their being supplanted. 'February 1936' makes a leaden winter day the portent of violence incubating:

> The unshed tears
> Of frost on boughs and briers
> Gathering wait discharge like our swoln fears.

In 'Bombers' and 'Newsreel' a 'womb-like sleep' resists the warning noise of aircraft in combat rehearsals.

Overtures to Death [the title-poem of the selection – Ed.], which follows, is a series of seven poems. They address, directly and with wit – the 'overtures' are preliminary negotiations – the death who is a menacing bystander in their ten forerunners. The first overture, without explicitly saying so, presents death as a 'remittance man', ignored by the family ('but in church sometimes / They seemed to be praying for you'), who 'had done well in the War', thereafter sought out by its survivors:

> Some of us went to look for you
> In aeroplanes and fast cars;
> Some tried the hospitals, some took to vice,
> Others consulted the stars.

In the second poem he is a bailiff,

> And he sits in our best room
> Appraising chintz and ornaments
> And the child in the womb.

The third poem pays tribute to 'one whose prowess in the bed and the battlefield / Have [sic] excited (and justly) universal comment'. Death has dominion over humanity, but a tolerable one: 'You are in nature.' To recognise and accept mortality is part of the human trial which only the elect – in another mountaineering image, 'Nearing the watershed and the difficult passes' (6) – can survive. But death alone has the right 'to deface the honoured clay' (4), not (the political moral) 'your free-lance and officious gunmen' (3), the despoilers of society who bring death prematurely to the weak. In the last poem the poor are the familiars of death ('We have come to think of you, mister, as / Almost the family friend'), waiting now to even old scores by becoming, in their turn, death's agents:

> When the time comes for a clearance,
> When light brims over the hill,
> Mister, you can rely on us
> To execute your will.

Most of the poems are in these sprightly quatrains. Their bouncy metre and laconically evasive personifications underplay the mordancy. The major theme of Day Lewis's poetry is engagements of mind and will in which death is the ultimate hazard to be faced. Characteristically, diction and imagery have an explicit and serious heroic tone. A different manner appears in 'Overtures to Death' [the title-poem of the 1938 collection – Ed.], where a number of the poems [in its sequence] endow the hero with something of the wisecracking self-containment of Hemingway's heroes. Beneath the assumed nonchalance the same exigent challenge remains effectively present.

This sequence discharged the depressive mood of the poems that precede it. Among those which follow it are 'When they have lost' and 'In the Heart of Contemplation', both returning to images of glowing light, expansive scenes. 'The Volunteer' is a tribute to the Spanish War volunteers, in spirit recalling the idealistic poems written early in the First World War and like them contrasting the alien battlefields with remembered pastoral scenes in England. It introduces 'The Nabara', the very fine narrative of a sea battle off the Basque coast in 1937. . . .

Overtures to Death and Other Poems reveals some of the outlines of Day Lewis's later poetry. 'Passage from Childhood' delicately unfolds the solitary evasions of a sensibility damaged in childhood. It anticipates the interest of 'Cornet Solo', 'O Dreams, O Destinations', 'Juvenilia' and other poems of youthful recollections issuing into later life with a significance not grasped in the original experience. There is a marked turning away here to a much more 'subjective' area of consciousness.

A number of the poems which conclude *Overtures to Death and Other Poems* suggest the same switch of attention. 'Behold the Swan' describes an October lake scene, its serenity abruptly shattered by the sudden out-thrust of energy as a swan takes off in noisy flight. At the end the poem says of the beating wings and stretching neck, 'They are a prophecy'. But like 'Maple and Sumach', 'February 1936' and 'Regency Houses' the poem is primarily descriptive, with the 'moral' appearing very briefly as a tailpiece. One can construe it politically only because of what one knows from the poetry generally. The poet has responded to a quality in the scene which awakens a fundamentally personal emotion. Any ulterior social attitude it might be used to signify pulsates much more weakly than the immediate personal feeling. In this collection, too, the style has shed or modified most of the features that previously marked it: the elliptical syntax, the reminiscences of Anglo-Saxon models, the syncopated rhythms. And with these the frequent echoes of Hopkins, Wilfred Owen, Eliot have faded also.

The later poetry is both more personal than the poetry Day Lewis was writing in the thirties and, in a way, more general. That is, it reflects personal feelings and concerns which are more a part of common experience than the dedicated political commitment. Recollections of past life ('The Album'), marriage ('Marriage of Two'), landscapes ('Seen from the Train'): these are the subjects of the post-thirties poetry, which contains them in their private alignments. Day Lewis has much stronger affinities with John Clare than, as is often suggested, with the Georgians: in his deep attachment to the rural English scene and to domestic situations; his natural style is far less modernistic than the manner he cultivated in the thirties. Yet the poetry he wrote then bequeathed useful instruction to its successor. His novitiate came, happily, in a period which emphasised the astringency and the hold on sensuous reality which the Georgians lacked.

His later poetry retains a strongly public element. He writes with assurance about 'public affairs' – as in his war poems; and the communal world of extrinsic objects and events is firmly present, as in the scenery of *An Italian Visit* [1953]. The colloquialism is toned down, but its idioms and intonations still invigorate the cadenced, lyrical periods and set in relief the more elevated style. We hear this counterpoint in 'Two Travellers' and the sequence 'Florence: Works of Art' in *An Italian Visit* adopts the vernacular off-handedness fashioned in the thirties. One in particular of its poems, 'Perseus Rescuing Andromeda: Piero di Cosimo' re-enters the world of updated myth and fairly tale which had harboured the ogres of the thirties. Its prefatory initials, W.H.A., are intended as a clue to the reader that like the other Florence poems it is deliberate Auden pastiche. The later poetry also maintains the heroic stance of the political poems. The seasons, the individual's experience of life appear still in images of movement and crisis. And again, the modern setting assumes the exemplary patterns of myth – 'The Image', 'The Revenant' – now without the specific political application.

Despite the evident differences between the two, the poetry Day Lewis wrote during and after the war is recognisably the descendant of the poetry he was writing in the thirties. The earlier verse does not fully represent his achievement – in translation, for example. But it is a distinguished body of poetry. It gives real emotional substance to the bickerings induced by Marxist dialectic and the crude simplifications of the party line. The literary debate though solemn, was not uniformly edifying nor even very sensible. Day Lewis's poetry, however, gives the abstractions – art as propaganda, the *bourgeois* predicament, documentary realism – a flesh and blood presence. They exist in the events, personalities and appearances of the time: the shabby towns of an industrial wasteland denied the machines of the new technology; in the sad landscapes of a countryside neglected or despoiled; in the heartless antics of the complacent or ill-disposed; and in the patterns of ideas and emotions which these formed in a troubled conscience not quite sure what was to be done but recording its dilemmas in terms of heroic conflict. The attitudes expressed are attractive; the passage of time has not obliterated their relevance. The poems uncover old myths in their images of the present; and refresh traditional forms – ballad, parable, narrative – with new techniques and contemporary language. It is not a 'communist' poetry; but it is a poetry which could hardly have existed without the communist entrance into the England of the thirties.

Source: extracts from ch. iii, 'C. Day Lewis: Between Two Worlds', in Maxwell's *Poets of the Thirties* (London, 1969), pp. 117–22, 124–6.

NOTE

1. The version in *A Time to Dance*, which ends 'He is what your sons could be, the road these times should take', perhaps shades the odds a little compared with the original ending. The poem appeared in *Left Review* for November 1934, when it was called 'The Communist', and ended: 'He is what your sons will be, the road these times must take'.

Geoffrey Thurley   On Spender: A Kind of Scapegoat   (1974)

If Spender is not the most unfashionable poet in the world at the present time, it is certainly difficult to think of a *more* unfashionable one. He is known universally as a Poet, and as a Social Poet. Yet there are reputable anthologies of middle twentieth-century verse which exclude him altogether, and in the universities he is likely to be scorned. Contempt rather than oblivion has been Spender's lot – contempt for the lapsed fellow-traveller, for the vegetated poet, for the confessor who never quite came clean. The *Encounter* association and divorce only reinforced the common image of the faded pink whose left hand was so ignorant of the right hand's doings that it could work for ten years against its own real interests.

Yet Spender was, I believe, Auden's superior as poet, and, with David Gascoyne, the most powerful English poet of his time: he became, not entirely through his own fault, the victim of the *maladie Anglaise*, a kind of scapegoat. His poetry assumes greater significance today: if we turn to Spender, to David Gascoyne and Dylan Thomas, ignoring both the more facile Pylon verse and the more gaseous New Apocalypse writing, a different picture of English poetry emerges from the thirties, one that suggests a new future and avoids the poverty of New Lines and The Movement. Such a tradition harks back to D. H. Lawrence rather than to Hardy, to Eliot's poetry rather than to his criticism, and to Wilfred Owen rather than to Edward Thomas; it develops through Ted Hughes rather than Philip Larkin. If such a tradition is a conscious construction rather than an actuality, so is any tradition in so far as that tradition affects the way people aware of it think and write. What inscape in the past we see there depends very largely upon what someone has taught or told us to identify and pick out. In such a re-casting of a poetic and critical tradition, then, a just appraisal of Stephen Spender assumes considerable importance.

Spender himself has largely connived at his own dereliction. He suffered the savage fate of a too early and too complete acceptance, that was based upon a serious misunderstanding – or rather upon an even worse half-understanding. For Spender was accepted as a triumvir, the author of 'The Pylons', a sidekick of Auden's. Scorned at Cambridge as the 'new Shelley', Spender sank into a curiously public decline, which he seemed willing to accept as heartily as anyone else. Thus, in his brilliant long story, *Engaged in Writing*, he catches himself beautifully, mirrored in the distorting pebbles of Sartre's glasses (the French philosopher is thinly anagrammed as Sarret):

They approached him as one attending the funeral of his career.
He did not altogether regret their sympathy.   (*Engaged in Writing*, p. 20)

– *Pauvre type!* Spender appears to have endorsed the verdict with dogged glee.

Yet he is much closer than Auden to what, for example, a Polish or a Spanish or a Russian poet or critic would regard as *a Poet* – and this fact seems to some extent to explain his fall from grace. The English do not like a Poet, unless he is Celtic: and Spender has always been 'being a Poet'. He has been both hampered and helped by this consciousness of role. Much of the self-conscious symbol-mongering of his later verse stems directly from it. He becomes, as one works through the *Collected Poems*, more and more 'literary' until he cannot open his mouth but to hold forth like a translation of Rilke or Seferis –

Again, again, I see this form repeated. . . .

At the same time, the appearance he has of being at all times 'a Poet' is not entirely a matter of mistaking the career of the man of letters for the activity later dubbed poetic, nor of laboriously impersonating the style and rhetoric of the classics. Spender appears 'more a poet' than either Auden or Empson because his verse strives more continuously than theirs for a unifying context both transcending and undercutting the immediate perception. Both in rhythm and body of verse, Spender's best poetry is more powerful and more deeply organised than Auden's. And this reflects the kind of serious commitment of himself that is inherent in the choice of the life of a poet. What is most important here probably is the awareness that a choice has been or has to be made.

It is the early verse, naturally enough, that demonstrates this best. *Poems* of 1933 seems now an impressive achievement. Less precocious than Auden's *Poems* of 1932, less dazzlingly sure of its indefinable subject-matter than Dylan Thomas's *Eighteen Poems* of 1936, it is still a declaration of promise which the later work was never wholly to fulfil. It is startlingly naïve: *viz*. 'How strangely this sun reminds me of my love', which is a good poem, in fact. But the naïveté *is* Spender, or at least an important part of him: it goes along with a genuine innocence of eye, and a capacity not only for being easily and deeply moved, but for honouring that emotion in strong and direct expression. But there is also a most impressive energy here, arching and bracing the stanzas with a strongly emotional physicality, which reminds one of Ted Hughes's *Hawk in the Rain* manner. (Spender's *Collected Poems* came out in 1953 – to be savaged in the Leavisite *Delta* – while Hughes was an undergraduate at Cambridge.) This is best seen in the poems which directly address the important question shelved by Auden and Empson in the interests of a vigilant self-awareness – the obligations inherent in the possession of poetic talent. Auden and Empson, as it were, pretend not to know they are poets. But the young artist is necessarily a hero-worshipper. Hence, Spender's quite legitimate tendency to think 'continually of those who are truly great'. The resignation and envy in the very title of this poem (it makes it clear the poet knows he isn't one of them) are significant in fact. But the awareness of the sort of spiritual quest involved is equally important: it is a far more mature recognition of the nature of the task confronting him than the sincere but inadequate social conscience the volume also flaunts. A more impressive instance of this *Kulturmythologie* is the frankly adulatory poem on 'Beethoven's Death Mask'. Once again, Spender puts a distance between himself and the 'truly great' man which is clearly going to incapacitate him for the sustained spiritual flight. But again, also, the acknowledgement of the peculiar role of genius is intelligent and constructive. It is also quite legitimate that Spender should explore the possibilities of the spiritual aspiration through the actual achievement of Beethoven – the transition from Scherzo to Finale of the Fifth Symphony in this case:

> Then the drums move away, the Distance shows;
> Now cloud-hid peaks are bared; the mystic One
> Horizons haze, as the blue incense heaven.

> Peace, peace. . . . Then splitting skull and dream, there comes
> Blotting our lights, the Trumpetter, the sun.

Spender's talent is far better exercised here, in the naïve imitation of a master (an Imitation of Christ, *mutatis mutandis*), than in the would-be sophisticated knowingness of 'An "I" can never be a great man', in which received twentieth-century ideas are crossed with Negative Capability in an image-less confusion.

Much more impressive than the latter poem in a related vein is 'What I expected' (poem XIV in the book), which makes an interesting parallel or contrast with Auden's contemporary allegories of the intellectual life – 'Atlantis', for instance, or 'The Quest'. Where Auden parabolised in studious disenchantment, Spender eschews the extended allegorical schema, confident in the capacity of a loosely connected sheaf of activities – climbing, struggling, fighting – to coalesce into a composite image of the spiritual experience:

> What I expected was
> Thunder, fighting,
> Long struggles with men
> And climbing.
> After continual straining
> I should grow strong;
> Then the rocks would shake
> And I should rest long.

The next stanza introduces us to the disabusement anticipated in the tense of the first, 'the gradual day / Weakening the will / Leaking the brightness away'; the third, to the objective causes of this process, 'the watching of cripples pass / With limbs shaped like questions / In their odd twist, / And pulverous grief / Melting the bones with pity.' It is these facts that inhibit the exercise of that sense of a personal destiny in the Romantic manner, and Spender speaks here for all the poets and intellectuals of his generation. The last stanza of the poem maintains the pluperfect disillusionment, but presents through the tense the redeeming image the whole poem is meant to embody – 'The created poem, Or the dazzling crystal'.

Structurally and methodologically, it is a beautiful piece of work, the parts related simply and subtly to the whole which they modify as they create it, yet still holding the air of an honest and honestly outraged personal testament. Like all the best poems Spender produced at this time, it embodies the message it enunciates: in pursuing the structural argument, one experiences the poem. And this capacity in Spender has a lot to do with his conception of the poem as an act, rather than as a statement. It is this which most distinguishes him from W. H. Auden, with whom he was fatally associated for so long. The Auden association seems to me to have been a disaster. No poet could have been better chosen to expose Spender's deficiencies and undermine his self-confidence than W. H. Auden. Nor, at the same time, could any poet conceivably be further removed from Auden in mind and ability than Spender. They are in fact polar opposites: as so often happens in the history of thought, two temperaments more or less exclusively contrasted become fixed in a polarisation at first stimulating, then destructive. As with Words-worth and Coleridge, the weaker character went under and suffered in the process more or less crippling damage to his self-esteem and identity. In the present case, the extraverted abreactive brain of Auden, scientific and sharply exact in its annotative habits, decisively demoralised the vacillating religiose vagueness of Spender. The decline of Spender's reputation set in when those who had bracketed him with Auden first realised how far he was from fulfilling the Auden norm, a norm he was hopelessly ill-equipped to attempt.

Like Day Lewis, Spender laboured hard to compete with Auden without ever understanding that Auden's 'precision' was based, as I have suggested above, upon an always semi-ideational mode, a conceptual 'case' argued with brilliant selection of instance. Thus, they did not see that the effect in Auden's verse of sharply focussed observation derived at least in part from the mental manipulation of 'idea', and that Auden, in short, rarely had to bother to get the precise visual phenomenon in its particular inscape: it was enough for him to introduce the typical instance – the pier pummelled by waves, the cave full of outlaws, the rioters in the square.

Spender never really understood this fact about Auden. His weakest lines are those which attempt to fix the politico-social facts with what he seems to have felt was an Audenesque precision. Now precision is exactly what Spender characteristically lacks – precision and swiftness: the movement of his verse is laboured, heavily stressed, bound up with its own rhyme echoes. If we compare a poem like the much-anthologised 'Fall of a City' with any of Auden's political poems, Spender will appear naïve and amateurish:

> All the posters on the walls,
> All the leaflets in the streets
> Are mutilated, destroyed, or run in rain.   ('Fall of a City')

Auden would, in the first place, hardly have bothered noting the observations down – he would not have *seen* them as 'images' at all. They are too much the earnest sixth former's great-eyed search for 'material'. At most, he might have noted the single detail of leaflets or torn posters in the rain. Now, Spender does little to really fix the impression: there is no distinguished touch to the lines. And yet the heavy-handed emphasis on the three verbs – 'mutilated', 'destroyed' and 'run-in-rain' – does something beyond and beneath the actual visual content of the words. In fact, what at first appears its embarrassing ineptitude (the fact that the three verbs together tell us little more than any one of them might have alone) emerges as its real strength: the compassionate pathos that rubs off or through onto the inhabitants of the city. More, the suggestion in these lines of tears is something Auden would either not have caught, or would have been embarrassed at: it is the limitation of very clever people that they can often only see suffering as a reason for pity, without being able to feel pity itself.

Auden's apperceptive rapidity – we remember that 'neural' is a favourite adjective of his – marshals the instances much more brilliantly and effectively than Spender's slow-moving introspection, but at the same time succeeds often in merely registering or demonstrating the 'truth' without the pity being generated. Spender's clumsiness, in the instance under discussion as in many others, derives probably from the fact that he had to make a conscious effort of will to focus the external facts (the posters and leaflets) from which Auden, bad eyes or no, would have extracted the essence in a trice.

Yet the difference between Auden's mind and Spender, lies deeper than this. I have already noted certain similarities in their use of allegory to express the struggle of the intellectual life. Another type of allegoric poem both poets liked to exploit concerns sexual and emotional situations. Here the allegoric narrative is replaced by a single symbol, as in Rilke's great poem 'Exposed on the mountains of the heart', from which both English poets, I fancy, learned something. Spender's 'Your body is stars whose million glitter here' recaptures much of the ecstasy of Rimbaud's *Illuminations* in its frank hyperbolic celebration of the act:

> Our movements range through miles, and when we kiss
> The moment widens to enclose the years.

The explorers invoked in the second half of the poem are not Auden's

jaded delinquents – swillers of rare liqueurs in Graham Greene bars –
but acolytes, 'explorers of immense and simple lines'. It is in fact, an
immense and simple poem, despite its post-coital deflation, which
seems less an intimation of disenchantment than a pain of exclusion
welcomed as part of a ritual:

> The promise hangs, this swarm of stars and flowers,
> And then there comes the shutting of a door.

Again, as in 'What I expected', Spender combines several loosely
associated images – beholders, explorers, the sky, branches, mountains, flowers – trusting to the validity of the emotion to fuse them all
into a coherent whole.

We note, by contrast, the purely 'literary' origination of the
mountain symbol in Auden's Sonnet, 'The Climbers': the poem
becomes a mere exercise, presenting the labours of love in terms of a
climb. Imagery of kitting-out, setting off on a gruelling expedition
which is not literal but figurative is, I have noted, a common property
of Auden's universe. The sonnet sequence 'The Quest' explores the
possibilities better than anything else of his perhaps; in a more overtly
allegorical form, 'Atlantis' provides another example of the genre, an
at times exciting mélange of school-boy adventure story (Hadath and
Henty), literary myth and Freudian double-think. 'The Climbers'
seeks to combine narrative and lyric. Yet it *is* allegory, and the
comparative facility of the medium contrasts badly with Spender's
more compact symbolism. Thus, Auden writes,

> with excuse concocted
> Soon on a lower alp I fall and pant,
> Cooling my face there in the faults that flaunt
> The life which they have stolen and perfected.
>
> ('The Climbers')

In spite of the apparent complexity of meaning (he cools his face not
in snow but in 'faults' that have 'stolen' the poet's life, and 'perfected'
it), the result of Auden's manipulation of the mountain-climb symbol
is to rob it of its immediacy and to return it to allegory. Spender,
forsaking the clever ramifications of the symbol, achieves a far greater
intensity and reality of experience:

> Here is our goal, men cried, but it was lost
> Amongst the mountain mists and mountain pines.
>
> ('Your body is stars whose million glitter here')

Something of Spender's greater relevance in the contemporary scene can be gleaned from a glance at Dom Moraes's beautiful 'Snow on a Mountain', which sustains the symbol with a narcissistic sensualism and an overall strategy not really present in Spender's more ambitious poem:

> One moment past my hands had run
> The chanting streams of her thighs;
> Then I was lost, breathless among the pines
>   ('Snow on a Mountain')

Auden's Sonnet could not have helped to midwife so fine and fresh a piece. One turns with a mixture of weariness and disgust, on the other hand, from the inevitable self-accusations of 'The Climbers': phases like 'Excuse concocted' and 'Cooling my face in the faults' amount almost to self-parody. Why, we ask ourselves, can Auden only prove his integrity by demonstrating his awareness of his own mendacity and failure? In spite of its confessional nature, Spender's poetry is free of this characteristic vice of ironist verse, and it is the consequent openness and fullness, coupled with the greater volume and rhythmic power of his poetry, that establishes his superiority over Auden. These particular quotations suggest, it is true, a disparity between their gifts that does not always obtain. Spender is not always that good, nor Auden often that bad. 'The Climbers' has been anthologised (in a collection containing not a line of Spender)[1] and appears at first glance a plausible enough offering. Only closer scrutiny shows Auden at an unusually weak moment: 'excuse concocted / Soon on a lower alp I fall and pant' is deplorably feeble *just as verse*: the words are slack, the lines lack all inner cohesion. By contrast, the Spender has an Olympian ease and strength: 'lost / Among the mountain mists and the mountain pines'. The placing of 'lost' really *does* something in and for the poem, and the following line expands with an impressive relaxation.

   In general Auden's actual versification *does* less, and it is probably this transparency of texture, through which the instances are meant to be seen, that has kept him in bad odour in circles where he ought to be admired, and which does in fact justify ultimate reservations as to his stature. By the same token, Spender's higher rate of prosodic 'work' earns him the higher Parnassian niche, and justifies an increased interest in his poetry today. The strenuousness of Spender's language and rhythm is easily demonstrated. It derives from the poet's slow involvement in his emotionally possessed and surrounded objects and observations. The strength and inner life of his metre explain – as they are explained by – that very naïveté and sluggishness which seemed initially to make him such a hopeless straggler in the thirties field:

> Only the world changes, and time its tense
> Against the creeping inches of whose moons
> He launches his rigid continual present.
>
> ('No Man's Land')

In these lines, Spender compels a slow, tensed-up reading – it is not possible to hurry the verse along in the way that Auden encourages us to hurry his, to glance at things in passing, without being really aware of the words being used. The strategic placing of 'tense', with its grammatical ambiguity, enforces a stiff concentration, much as the shadow creeps across the 'rigid continual present' ('continual' is possibly just an oversight, but certainly its implication of something nagging, wearying, suits the mood of the lines better than the correct 'continuous'). The slow strenuous movement of the time is maintained in the following triplets by means of the cinematic concentration on the growth of grass, which is finally seen piercing the skin of a dead soldier 'as through a drum'. Much of the tension of the piece stems from the contrast between what is normally felt to be a gentle sensationless process (the moon shining, the grass growing) and the immense physical restraint Spender exercises on his verse. I submit that there is nothing in Auden of comparable weight.

The Spanish Civil War poems are probably on balance the most satisfying in the Collected Spender.[2] Significantly, the fighting and death afforded Spender a profounder vision into reality than they afforded Auden. Where Auden communicates an exciting sense of disaster and anarchy, Spender sees both sides engaged in a conflict which ultimately transcends their partisan differences; he achieves the classic serenity that marks off the merely good from the momentarily great:

> Clean silence drops at night, when a little walk
> Divides the sleeping armies, each
> Huddled in linen woven by remote hands.
> When the machines are stilled, a common suffering
> Whitens the air with breath and makes both one
> As though these enemies slept in each other's arms
>
> ('Two Armies')

The last line suggests that Spender can achieve maximum engagement in a poem only in the presence of a near erotic element. Certainly, some of his finest pieces stem directly from personal relationship. 'The Room above the Square', for instance, presents its 'shatteredness' with an impressive straight-forwardness:

> Now I climb alone to the high room
> Above the darkened square
> Where among stones and roots, the other
> Unshattered lovers are.

The powerful slowing vowel-structures ('alone – room – darkened – square – stones – roots – lovers – are') strengthen the stanza-structure (note the excellence of the 'square-are' half-rhyme) in a manner quite unknown to the reader of Auden. Essentially, though, it is that same capacity for the open gaze as we observed in 'Fall of a City', sensitised by Spender's almost professional capacity for being wounded, which lends his relationship poetry its force. 'A Separation', hardly less successful than 'The Room above the Square', treats its eminently representative situation with equally admirable directness (it is the naïveté, of course, that makes this possible):

> Yes. The will decided. But how can the heart decide,
> Lying deep under the surface
> Of the level reasons the eye sees.

The heart cannot, of course, and the body must endure along with it the consequences of the will's decision:

> Under sleep, under day,
> Under the earth, in the tunnel of the marrow,
> Unchanging love swears all's unchanged, and knows
> That what it has not, still stays all it has.

The heart-reason distinction the poem is based on is hardly promising; yet Spender has made it his own, and given it verbal embodiment, precisely because he uses it to make sense of an actual situation: the distinction serves the moment, the poem does not embroider the distinction.

Spender's successes come when he has forgotten the wrangle with symbol and image that bogs down so much of his verse; conversely, his poetry loses its point when the symbol takes over. This almost wrecks the central stanza of 'The Room above the Square'; in 'Meeting', the strikingly original opening section is suffered to give way to the studied preciosity of this kind of Metaphysical riddling:

> Distances between us are of crystal
> Traversed with diagonals of rays
> In which our eyes meet when, near or far, they gaze.
>   . . .

Yet despite the strength of the poetry of relationships, some of Spender's most powerful writing has been dictated by his peculiarly emotional apprehension of political situations. At moments in the Second World War poems, he attains to the hard transcendentalism of the best Spanish Civil War poems. 'June 1940' fumbles its way through a good deal of inconclusive dialogue to reach a cold visionary statement that might have come out of the underground limbo of Owen's 'Strange Meeting':

> I am cold as a cold world alone
> Voyaging through space without faith or aim
> And no Star whose rays point a Cross to believe in,
> And an endless, empty need to atone.

The 'need to atone' of course derives very much from the Spenderian psyche: confession, atonement, abasement – these are emotions he understands and even relishes. Yet here he has struck through to an impersonal layer of generality, as indeed he does in the amazing 'Rejoice in the Abyss', surely one of the finest examples of Blitz poetry. The tone of Christopher Smart penetrates Spender's sleep in a weirdly prophetic ecstasy:

> I saw whole streets aflame with London prophets,
> Saints of Covent Garden, Parliament Hill Fields,
> Hampstead, Hyde Park Corner, Saint John's Wood,
> Who cried in cockney fanatic voices:
> 'In the midst of Life is Death!'

The poem opens powerfully – 'The great pulsation passed' – and throughout a somewhat haphazard, quasi-rhapsodic development, manages to sustain a queer dream-like momentum:

> Then in the sky, indifferent to our
> Sulphurous nether hell, I saw
> The dead of all pasts float on one calm tide
> Among the foam of stars
> Above the town, whose walls of brick and flesh
> Are transitory dwellings
> Of spirits journeying from life to death.

Like 'Beethoven's Death Mask', 'Rejoice in the Abyss' breaks through to a visionary world in which a voice speaks that is not the poet's own, one possessed of a felicitousness unknown to the waking man:

> For hollow is the skull, the vacuum
> In the gold ball under Saint Paul's gold cross.
> Unless you will accept the emptiness
> Under the bells of fox-gloves and cathedrals,
> Each life must feed upon the death of others

The felicitousness of 'Under the bells of fox-gloves and cathedrals' goes along with the authoritativeness of the moral mandate – 'All human aims are stupefied denial'. To penetrate so far beyond his habitual diffidence represented a considerable victory for the demonic principle within Spender, unless that diffidence is itself less than ingenuous.

The strenuousness (body, rhythmic strength), which I have tried to illustrate in Spender, ties in with his genius for metaphor, or his weakness for it, as it often appears. Metaphor is not only Spender's most natural mode of expression; it is part of his conceptual apparatus – everything is seen in terms of something else. Each image breeds an analogical double. Spender has often been described as 'introspective', usually in a loose way, referring to his awkward self-consciousness. It is not merely his penchant for thinking 'continually of those who were truly great', however, that justifies the label. Spender's mind is introverted in a more precise sense, that relates to his actual manner of perceiving reality. Certainly it is no accident that so many of his successful poems take the form of a commentary on his prolonged rumination (it is this, rather than meditation). 'I think continually' is a much more Spenderian poem than many of the political pieces contained in the same volume. 'Beethoven's Death Mask' and 'Dark and Light', also exemplify the ruminative envelope within which so much of his poetic thinking takes place, and which it tries so hard to break out of. Another, slightly different, example is the sympathetic piece he wrote on the thirties unemployed, 'Moving through the silent crowd'. This poem is carried off largely in the social imagery of the kind more brilliantly handled by Auden:

> Moving through the silent crowd
> Who stand behind dull cigarettes. . . .
>
> They lounge at corners of the street
> And greet friends with a shrug of shoulder. . . .

The technical immaturity (the articles omitted for reasons of scansion) in this case suits well with the awesome naïveté of feeling – 'Now they've no work, like better men / Who sit at desks and take much pay' – which suggests the direct influence of Wilfred Owen. But what makes the poem specifically Spenderian is the final move, when, the objective scenes behind him, Spender returns to his interior silence:

> I'm jealous of the weeping hours
> They stare through with such hungry eyes
> I'm haunted by these images,
> I'm haunted by their emptiness.

The first couplet skilfully places Spender's own position – the well-heeled young poet, over-emotional, and envious of the Romantic despair of the unemployed. In the last couplet, when the withdrawal into the inner world is complete, we accept fully and in good faith his assertion that he is 'haunted'. In one way, the superiority of the poem over so many of Auden's much more impressively adroit social poems could be expressed quite simply by stating that it transmits a far greater 'pity' than is ever present in Auden. Yet what is really interesting about Spender's poem is that emotionally it is *more* sophisticated than Auden's poetry on comparable themes: Spender pursues his compassion with an almost erotic avidity. The poem woos the workers with a woman's softness. The flow of the verse, too, testifies to the technical skill that underlies so much of Spender's almost willed gaucherie.

Spender's genuine introversion of temperament is much better suited to interiorisation of this kind than to the kind of reportage attempted in the popular 'Landscape near an Aerodrome'. This poem, like the equally often anthologised 'Elementary School Classroom', though not offensive in its class-attitudes, remains heavily 'descriptive', its emotion really squirted on to its somewhat turgidly 'precise' observation: fundamentally, Spender remains unengaged. The opening stanza of the 'Landscape' is certainly well achieved with its characteristically tender animism (the 'moth' image, with its 'furry antenae' could only come from Spender), and he has 'done' the aircraft descent for us. But beyond its general accuracy, it fails to justify an interest in the moral indignation that follows. In this case, the indulged sensualism of the animistic metaphor clashes with the social compassion: we get an exercise in social criticism instead of the strongly motivated emotionalism of 'Moving through the silent crowd', in which the poet's near-erotic engagement in the subject fuses into or identifies with the social sympathy. In the present case, the Dickensian social protest – 'Figure frightening and mad' and 'squat buildings / With their strange air behind trees' – is artificially yoked to the beautiful descent imagery of the first stanza, so that the final Blakean warning – 'Religion stands, the Church blocking the sun' – falls with a platitudinous thud.

The successful interiorisation of 'Moving through the silent crowd' and the animistic moth image at the beginning of the 'Landscape' represent two aspects of Spender's introversion of temperament. For the animism could be predicted of his mind. Metaphor itself represents an attempt to activate or vitalise phenomena. It is often implied in critical writing that such an act of animism informs all metaphor in poetry, but as I have tried to show with Auden, this is not really so. In a poet like Spender, we see at work something like the primitive animism, almost fetichistic in its intensity, that galvanises the descriptive writing of Dickens. The moth image at the beginning of the 'Landscape' assumes an alarming furry reality: the 'plane becomes a moth, just as the harbour walls of Port Bou, in the poem of that name, become a child's hands holding a pet. The pet is the sea, trapped in the harbour that

> looks through the gap
> To outer freedom animal air.   ('Port Bou')

The pent-up energy in the clutched animal is transferred to the sea, thus lending the 'description' animated vitality it could not otherwise have had.

This kind of energy-transference, the province often of the witch-doctor or the psychoanalyst, is radical to Spender's metaphor. At its best it is charged alternately with a tremulous tenderness, or a circumscribed virility. At its worst, it merely seeks some objective justification in the given image for the metaphoric transformation the poet automatically needs to effect upon it. 'Seascape', for example strives for the symbolic immanence of Valéry's 'Cimetière Marin' (though the feeling is closer to Shelley), and succeeds only in laboriously establishing average-to-good analogies: the ocean, for instance, is like 'an unfingered harp'. Such *Correspondences*, of course, have been the goal of the poet ever since Baudelaire, although the source for an English poet is directly available in Wordsworth. In

'Cimetière Marin' Valéry lifts the entire plan of his dazzlingly Platonist poem to an exalted spiritual revelation by means of a *Correspondence* between the sails of the ships at sea and the sight of doves pecking upon a roof.

The latent academicism of Spender's symbolist programme in 'Seascape' is mitigated and in part redeemed by the image of the 'motionlessness of the hot sky' that 'tires' to produce the 'sigh, as a woman's' from inland. There is also the characteristically tender image of the two butterflies 'like errant dog-roses' that get themselves drowned (a narrative awkwardness Valéry would have shuddered at, yet somehow carried off by Spender). It is the true naïveté of such images here that keeps Spender from stiffening into an academic symbolist laboriously culling the analogies that have long since lost their Symbolist resonance. The lines following the drowning of the butterflies shockingly betray his naïveté –

> Fishermen understand
> Such wings sunk in such ritual sacrifice.   ('Seascape')

The modish interest in 'ritual' (there is nothing ritualistic about the episode as narrated by Spender) effectively mars the naïveté, and in doing so, underlines it. The final stanza of the poem gives everything up for a mélange of literary echoes involving visions of Atlantis, the sea-change, *The Tempest*.

It was Rilke, however, and not Valéry, who set for Spender the most dangerous precedent, for it was Rilke rather than Valéry who made the most absolute claim for the symbolist *Correspondences*. The *Duino Elegies* are the Koran of symbolism and their success or failure must be held to refute or confirm the acknowledgement of bankruptcy declared in *Une Saison en Enfer*. As we move through the *Collected Poems*, the hand of Rilke exercises a more and more inhibiting restraint upon Spender's native metaphorical sense. He displays a greater and greater concern for finding analogical correlates for phenomena which do not especially seem to have struck him, and his own natural metaphorical animism gives way to an increasingly literary symbolism.

Ultimately the effort to compete with Rilke (this is how it registers) broke Spender. The single image in which he most seriously strives after a Rilkean universality – 'The Vase of Tears' – unequivocally announces the failure of Spender's adoption of Rilkean profundity:

> And one by one these bitter drops collect
> Into my heart, a glass vase which reflects
> The world's grief weeping in its daughter.

A co-translator of the *Duino Elegies* ought to have been more aware of the care with which Rilke ensures a feasible analogical form for his symbols. The cause of Spender's failure in these lines is the absence of any visual or other actual support for the symbol. To call his heart 'a glass vase' was bad enough – the metaphor lacks any real analogical basis. But to go on to picture the vase *reflecting* was disastrous: we are forced to conclude that Spender was leaning entirely upon the reader's stock response to the loaded words – heart and tears.

'The Vase of Tears' was published in the 1937–9 collection, *Love and Separation*. Thereafter the imagery and metaphor show an increasing self-consciousness that borders often on the mechanical. The metaphors and similes succeed more and more in fixing only a limited visual effect. An air raid at Plymouth for example, provokes Spender only to a series of more and less successful parallelisms – the searchlight-beams 'fuse in a cone', or smash the aircraft's image like a cup; they are like fencing swords, or they make geometrical patterns, trying to mark the spot with a cross of doom. The cross they make is of course at once a geometrical intersection, an omen of doom, and then the cross that marks the pilot's grave. This kind of ingenuity betrays the gravity of the events observed. The concern for analogical accuracy destroys or precludes any serious feeling Spender might have entertained. He might be describing a firework display or a circus instead of a struggle in which somebody – the aircrew or the inhabitants of Plymouth – is likely to get killed. The last stanza's Christian sermonisings do not ease matters: on the contrary, the laboured accuracy now connives at a knowing wit – 'the waves/ Chuckle between the rocks'! No-one who has read Edith Sitwell's 'Still falls the rain' is going to be impressed, either, by Spender's final crucifix reference:

> Man hammers nails in Man
> High on his crucifix.

This kind of image-hunting is still more shocking when the subject is Belsen or Buchenwald. The pilot was out of sight, and after all he was a Nazi. Confronted by the living skeletons of Belsen, Spender – who has shown himself so enormously compassionate, so profoundly moved by suffering in poem after poem; who is dangerously vulnerable to emotion, and half-Jewish at the same time – retreats into a hunt for the appropriate image that genuinely appalls: their skin 'tars the bones' with a 'thin varnish'; their faces are like 'clenched despair' 'Knocking at the birdsong-fretted air'.

Failure in the face of Belsen and Hiroshima cannot be held against any artist: they are beyond sympathy. The attempt to treat them in artistic form is at best misguidedly immature, at worst presumptuously self-important. It was inevitable that someone of Spender's endowment – tremulously emotional and accessible to suffering – should be forced into a total withdrawal of himself in the face of the Nazi camps. Hence, his poem on the subject (self-mockingly called 'Memento') not only reveals no evidence whatever of genuine emotional response, it is positively offensive in its unscrupulous seeking after effects: 'birdsong-fretted' in particular, with its Shakespearean overtones, hits an unpleasantly literary note. We resent this display of technique in the context of such suffering, just as we reject the elegance of Sydney Nolan's Auschwitz drawings, and the pious pomp of Britten's War Requiem. All of these performances seem insulting in the circumstances, their 'sincerity' an impertinence, their articulations heartless. Only silence will do, and silence is a failure.

SOURCE: ch. 5, 'A Kind of Scapegoat: A Retrospect on Stephen Spender', in Thurley's *The Ironic Harvest: English Poetry in the Twentieth Century* (London, 1974), pp. 79–97.

NOTES

1. Maynard Mack et al. (eds), *Modern Poetry* (New York, 1952).
2. [Ed.] Spender's poetic response to the Spanish Civil War is discussed by Samuel Hynes in section 2, below.

2. POETS AND WARS

Samuel Hynes On Spender, Auden and Day Lewis (1976)

. . . Spender . . . went to Spain as a propagandist – he was to broadcast from Valencia – and both the propagandist role and the non-combatant status must have created problems. And so, surely, did his poetic sensibility, which was naturally lyrical and emotional, and not inclined to deal in history and abstractions.

From the first, Spender reacted strongly against the distortions of reality that propaganda required. In April 1937, he wrote to the *New Statesman* from Madrid: '. . . to say that those who happen to be killed are heroes is a wicked attempt to identify the dead with the abstract ideas which have brought them to the front, thus adding prestige to those ideas, which are used to lead the living on to similar "heroic" deaths.'

This is a strong statement of [the] recognition . . . of the gap between the big words and the real thing; it is also virtually a programme for Spender's war poems. Spender did not try, as John Cornford had, to include both terms of this dissonance within his poems; rather, he separated individuals altogether from history and ideas. In his Spanish poems no distinctions are made between one side and the other; there is no enemy and no clear cause; there is not even, in most of them, an observing self. What remains is suffering individuals, and an overwhelming, unqualified compassion for them.

The poetry, then, is in the pity. Of all the English poets of the Spanish war, Spender was most clearly indebted to the example of Wilfred Owen, and he was clearly conscious of his debt. In an essay published in the summer of 1937 (not long after his return from Spain), Spender called Owen the greatest English war-poet, and praised his anti-heroism and his truthfulness. What Owen opposed, Spender wrote, was 'the propagandist lie which makes the dead into heroes in order that others may imagine that death is really quite pleasant'.[1] This is very close to the language of Spender's report from Madrid; what it does is to claim Owen as an ancestor, a model of how to write war poetry that avoids propaganda and tells the essential truth, that 'for most of those who participate in it, a war is simply a short way to a beastly death'. Owen was not, for Spender, a technical influence (as he was for Cornford); his example was a moral one, a matter of truth-telling.

One can see Owen's influence in a poem like 'Ultima Ratio Regum', which was published shortly after Spender's anti-heroic report from Madrid, and which is clearly a product of the same experience. The title of the poem comes from the motto that was embossed on the cannons of Louis XIV: force is the final argument of kings. The poem dwells on the disparity between the powerful war-making world of money and arms, and the death of one boy.

> The guns spell money's ultimate reason
> In letters of lead on the spring hillside.
> But the boy lying dead under the olive trees
> Was too young and too silly
> To have been notable to their important eye.
> He was a better target for a kiss.

Spender uses none of the brave abstractions that supported Cornford in his fears; the boy has no consciousness of causes, he is simply a natural thing, like the grass and the leaves, and like grass and leaves he dies. He dies for no principle, one cannot tell which side of the battle he was on, or even whether he was Spanish. He has no connection with the poet – he is neither a comrade nor an enemy – nor even with the battle in which he died: his death has no consequences.

To be truthful as a poet, Spender wrote of Owen, is to be truthful to your own experience. He, too, had experienced a war – that is, he had gone there, he had seen the dead – and his reaction was, like Owen's, one of undiscriminating pity for the victims of war. Like Owen, his pity extended even to the dishonoured dead (compare for example his 'The Coward' and 'The Deserter' with Owen's 'S.I.W.'). Like Owen, he wrote war-poems that do not contain history, or take sides, or deal in ideologies. But behind these similarities there is the deep difference: Owen had shared the experience of war, but Spender only observed it. This is not a point of morality or courage or any such personal judgement, but of poetry. There is something missing from Spender's war poems, some authority for the right to pity; without that authority, which perhaps a poet must earn by sharing in suffering, pity becomes a patronising, distant attitude. Spender's experience of war had been compassion for those who fought, and anger for those who made propaganda, but these feelings had been distanced by the fact that Spender was neither a soldier nor a Spaniard. His compassion is in the poems, but so is the distance. They are, even the best of them, the war poems of a tourist.[2]

Spender wrote many poems about the Spanish war, over several years; Auden wrote only one – 'Spain'. He wrote it immediately after his return from his one visit to the war, and he seems to have got everything he had to say about the issue into it. Auden had departed for Spain in January with a certain amount of left fanfare; the *Daily Worker* announced on 12 January that:

W. H. Auden, the most famous of the younger English poets, co-author of 'The Dog Beneath the Skin', recently produced in London, and a leading figure in the anti-Fascist movement in literature, has left for Spain.
  He will serve as an ambulance driver.[3]

But he didn't; he visited Barcelona and Valencia, and then quietly returned to England. He had little to say at the time about his experiences in Spain, but many years later he recalled one surprising reaction. 'On arriving in Barcelona,' he wrote,

I found as I walked through the city that all the churches were closed and there was not a priest to be seen. To my astonishment, this discovery left me profoundly shocked and disturbed. The feeling was far too intense to be the result of a mere liberal dislike of intolerance, the notion that it is wrong to stop people from doing what they like, even if it is something silly like going to church. I could not escape acknowledging that, however I had consciously ignored and rejected the Church for sixteen years, the existence of churches and what went on in them had all the time been very important to me.[4]

This is reminiscence after nearly twenty years, and perhaps it is coloured by Auden's subsequent return to religion, but something certainly happened in Spain that diminished his commitment to the left line (which had never been very strong). The poem that he wrote after his return is the best of the English war-poems from Spain, but it is also the least partisan, the least passionate, the least concerned with actual war, and the least Spanish. The war in Spain is indeed not so much the subject of the poem as the occasion. What the subject is we may define by recalling Auden's remark about poetry in *The Poet's Tongue*:

. . . Poetry is not concerned with telling people what to do, but with extending our knowledge of good and evil, perhaps making the necessity for action more urgent and its nature more clear, but only leading us to the point where it is possible for us to make a rational and moral choice.[5]

This is what Auden's poem does: it extends our knowledge of the crucial moral choice of the thirties – the choice between fascism and its opponent – by examining that choice as it was manifested in Spain in 1937. But it does not *make* the choice: its subject is moral decision, not political action.

Like [John Cornford's] 'Full Moon at Tierz', 'Spain' takes its form from a theory of history. Auden begins, as Cornford did, with a long perspective view of the process of historical change. He starts where European economic history starts, with 'the language of size / Spreading to China along the trade routes', and moves through the Middle Ages, the Renaissance, and the Counter-Reformation, to nineteenth-century science and engineering, seeing the European past as a record of consciousness altered by economic change.

At the fourth stanza the present begins to enter contrapuntally: 'Yesterday the Sabbath of witches; but to-day the struggle.' *Struggle* is a heavily ideological word, but in the poem it carries a meaning that is more general, ,and less specifically polemical, than simply *class-struggle*; it is rather the struggle or moral choice that goes on occurring *every* today, because in the present in which men live they must choose and act: the present is the point of intersection in time where Freedom becomes Necessity, and Choice becomes History. Though individuals (the poet, the scientist, the ordinary poor) and nations invoke the life-force to intervene and act for them, life only replies: 'O no, I am not the mover; Not to-day; not to you . . . I am whatever you do . . . I am your choice, your decision.' In 1937, that determining decision would be a decision about Spain, but the conception is one of general morality, not of particular politics.

In Auden's terms, every moment is a border-situation in time, a frontier between the known past and 'perhaps, the future' – *perhaps*, because the future depends on the decision made now, as the frontier is crossed. The future is therefore rendered in the poem in random images of peace, some solemn, some rather comical or ironic: the rediscovery of romantic love, the photographing of ravens, the bicycle races through the suburbs on summer evenings, 'all the fun / Under Liberty's masterful shadow'. They are random, because the future is composed of unselected options – it is perfectly free, because it is not yet history. There is no implication in the poem that the future will take any particular political form, or that it will be different in details from the present and the past; it will simply be people doing what they like.

But between past and future lies today, and today's choice, which waits in Spain to be made:

> On that arid square, that fragment nipped off from hot
> Africa, soldered so crudely to inventive Europe;
>   On that tableland scored by rivers,
> Our thoughts have bodies; the menacing shapes of our fever
>
> Are precise and alive. For the fears which made us respond
> To the medicine ad. and the brochure of winter cruises
>   Have become invading battalions;
> And our faces, the institute-face, the chain-store, the ruin
>
> Are projecting their greed as the firing squad and the bomb.
> Madrid is the heart. Our moments of tenderness blossom
>   As the ambulance and the sandbag;
> Our hours of friendship into a people's army.

The striking thing about these lines is that they treat the Spanish war in psychological, not political terms, as an eruption of the sickness of modern society: in Spain, the enemy is *us* – our fears and greeds (as usual, Auden involves himself in the class he condemns); and the people's army is psychological, too, a sort of metaphor for loving feelings. It is more than a metaphor, though; in Spain 'our thoughts have bodies', what was mental has become physical, and therefore mortal.

The struggle, then, is a struggle between sickness and health, and Spain is a case. The treatment is immediate choice, commitment to some form of action:

> To-day the deliberate increase in the chances of death,
> The conscious acceptance of guilt in the necessary murder;
>   To-day the expending of powers
> On the flat ephemeral pamphlet and the boring meeting.

A chance of death, guilt, wasted time, boredom – these are random, unheroic, and not explicitly political (which side does one write the pamphlet for?). But they are actual commitments that a young poet might make or reject, occasions for moral choice.

At the end the poem returns to that abstract theme, to re-state it as directly and bluntly as the moral of a fable:

> The stars are dead. The animals will not look.
> We are left alone with our day, and the time is short, and
>   History to the defeated
> May say Alas but cannot help nor pardon.

Auden has since condemned this passage as 'wicked doctrine', on the grounds that it equates goodness with success. But in fact it does nothing of the kind; what it says is simply that History is Necessity, and that it is made by men's choices. Once it is made, help and pardon are irrelevant. It is a harsh morality, for a harsh time, but it is nevertheless a morality, and not a wicked one.

'Spain' is an extraordinary war-poem – diagnostic, abstract, detached, lacking all the particularities and feelings that defined the genre in the First World War and were continued by poets like Cornford and Spender. There are no battles in the poem, no dead boys or screaming women, no grisly details, and no personal voice testifying to war's hideousness. Not only is there no 'I' in it, there is no suggestion of direct observation at all; Auden's Spain is a shape on a map, or the earth seen from a great height, not a landscape. It is a pitiless poem; the poetry is in the pitilessness.

It is also an open and unresolved poem. This is partly inherent in the theme: moral choices must be made *now*, but the consequences are never clear. But it is also partly a function of the poem's date: in the spring of 1937, the future of the Spanish war, and the future of Europe that seemed to hang on it, were still uncertain. And it was partly an expression of Auden's own unideological position: he was certainly pro-Loyalist, and that shows in the poem, but he was unwilling to assign good and evil to causes in the simple way that other war-poets did, or to pretend that a good cause was necessarily a successful one. What he wrote instead was a poem expressing the difficulty and necessity of making moral choices in a disastrous time. . . .

. . . The Munich Crisis of September 1938 was a symbolic event equal in its effect on literary consciousness to Hitler's rise to power in 1933, or the beginning of the Spanish Civil War in 1936. After Munich, writing in England has a different tone: the last calls to political commitment had been sounded, and had failed, and there would be no heroic actions. The waiting for the end could begin in earnest.

This was more than a matter of literary sensibility – the tone of all English life changed during those late September days. While Chamberlain negotiated, England made preparations for war;

trenches were dug in the London parks – in Kensington Gardens and
Hyde Park, in St James's Park, and in Lincoln's Inn Fields – and
passers-by paused to see how it was done, and then went home to dig
their own air-raid shelters. Gas-masks were issued to civilians, and
the evacuation of children began. Blackout precautions were issued,
and air-raid wardens were recruited. The quality of life became
essentially that of a nation at war.

A clear example of this change of tone is in the reception given to
Day Lewis's new book of poems, *Overtures to Death and Other Poems*,
when it appeared in October 1938. Like the earlier collections of his
short poems, this one shows the two conflicting sides of the poet's
mind: his Georgian, nature-poet sensibility, and his political mili-
tancy. But it also contains a third kind of poetry – poems of passive
waiting for disaster that one might call his 'post-political poems', such
as 'Bombers', 'Newsreel', and the long title poem. The effect of the
whole is more sombre, and more private, than the earlier Day Lewis
had been; even the political poems seem less strident (the longest
poem, 'The Nabara', a narrative account of a Spanish sea-battle, has
the retrospective, historical quality that the narrative poems of
Newbolt and Chesterton have).

John Lehmann reviewed the book in the *Daily Worker*, and, as one
might expect, praised it. But his praise struck a new note. Day Lewis,
he said, had withdrawn into himself, but he did not take this to be
wrong:

When I say he has withdrawn into himself, I do not mean he has ceased to be
interested in the immediate problems of society: far from it. The chief
impression which the collection gives is of painful, rigorously honest
self-examination, of bitter foreboding of impending disaster for the life
around him, of struggles to decode questions of choice and action which
experience has shown to be far harder and more complex than first
enthusiasm counted.

But this mood seems to me the real 'iron' which Day Lewis had not yet
achieved in *From Feathers to Iron* [1931], and to create a poetry which is truly
adequate for a thinking, civilised being face to face with the terrible future
that the convulsions of capitalism are preparing for us.[6]

And he quoted, from 'February, 1936', and 'Bombers', passages
which seemed to him 'the grim essence of thoughts and feelings which
only came to most people in the "dream-house" for about three days
at the end of September'. So the poems express the mood of Munich,
and Munich confirms the poems.

Elizabeth Bowen also reviewed the book, and like Lehmann she read it as topical and necessary to the time. 'At any time,' she wrote,

the appearance of a new collection of poems by Mr Day Lewis is an event. But coming in this present unhappy autumn, *Overtures to Death* has an importance outside literary experience. Above the too many confused, urgent, uncertain voices we wait to hear the poet lift his note of authority. Stress, tension have tuned us up to listen: it is essential for us that what *is* essential should now be said. Where, under this constant threat to peace, do we stand – in our relation to the outside world, in our relation to ourselves? We hardly even know what questions to put to our own hearts. And at this moment when we must need vision, the everyday man's vision is cruelly blurred. Art keeps its immutable values, but if we are to draw strength from art (and we do need strength) we must have art that speaks in our own terms, that comprehends our entire experience. Mr Day Lewis's poems seem most great now because of their double relevance – they have a poetic relevance to all time, and are at the same time relevant to our perplexing day.[7]

This sounds surprisingly like *The Times* leader-writer on 'Poets and the Crisis', though its example is a poet whom *The Times* would scarcely be expected to approve. The point is that in this mood, in this 'unhappy autumn', old and young, Right and Left were not essentially different in their notions of the poet's task: for both, art could only play a passive role – comforting, but not directing. No one could demand any longer that the writer 'make action urgent and its nature clear', for action no longer seemed possible. As the *TLS* said, Day Lewis's poems were 'dreadfully apposite at the moment; they are written under the stimulus and fear of death by air-raid'.[8] And what action should a poet urge against that destiny? . . .

SOURCE: extracts from chs VIII and IX of *The Auden Generation: Literature and Politics in England in the 1930s* (London, 1976), pp. 248–55, 334–7.

NOTES

[Reorganised and renumbered from the original – Ed.]

1. Stephen Spender, 'Poetry', *Fact*, 4 (July 1937), p. 26. [Extracts from this essay are given in section 1 of Part One, above – Ed.]

2. It is perhaps this aspect of Spender's relation to the war in Spain that led Hugh Kingsmill and Malcolm Muggeridge to satirise his war poems in their *1938: A Pre-view of Next Year's News* (London, 1937). The book is a series of imaginary news items for the year ahead. The item for 20 June reads:

At a literary luncheon in the Holborn Restaurant yesterday, the guest of honour, Mr Stephen Spender, gave readings from poems written while on active service in Spain. Proposing a vote of thanks, Miss Maude Royden said that whatever their political views might be, they must all surely recognise in the poems they had just listened to the most poignant expression, since Rupert Brooke, of youth going gallantly into battle. Certain lines of those they had just heard would, she knew, for ever linger in her memory:

> If I die in Spain
> I do not die in Spain
> I die in the future
> And shall live again
> When the future has overtaken the past.

3. *Daily Worker*, 12 Jan. 1937, p. 3.

4. W. H. Auden, in *Modern Canterbury Pilgrims*, edited by the Dean of New York (London, 1956), p. 41.

5. W. H. Auden and John Garrett (eds), Introduction to *The Poet's Tongue: An Anthology* (London, 1935), p. ix. [Extracts from this Introduction are given in section 1 of Part One, above – Ed.]

6. John Lehmann, 'The Advance of C. Day Lewis', *Daily Worker*, 19 Oct. 1938, p. 7.

7. Elizabeth Bowen, 'Overtures to Death', *Now and Then*, 61 (Winter 1938), pp. 32–3.

8. 'A Poet of Warfare', review in *Times Literary Supplement*, 8 Oct. 1938, p. 637.

3. POETRY AND THE THIRTIES

Francis Hope   The Thirties   (1964)

Clichés drive out clichés: in the process, we hope, truth is approached. Five or ten years ago it was a commonplace to see the Thirties as the Pink Poet's decade, when some fine talents were marred, and a few ruined, by an extreme concentration on externals dictated by the party line; when an all-pervading concern with politics swept into literature. Today it is becoming a commonplace to see it as the reverse: a period, as Mr Philip Toynbee wrote, of 'intense literary excitement' first and foremost, when an all-pervading concern with literature even swept into politics.

For the truth is that the 'political' thirties were nothing like so heavily political, for the readers of little magazines, as the past ten years have been. Or rather it is fair to say that the politics of middle-class intellectuals in those days were really a kind of hobby – a passionate stimulant rather than a burdensome and cruel necessity. With perfect propriety the poets and novelists of that time took only what they wanted from a political scene which was still remote from them.

Defending themselves against journalistic charges of journalistic practice, the Thirties poets have established how few of their poems were in fact concerned with political subjects; how little of an organised group they actually formed (the Big Four rammed together under Roy Campbell's contemptuous pseudonym Macspaunday were only once, during the whole decade, simultaneously all in the same room); how much the trade of pure literature owes to them. Time, which is indifferent to the Oxford collective poem or *Poems about the Spanish Civil War*, has invested Auden with a retrospective faith and promoted MacNeice for honest doubt. Indeed, the advance of MacNeice's reputation marks the current valuation of the Thirties as surely as mercury in a thermometer: the higher this uncommitted urban lyricist, modern but not contemporary, the further we are from the Left Book Club and the International Brigade. The real Thirties, now, are sought beneath the political surface, in the timeless springs of good writing: we do not accuse that lost-and-found generation of politicising literature, but of putting too literary a gloss on politics. And out of their own mouths many a middle-aged mellow retrospective glance confirms this diagnosis. Day Lewis's *The Buried Day* [1960] is a fine but not a unique example.

Should we take it, and leave it, at this? Surely the Depression and the War, armaments and anti-fascism, China and Spain, have been unburied often enough?

> The Anschluss, Guernica – all the names
> At which those poets thrilled or were afraid
> For me mean schools and schoolmasters and games;
> And in the process something is betrayed.

Separate the poets from the ballyhoo, Auden recently urged on television; judge the tree by its fruits, not by the slogans that someone else has pinned on the orchard. Even if it means accepting those neo-Poundians who dismiss the Thirties as a literary irrelevance (another strong 'revisionist' interpretation now going the rounds), shouldn't we keep to the poetical texts?

Certainly some quiet empiricism seems in order. The cross-currents of the period were more complicated than elementary stratifications allow. *New Verse*, for example, published a variety of poets from Dylan Thomas and Philip O'Connor to Norman Cameron and David Gascoyne, as well as Auden, MacNeice, Spender, Allott, Madge, Fuller, Prokosch and Bernard Spencer. It also rarely missed an opportunity to denounce Day Lewis for lickspittle fellow-travelling. (It rarely offered total freedom from denunication to anybody, which may provide an artificially easy ground for seeing internecine differences.) The personalities of the decade altered their views as the decade wore on: by 1937 Edgell Rickword was upbraiding Auden for having abandoned 'that sensuous consciousness of social change which made his early poems such exciting discoveries'. Spain quenched almost as much enthusiasm as it kindled; even Baldwin's government either introduced or was blessed by some economic recovery. In Spain itself, as Julian Symons has recorded, the majority of English combatants were workers, not middle-class intellectuals. His book on the Thirties also does the useful service of pointing out how small the numbers actively involved in intellectual life were: Auden's *Poems* sold 3,500 copies in seven years; *The Orators* sold 2,000 in eleven. Respectable, but hardly remarkable. The famous silences of the Forties ('where are the war poets?') marked not only the expiring hopes of a clever, dishonest decade, but a turning away from politics which went deep into the decade's second half. In MacNeice's *Autumn Journal* the spirit of post-war liberalism is already beating strong.

> Nettlebed, Shillingford, Dorchester – each unrolls
>   The road to Oxford; *Qu'allais-je faire* tomorrow
> Driving voters to the polls
>   In that home of lost illusions?
> And what am I doing it for?
>   Mainly for fun, partly for a half-believed in
> Principle, a core
>   Of fact in a pulp of verbiage,
> Remembering that this crude and so-called obsolete
>   Top-heavy tedious parliamentary system
> Is our only ready weapon to defeat
>   The legions' eagles and the lictors' axes. . . .

And as well as empiricism, modesty might temper our hindsight. Once past 1945, Attlee's brand of socialism may seem acceptable and eminently realistic; in 1933 the coming death-agonies of capitalism and social democracy were a more probable bet. We tend to think that because we know that the Great Crash of 1929 was important, we also know what living through it was like, and to measure the intellectual appeal of Marxism by the crudities of the *Daily Worker* or the sibylline obscurities of *New Left Review*. Claud Cockburn, John Strachey and Christopher Caudwell were not fools, and those who were influenced by them can hardly be said to have ignored all the real issues of their time. Early Stalinism was swallowed, the New Deal was wrongly ignored (though not by Cockburn), and books like Geoffrey Gorer's *Nobody Talks Politics* provide rich material for a *sottisier*. All the more credit to people like Orwell or D. W. Brogan, who were isolatedly right. But one cannot dismiss the 'left-wing orthodoxy' as a touching blind alley, nor as a marginal interference. It was a more political – or at least a more politically hopeful – period than the present; we enjoy different circumstances, but not necessarily better judgement. Until we outgrow the illusion that the politics can be dismissed we shall not get very far with the poetry; we shall impose our presuppositions on them as surely as they sometimes imposed theirs on history.

It is commonly asserted now (and was then) that as middle-class radicals they failed to connect political ideas with anything that touched them very deeply. Allen Tate, in 1937:

> The well-brought-up young men discovered that people work in factories and mines, and they want to know more about these people. But it seems to me that instead of finding out about them, they write poems calling them Comrades from a distance.

A judgement vindicated by examples too numerous to quote and, in some cases, too obvious to refute. One of the attractions of the Spanish cause may well have been the classlessness which foreigners always miraculously acquire: the embarrassing gulfs between a socialist poet and an English industrial worker were transmuted to a picturesque starkness when the worker was replaced by a Catalan peasant. But one cannot accuse Julian Bell, or Caudwell, or John Cornford of frivolously dabbling in a world to which they had no real commitments. Death in battle is a solider guarantee of sincerity than the most impeccable working-class pedigree. It was political doctrine, rather than social authenticity, that motivated the pre-war left. Today the balance has shifted.

Admittedly, Thirties parties were not free from arguments about whose parents' house had a bathroom, but they tended to be of a rather academic kind. There was proletcult, but few real proletarians: this led to the insincerity Tate deplored, and to such vagaries of bourgeois Marxism as the snobbish assertion that the lower-middle class represented the real scourings of capitalist society; the barrister's son sneered at the clerk's, and called it socialism. (Today the lower-middle class has provided far too many of the new intelligentsia for such sentiments to gain wide currency.) But all this didn't occupy quite the front rank that class-obsessed moderns may give it. Some solid political interest and information underlay it – far more, I think, than CND ever dispersed, and CND is the nearest thing to politics that post-war Britain can show. A friend of Spender's once complained to me that he (Spender) had been attacked for crusading in politics without understanding them. 'They say that now we have writers like Wesker, who tell us what the working-class is really like, we can see what rubbish Stephen was talking. And after *Roots*, they still think that Wesker knows about politics. Compare him with Stephen, who really did know – who could tell you what a Viennese Social Democrat was.' Between the conception of politics as being in resonance with one's own country's working-class, and the conception of politics as knowing what a Viennese Social Democrat stands for, there is a deep and important gulf. The Thirties' political commitment, like that of well-off English radicals from Byron on, was a European one: and that is now simply unfashionable. We read foreign languages, and travel, less; American academic grants, not the European purchasing power of the pound, are the main prop of the contemporary poet's *wanderjahre*, if he has any. Our horizons are either too small for Europe, or too wide; our own concerns don't straggle beyond Dover and our headlines take in the whole world.

Most literary radicals of the Thirties, I believe, were in a very different situation. For them politics and Europe were almost interchangeable terms. Both were urgent, tragic, and yet liberating areas to explore; fields of great importance, which the old and powerful were too stupid to understand but where the future of civilisation would be settled, and settled soon. Time and again in the poems of the period one finds Europe used as the symbol of political struggle. As Allott wrote:

> From this wet island of birds and chimneys
> who can watch suffering Europe and not be angry?

These Anglo-Eurocentric attitudes may explain their ignorance of American culture as well as American politics. It may also account for the frequent glossing of Soviet crimes as something only to be expected from a primitive, semi-Asiatic nation: Auden (again, on television) ruefully remarked that his contemporaries had felt that the Russians 'weren't white folks' and therefore should not be judged too harshly.

If this led them to ignore today's '*supergrands*', it also led them to ignore the Empire. So did anti-patriotism, an emotion for which First World War schooldays must have provided a firm, almost an objective foundation. In one of *Encounter's* interminable symposia on entering the Common Market, Auden wrote:

Beneath the arguments Pro and Con lie passionate prejudices and the eternal feud between the High-Brow and the Low-Brow. . . . I know Europe at first hand, and as a writer I cannot conceive of my life without the influence of its literature, music and art. The Dominions, on the other hand, are for me *tiefste Provinz*, places which have produced no art and are inhabited by the kind of person with whom I have least in common.

For the Low-Brows . . . the Dominions are inhabited by their relatives and people like themselves, speaking English, eating English food, wearing

English clothes and playing English games, whereas 'abroad' is inhabited by immoral strangers – a French novel is synonymous with pornography . . .

A bit quirky? But isn't it also true that one of the great disasters of the period was that British policy was in the hands of men who really were more interested in Empire than in Europe, and that they were too old or too stubborn to change their focus? Ideally an intermediate generation should have forced up a way under them; but nobody, in this Commemorative Season of 1914, needs to be told where that generation was. Some arrogant and prickly certainty, some conviction that only radical change would do, some contemptuous insistence on the war between young and old, is no more than one would expect from a generation without elder brothers. Once again their situation was very different from our own: a mere application of the commonsense of the Sixties doesn't highlight solutions they were too stupid to see.

The difference cuts both ways, making nonsense of nostalgia as well as the wisdom of hindsight. As always, the lesson of history is not to assume lightly that history repeats itself. A return to the spirit of the Popular Front is not going to revivify either our poetry or our politics. We know our situation as they knew theirs, and react accordingly; to revamp an old Thirties slogan – and one that may be quite compatible with Toynbee's argument – liberalism is the knowledge of impotence. That superb confidence which is the main virtue of the Thirties poets was not all of it misplaced confidence. It was in part the inherited moral capital of a class: of that overlapping ground between the English gentry and the bourgeoisie which was so supremely sure of its right and ability to teach, cure, preach to and administer its own inferiors at home, or whole nations overseas. It was in part the product of a specific political situation: a country governed by old men, apparently indifferent to the problems to which the poets' inclinations, education, friendships and knowledge all drove them. It was partly a matter of individual temperaments: Auden's schoolmasterly certainty combined with a streak of *enfant-terrible* desire to make the grown-ups' flesh creep with imaginary horrors (he once told me in conversation that he had always been the youngest child and the youngest grandchild in family gatherings, and still tended to look on himself as the youngest person in any room); or that Wykehamist rectitude that has often infuriatingly protected Labour Party leaders from being irritated by criticism. It did not even survive their own decade. But it was more than an error which time has disproved; more than a passing eccentricity which we luckily will not have to go through, and which we can ignore in our comments on them. It is not a question of what 'real poetry' we can salvage from the wreck of convictions, but of hiving off the good from the bad in what the convictions produced. They were indeed, as they claimed, involved with history. Consequently, the worst of their poems may only be read for the light they throw on their decade; but the study of their decade will continue to throw some light on even the best of their poems.

SOURCE: essay first published as 'Then and Now' in *The Review*, 11–12 (1964); reproduced with the title 'The Thirties' in Ian Hamilton (ed.), *The Modern Poet: Essays from 'The Review'* (London, 1968), pp. 83–9.

Martin Dodsworth   'The Poetry of Addition': on Bernard Spencer and Others   (1964)

Bernard Spencer was fifty-three when he died in an accident in 1963; his second book of poems, *With Luck Lasting*, had only just been published. It received little notice, and despite the efforts of the Third Programme and *The London Magazine* it is quite possible, things being what they are, that it will soon be forgotten. That would be a pity because Spencer was a good poet. He belongs, perhaps, with those writers who have cultivated a single talent rather than a handful – poets like Norman Cameron or Andrew Young – but that is not a place without honour. Spencer fills it with an authority that I find lacking in either Cameron or Young. Furthermore, his poetry is more clearly related to the poetry of his own generation than is the case with either of these other two; it achieves in its own clear way something that most of his contemporaries were fumbling for in their poems.

His first book did not appear until 1946, at so late an hour that you might think he didn't have much to do with the Thirties at all, especially as its title, *Aegean Islands*, smacks more of Mediterranean luxury than of social concern. But then we have some odd ideas about these poets anyway: for example, we relegate Dylan Thomas and George Barker to the Forties, as though they weren't as much part of the post-Eliot scene as Auden or MacNeice. No: Spencer was a poet of that generation all right – born the same year as Louis MacNeice, and first published noticeably in *New Verse*, of which he was for a while co-editor. The pedigree is impeccable.

Kenneth Allott has said that Spencer's poem 'Allotments: April'

might very well represent the kind of poem for which *New Verse* stood: straightforward but unpedestrian language, feeling expressed through obser-vation, intelligence reflecting on observation and awake to the implications of feeling.

The poem is in part an attempt to revise literary convention; it is about spring, but spring is no longer 'the only pretty ring-time', for now 'love detonates like sap / Up into the limbs of men and bears all the seasons / And the starving and the cutting . . .' We have given up songs of spring, and our sense of it is diminished further by our no longer believing in a God: 'Lost to some of us the festival joy / At the bursting of the tomb . . .' April only means now the boys playing out of doors again and the gardeners working in the allotments:

> they make a pause in
> The wireless voice repeating pacts, persecutions,
> And imprisonments and deaths and heaped violent deaths,
> Impersonal now as figures in the city news.

It cannot expunge the poet's consciousness of 'real poverty, / The sour doorways of the poor';

> Rather it adds
> What more I am; excites the deep glands
> And warms my animal bones as I go walking
> Past the allotments and the singing water-meadows. . . .

It is not only the qualities of observation and intelligence noted by Mr Allott, or the way the poem works against literary convention, or its awareness of 'real poverty', that makes it typical of its time (it was printed in *New Verse* for June–July 1936); it is also the very structure and conclusion of the poem 'Rather it adds . . .'

'Allotments: April' begins with a question: 'In what sense am I joining in / Such a hallooing, rousing April day . . . ?' After the question, possible answers are rejected, for the old ways of thinking about the season are outdated. The poet's situation is described, and finally an answer is given. Spring is no longer seen as a force that transforms sensation; it merely adds to existing sensations the sense of 'what more I am'. Just as the feeling of spring is reduced by the poet to the same level as other feelings, so the poem's conclusion seems to have an equal weight with its other parts. It is equally important for the poet to say what April is not as what it is. There is an equal stress on the descriptive part of the poem as there is on the part which attempts to answer the question which ostensibly prompts the poem. Finally, there is an impression of arbitrariness in the order of the parts of the poem that separate the question from its answer, and this may be attributed to the poet's refusal to value one rejected answer above another. He wants his rejected answers, as it were, side by side. I would like to argue that this poetry of addition, as it might be termed, derives from the general tendency of the Thirties poets to employ catalogues of objects or similes in their poems, and especially from the kind of feeling that drove them to do this.

These poets were attempting to make the subject of their poetry a vastly more complicated world than had for a century or so seemed to be in its affinities poetic. They wanted to get into their poems direct experience of a largely mechanised society viewed in the light of current political and psychological theory, and that implied, in effect, a development of poetic practice in two directions at once. Firstly they had to extend the subject-matter of their poems to include a way of life under industrial conditions to a large extent unfamiliar to their likely readers, if not to themselves; and secondly they had to develop a style capable of expressing the complication and depth of motive which had brought that way of life into being. Day Lewis's *The Magnetic Mountain* is a good example of the poet's staking of claims in new territory; so is Charles Madge's poem 'Drinking in Bolton', with its curious air of being a report from country hitherto unexplored:

> Not from imagination I am drawing
> This landscape (Lancs), this plate of tripe and onions. . . .

A lot of the poetry was a kind of literary equivalent to Mass Observation: a poetry that accumulated detail in the present tense, adding clause to clause in a theoretically endless because arbitrarily related series:

> The streets are brightly lit; our city is kept clean:
> The third class have the greasiest cards, the first play high;
> The beggars sleeping in the bows have never seen
> What can be done in staterooms; no one asks why
>   (W. H. Auden, 'The Ship')

If one wanted to group the poets of the Thirties in a way that would make useful generalisations possible, it would not be utterly foolish to distinguish between those who, like Empson or Dylan Thomas, employed a syntax that was complex, argumentative and intensive, and those who, like Auden or MacNeice, used syntax that was simple and direct, but sought to hint at the intricacy of their subject matter by leaving the relation of statements to each other obscure. Auden, it is true, is a poet of such large sympathies that it is hard to pin him down to one method rather than another. Nevertheless, the cumulative style has played an important part in the development of his verse. It is, after all, the foundation of 'Spain':

> Yesterday all the past. The language of size
> Spreading to China along the trade-routes: the diffusion
>   Of the counting-frame and the cromlech;
> Yesterday the shadow reckoning in the sunny climates.
>
> Yesterday the assessment of insurance by cards,
> The divination of water, yesterday the invention
>   Of cart-wheels and clocks. . . .

Many of his recent poems, too, are indebted to this style of thinking and writing, since they consist largely of heaps of facts – the 'Bucolics' in *The Shield of Achilles*, for example, or more startlingly 'Encomium Balnei' and 'The Cave of Nakedness' (*Encounter*, August 1962 and December 1963).

Of course, to observe that the Thirties poets have such a rhetorical characteristic is to say nothing of the value of it poetically; the *kind* of use to which it is put differs vastly with each poet. Generally, it seems that wherever speech was reduced to a series of names of objects or simple statements not obviously connected by discursive logic it became necessary for the poet to emphasise the tone of voice in which he was speaking; both the examples from Auden show this. There is a similar stress laid in those poems of MacNeice that demonstrate this cumulative style; 'Bagpipe Music' is almost entirely a matter of the tone of voice:

> It's no go the picture palace, it's no go the stadium,
> It's no go the country cot with a pot of pink geraniums,
> It's no go the Government grants, it's no go the elections,
> Sit on your arse for fifty years and hang your hat on a pension.

There is no argument or progression here; the poem depends for its success entirely on the voice that we catch between the lines. The poem stands still as the music gets wilder and wilder – that is the point. But it needn't be; other poems pile up names and statements with this frenetic effect, and almost disguise the fact that the same device is being used:

> Down in Europe Seville fell,
> Nations germinating hell,
> The Olympic games were run –
> Spots upon the Aryan sun.
> And the don in me set forth
> How the landscape of the North
> Had educed the saga style
> Plodding forward mile by mile.   ('Postscript to Iceland')

The point about the way cumulative effects are used by the Thirties poets is that they resist being pinned down as part of one mode of expression at all because they can be made to serve so many different ends. For example, it would be tempting to explain their use as springing from the comparatively simple attitudes politically committed poets had to express; continually to add to the non-essential, non-argumentative parts of a poem might be a means of hiding the crudity of emotion and paucity of ideas implicit in the committed message. This might be true of 'Spain', for example, though one can applaud both the superficial liveliness of the poem and its right-mindedness; it might be even truer of Spender's 'Vienna'. But one has to bear in mind other uses of the trick: for instance, the effect is not simple in the conclusion of a poem like Michael Robert's 'Elegy for the Fallen Climbers':

> The pause, the poise between two worlds, returning –
> Rivers, communications, railroads, frontiers,
> The valley, and white saxifrage and gentians,
> Soft evening light upon the lower hills,
> Returning –
>
> The chouca turning in the air, the dazzling ice,
> The massive broken peak, the world unfolded.
> Darkness like an anguish, falling,
> The eyes, the fingers black with frostbite,
> The substance or the shadow, turning, twisting?

The landscape is at least half Auden – valley, frontier and gentians – but the intonation is Roberts's; far more even than the grating repetitions of 'Bagpipe Music' these lines depend on our noticing the kind of voice that underlies their grammatical haziness. The gradual mounting-up to an indefinite conclusion – 'turning, twisting?' – is parallel to the oncome of 'Darkness like an anguish falling', but the parallel is not made explicit in this series of phrases like beads on a string. Faced by a descriptive technique used for such different purposes as we find in Roberts and MacNeice, we must be content with the explanation that it derives from the poets' awareness of a wider world to look at, in the largest sense; a similar explanation can be offered for the similar technique in Whitman. It is not a striking generalisation, but it does not risk too much.

'Allotments: April' uses the cumulative style in a way that suggests on the part of the poet the discovery of a hitherto uncomprehended complexity in his feelings, together with an apparently artless honesty that withholds nothing from the reader. 'Rather it adds / What more I am . . .' Spring is Spencer's consciousness of his own self set off against his awareness of things that call him out of himself – 'imprisonments and deaths' and 'real poverty' – and he sees it as part of a larger movement in the world of which he is only one inhabitant. The personal conclusion and tone of voice suggest the individual, whilst the collection of descriptive facts suggests the world in which the individual is only another fact. The poem depends on the balance of these paradoxical feelings, and employs an equalising style to express them; finally, it evades any false solution to the paradox by a beautiful, gliding movement that passes from the individual to the nature that surrounds him to the nature that echoes his situation ambiguously:

> April warms my animal bones as I go walking
> Past the allotments and the singing water-meadows
> Where hooves of cattle have plodded and cratered, and
> Watch today go up like a single breath
> Holding in its applause at masts of height
> Two elms and their balanced attitude like dancers,
>   their arms like dancers.

'Once in Greece he started to carve out quite new kinds of poem, and indeed it is within the context of Greece that his work is best judged.' Spencer went to Greece in 1938, and it is true that from that date on his poems are immediately recognisable as his; yet we don't need to concur with the second half of what his friend Lawrence Durrell has to say. His development owes as much to the English literary scene in spirit as it does to the Greek and Mediterranean landscape in subject-matter. The intensity of the Southern light and atmosphere seems to have driven him to an extreme objectivity in his verse that almost squeezes personality out of the poem. But there is always the poet's special tone of voice to assure us that his interest is a human one. . . .

. . . Reading his poems reminds one that the Thirties was not a time of entirely political verse but of some of the most humanely concerned poetry in English.

SOURCE: extract from 'Bernard Spencer' in *The Review*, 11–12 (1964); reproduced in Ian Hamilton (ed.), *The Modern Poet: Essays from 'The Review'* (London, 1968), pp. 90–6, 100.

Bernard Bergonzi   'The Audenesque'   (1978)

. . . Auden's *Poems* of 1930 contained poems that resisted wide imitation, particularly the love poems, or the cryptic reflective pieces written in short lines, with a compact or repetitive syntax. It is only in his second collection, *Look, Stranger!* (1935), that one sees the full emergence of the Audenesque, by which I mean that particular manner of Auden's that became a collective idiom. Cecil Day Lewis was Auden's first unabashed disciple and imitator. They became acquainted at Oxford, where, although Auden was three years younger, Day Lewis succumbed heavily to his influence, particularly in 1927–8, when Auden was in his final undergraduate year and Day Lewis, having already graduated, was teaching in a prep school in north Oxford. Under Auden's dominance Day Lewis's verse changed rapidly from a neo-Georgian to an Audenesque manner; one of the sections of Day Lewis's *Transitional Poem* of 1929 contains an epigraph from Auden, while *The Magnetic Mountain* (1933) closely imitates Auden for long stretches at a time. By contrast, Stephen Spender, also much influenced by Auden at Oxford, possessed a tougher and more individual poetic personality; Auden's influence was more thoroughly absorbed and was more apparent in themes and choice of subject than in verbal mannerism, although an occasional line like 'Northwards the sea exerts his huge mandate', from 'The Port', in Spender's *Poems* (1933), is a pure example of the Audenesque. Louis

MacNeice, who is often placed with Spender and Day Lewis as part of the 'Auden group', seems to have known Auden only casually at Oxford and to have developed independently as a poet. His close contact with Auden did not begin until they collaborated in *Letters from Iceland* in 1936.

It was the anthologies *New Signatures* (1932) and *New Country* (1933) that found Auden a wider audience and spread his influence. One of the contributors to the latter, Charles Madge, wrote in his 'Letter to the Intelligentsia',

> But there waited for me in the summer morning
> Auden, fiercely. I read, shuddered and knew
> And all the world's stationary things
> In silence moved to take up new positions. . . .

The Supplement to the *Oxford English Dictionary* cites the first occurrence of 'Audenesque' in a quotation from *Scrutiny* in 1940. This is far too late: the word occurs much earlier, in the title of Gavin Ewart's 'Audenesque for an Initiation' published in *New Verse* in December 1933. (Admittedly the word is generally an adjective, while Ewart here used it as a noun, similar to 'humoresque'. Graham Greene used it as an adjective in a film review in 1936.) This poem, a remarkable achievement for a schoolboy of seventeen, as Ewart then was, is a witty and spirited imitation of Auden's 'Get there if you can . . .' from the 1930 *Poems* (itself, of course, a parody of Tennyson's 'Locksley Hall'). A few months later Ewart gave further evidence both of his own fascination with Auden and of the way in which Auden's name and influence were increasingly taken for granted. In 'Journey' (*New Verse*, April, 1934) Ewart wrote,

> Where do I want to go? Let me see the map.
> All these roads arc Auden's, old chap.
> I've been over them once, following his tracks;
> The private paths are Eliot's, stony and complex. . . .

In using the image of the map, Ewart shrewdly directed attention to a major feature of Auden's imaginative universe, and one of the most influential. Landscapes and maps, lists and catalogues, were indeed a recurring element in Auden's poetry. But to make the point too baldly is to emphasise content rather than form; critics of Auden have written freely about industrial landscapes, abandoned workings, or the airman's eye-view, but have not looked very closely at the way his style worked and what its implications were. One critic who did have an accurate understanding of the Audenesque, considered primarily as style, was G. Rostrevor Hamilton, whose short book *The Tell-Tale Article*, published in 1949, contains some acute if generally unsympathetic criticism of Auden. Hamilton drew attention to the heavy concentration of definite articles in Auden and other twentieth-century poets, and supported his analysis with some comparative statistics. After working through an anthology of English poetry in several volumes Hamilton noted that, whereas from the eighteenth century to the early twentieth the percentage of definite articles remained constant at about 6 per cent, in the volume devoted to modern poetry the percentage increased to $8\frac{1}{2}$ per cent, and rose to 10 per cent each for Eliot and Auden. By contrast, in the poetry of the sixteenth and seventeenth centuries the use of the definite article averages 4 per cent, while in a large sample of Donne it is as low as 2 per cent. Hamilton argues that before the eighteenth century poetry was less concerned with reflection and description and more with enacting relationships, whether with God or man or woman, a mode that makes much less of the definite article. On the other hand, in eighteenth century descriptive poetry the percentage is of modern proportions. 11 per cent for Thomson and 9 per cent for Crabbe.[1]

The definite article points to the recognisable if not to the already known. It recalls an actually or possibly shared experience, as well as, in its twentieth-century uses, reflecting the preference of modernist poetics for the particular against the general. This, as Hamilton points out, may be based on a confusion, assuming that the opposition 'particular / general' is the same as the opposition 'sharp / vague', which is not necessarily true. If Eliot and Auden each show a high percentage of definite articles, their reasons for doing so are fundamentally different, even though Eliot exercised a potent influence on the young Auden:

> But Eliot spoke the still unspoken word;
> For gasworks and dried tubers I forsook
> The clock at Grantchester, the English rook.
>
> ('Letter to Lord Byron', iv)

A line like 'The simple act of the confused will' (from Poem xxvii in *Poems*, later 'The Question' in *Collected Shorter Poems*, 1966), to which Hamilton draws attention, seems to be directly imitated from lines in Eliot's exactly contemporary *Ash Wednesday*, such as 'The vanished power of the usual reign' or 'The infirm glory of the positive hour'. But this syntactical formation is rare in Auden and can be regarded as an early, unassimilated influence. In Eliot the use of the definite article attempts, wistfully or urgently, to affirm the possibility of shared experiences and feelings recalled out of a fragmentary and chaotic past:

> But only in time can the moment in the rose-garden,
> The moment in the arbour where the rain beat,
> The moment in the draughty church at smokefall
> Be remembered. . . .

The experiences thus recalled are personal but not remote or esoteric, and they seek an echo in our own pasts. Auden, by contrast, can present bafflingly private experiences in a similar way, so that the attempt to participate either recoils or leads one on to speculative fiction-making:

> A choice was killed by every childish illness,
> The boiling tears among the hothouse plants,
> The rigid promise fractured in the garden,
>   And the long aunts.
>
> (Poem xxi in Look, Stranger!; 'A Bride in
the Thirties' in Collected Shorter Poems)

The effect is, as Hamilton disapprovingly remarks, 'as though an entire stranger were claiming our acquaintance'. More often, however, Auden's use of the definite article arises from his sense of reality as known and charted and intelligible, where all elements are potentially at least capable of classification. To quote Hamilton once more: 'We have seen the fondness of Eliot and Auden for the particular image, Eliot lighting up the fragments of what is, or is supposed to be, our common experience, while Auden indicates the marks by which we may recognise this or that type of person, and diagnose his disease.' Auden's classifying tendency was familiar to his friends from the beginning. In Christopher Isherwood's *Lions and Shadows*, where the young Auden appears as 'Weston', the narrator thinks, on a seaside holiday, 'Suppose Weston were here . . . he would know the names of the different species of gull – and, by naming them, would dismiss them to the proper recognized unimportant place in the background of the poet's consciousness. . . .'

Another stylistic feature which Auden derived from Eliot but used with a significant difference is the bizarre or unexpected smile, as in the famous opening of 'Prufrock': 'When the evening is spread out against the sky / Like a patient etherised upon a table'. In Eliot the simile is startling but not unintelligible; the underlying idea is of the cessation of consciousness, and we are invited to recognise the strangeness of a sensibility that interprets common experience in such a clinical way. There is, too, the conviction of the early modernist poet that we should think and feel differently about such a hallowed Romantic property as 'evening'. In Auden this impulse is systematically taken to the point of diminishing, even trivialising, large, potent concepts or images by comparing them to something everyday or banal. One example is 'Desire like a police-dog is unfastened' (Poem x, *Look Stranger!*); another is the treatment of the moon in Poem II of *Look, Stranger!*:

> Into the galleries she peers,
> And blankly as an orphan stares
> Upon the marvellous pictures.

In the revised version of this poem, 'A Summer Night', the comparison is made even more reductive: 'And blankly as a butcher stares'. This stylistic device became more frequent as Auden developed during the thirties; it is rare in *Poems*, moderately common in *Look, Stranger!* and a repetitive trick in *Another Time* (1940). 'Brussels in Winter' from the last volume is representative, with four similes in fourteen lines: 'Wandering the cold streets tangled like old string'; 'The winter holds them like the Opera'; 'Where isolated windows glow like farms'; 'A phrase goes packed with meaning like a van'. Such repetitions deaden whatever startling impact the device might have; it was, however, widely imitated, and became a major element in the collective Audenesque manner.

Equally influential was Auden's reliance on adjectives and adjectival phrases. These are sometimes scientific or clinical. But others – not all of them used frequently, but with a particular tactical emphasis – are partly descriptive, partly affective, with the exaggerated overtones of a familiar register in English middle-class speech: 'wonderful', 'marvellous', 'lovely', 'horrible', 'appalling', 'tremendous', 'ridiculous', 'doubtful', 'enormous', 'absurd'. When applied to natural objects, or to unlikely human artefacts or institutions, the effect, as with the similes, is reductive, suggesting that there is nothing in reality that cannot be contained within the conceptual and verbal confines of the poet's world of discourse. The effect is similar to

Weston's hypothetical classifying of seagulls as described by Isher-wood. . . .

. . . [Other key words], one might add, are 'Love' and 'Europe', though 'History' was peculiarly obtrusive and influential. There is a striking antecedent in Eliot's 'Gerontion', where 'History has many cunning passages, contrived corridors'. In Auden's own poetry it occurs in rhetorically significant places rather than with great statistical frequency. One instance is in the final lines of Poem xxx from *Look, Stranger!*:

> And all sway forward on the dangerous flood
> Of history, that never sleeps or dies,
> And, held one moment, burns the hand.

Another is in the celebrated conclusion of 'Spain', which Auden later came to regard with abhorrence: 'History to the defeated / May say Alas but cannot help or pardon.' As a concept, 'History' has obvious Marxist implications, but as used in this personified way may have been suggested to Auden by Edward Upward. Upward's story 'Sunday' was written as early as 1931 and first published in *New Country* in 1933 together with Auden's poems. This didactic Marxist fable presents 'History' as a recurring personification, with a characteristic listing of disparate items:

History is here in the park, in the town. It is in the offices, the duplicators, the traffic, the nursemaids wheeling prams, the airmen, the aviary, the new viaduct over the valley. It was once in the castle on the cliff, in the sooty churches, in your mind; but it is abandoning them, leaving with them only the failing energy of desperation, going to live elsewhere.[2]

Upward seems to have been long preoccupied by 'History'. In *Lions and Shadows* Isherwood quotes a letter from 'Chalmers' as a Cambridge undergraduate: 'Beware of the daemon of history: it is merciless, it casually eats the flesh and heart and leaves the bleaching bones. History, history, hysteria.'

In addition to Auden's use of the personified abstraction, some-times given emphasis by the use of a possessive, as in 'And love's best glasses reach / No fields but are his own', one can note his use of the vocative – 'O love, the interest itself in thoughtless Heaven' – and of phrases in apposition, like 'New styles of architecture, a change of heart', both noticeable features of the Audenesque. In the 1930 *Poems* we find Auden experimenting with an elliptical, 'telegraphese' manner, by omission of the definite article. This characteristic is at the opposite pole to what became Auden's normal practice, but, as G. Rostrevor Hamilton remarked, 'it is clear that Auden is *the*-conscious, and that, in playing with the English language, he often deliberately avoids the article, elsewhere so profuse in his work'. In fact, the articleless manner became less noticeable after the 1930 volume. It was extensively used by Cecil Day Lewis in *The Magnetic Mountain*, and occurs in Spender's poetry. But it was not widely imitated. In general the characteristics of the Audenesque in syntax and diction seem to me to be those described above: copious use of the definite article; unusual adjectives and adjectival phrases, and surprising similes, which have a reductive or trivialising effect; and personified abstractions. These features are functions of Auden's imaginative universe, which regarded reality as actually or potentially known and intelligible, without mysteries or uncertainty. Experience could be reduced to classifiable elements, as a necessary preliminary to diagnosis and prescription. It is in terms of this predisposition that Auden's early allegiance to Marxism and psychoanalysis can best be understood; both were attractive as techniques of explanation. Unifying all stylistic elements, and much less easily imitated, was Auden's characteristic tone, of calm certainty and total self-confidence. The opening of 'Let History Be My Judge' is representative:

> We made all possible preparations,
> Drew up a list of firms,
> Constantly revised our calculations
> And allotted the farms. . . .

. . . The central paradox about the Audenesque is that, although by the end of the thirties it was disseminated throughout the English-speaking world, and can be called a collective style, its origins lay in one man's very personal, even idiosyncratic vision of reality. As, indeed, Shapiro acknowledged:

> The personal development of an English poet
> Became almost immediately the folly
> Of all who wrote in verse.[3]

If Auden was widely and rapidly imitated, at least in his most evidently imitable stylistic and structural devices, it was, I believe, because there was a general readiness to look at the world in Auden's categories. At a time of world economic depression there was something reassuring in Auden's calm demonstration, mediated as much by style as by content, that reality was intelligible, and could be studied like a map or a catalogue, or seen in temporal terms as an inexorable historical process. Hence the instant appeal of the classificatory vision, the reliance on definite articles and precise if unexpected adjectives, which placed and limited their subjects. Indeed, Auden's view of things was in a sense already in the air, as in the general admiration for the supposed virtues of the Soviet Five-Year Plan. If Auden liked lists, so too did the practitioners of that primitive kind of sociological enquiry called 'Mass Observation', which tried to understand social behaviour by accumulating disparate observations about what given groups of people were doing at any one time. 'Mass Observation' was sponsored by a poet and sociologist, Charles Madge, and its activities were sympathetically described in *New Verse*. One may compare the title of Geoffrey Grigson's first book of poems, *Several Observations* (1939); some of the early poems of Grigson and Kenneth Allott make use of lists in a way that recalls sociological investigation as well as Auden's models. There is a curious example in Kenneth Allott's 'Signs', published in *New Verse* in 1936:

> the letter to write
> the seaside cruet
> the magic flute
>
> goldbearing quartz
> the speeding fox
> the last waltz
>
> the rising gale
> the flowered voile
> the schoolbell . . .
>
> the flying start
> the dish-clout
> the murdered heart.

There are other possible sources for this manner, quite independent of Auden's poetic practice: some of the most famous and enduring popular songs of the thirties, for instance, like 'You're the Top' and 'These Foolish Things', were made up of lists of random items.

By 1936, when the Spanish Civil War broke out, the Audenesque had become an established idiom, as we see in 'Full Moon at Tierz: Before the Storming of Huesca', written by the young Communist poet John Cornford not long before his death in Spain. The first section contains the almost obligatory reference to 'history':

> And history forming in our hand's
> Not plasticine but roaring sands,
> Yet we must swing it to its final course.

The final section opens with a remarkably assured example of the Audenesque, with the characteristic geographical sweep, the reductive adjectives, the personifications, and the use of the vocative. It is nicely sustained for two stanzas, but in the third Cornford shifts into a more directly hortatory manner:

> Now the same night falls over Germany
> And the impartial beauty of the stars
> Lights from the unfeeling sky
> Oranienburg and freedom's crooked scars.
> We can do nothing to ease that pain
> But prove the agony was not in vain.
>
> England is silent under the same moon,
> From the Clydeside to the gutted pits of Wales.
> The innocent mask conceals that soon
> Here, too, our freedom's swaying in the scales.
> O understand before too late
> Freedom was never held without a fight.
>
> Freedom is an easily spoken word
> But facts are stubborn things. Here, too, in Spain
> Our fight's not won till the workers of all the world
> Stand by our guard on Huesca's plain
> Swear that our dead fought not in vain,
> Raise the red flag triumphantly
> For Communism and for liberty.[4]

The most famous poem to emerge from the Spanish Civil War, and one which seems to me the apogee of the Audenesque, was Auden's own 'Spain'. First published as a pamphlet in 1937, it was reprinted in a revised form in *Another Time*, but was finally dropped from the *Collected Shorter Poems*. Among other things, 'Spain' is a catalogue poem where, as G. Rostrevor Hamilton showed, the percentage of definite articles is no less than 20 per cent. Hamilton was altogether too dismissive about 'Spain', calling it 'a succession of calculated phrases without any backbone of verbs: the degeneration of syntax'. Despite its accumulative method the poem does have, as C. K. Stead has pointed out,[5] a coherent structure, with the form 'Yesterday all the past' / 'Tomorrow perhaps' / 'But today the struggle'.

In 'Spain' the geographical images are no longer the occasion of dispassionate surveys; the map has become the location for a violent, cataclysmic struggle:

> On that arid square, that fragment nipped off from hot
> Africa, soldered so crudely to inventive Europe,
>   On that tableland scored by rivers,
> Our fever's menacing shapes are precise and alive.

'Spain' is an immensely interesting poem, where Auden tries to meet a new and urgent situation with a method that was more suited to the calm analysis and diagnosis of historical and social disorder than to facing so immediate a challenge. It has given rise to arguments about the nature of political poetry, and about such particular contentious points as the phrase, later amended, 'the conscious acceptance of guilt in the necessary murder'.[6] But in the end the interest seems to me more historical than literary, despite C. K. Stead's careful advocacy of the poem's merits. For all its local brilliance 'Spain' looks strained and unconvincing and, perhaps, unconvinced; I find it a lesser achievement than many of the poems that Auden wrote earlier in the decade. Most significantly, 'Spain' shows signs of self-imitation, of Auden becoming self-conscious in his employment of the Audenesque, possibly by feedback from his imitators.

Certainly 'Spain' gave a powerful boost to the development of the Audenesque in the late thirties, particularly in the portentous references to 'History'. Auden himself continued to write in the familiar idiom but, as some of the poems in *Another Time* indicate, in an increasingly insensitive manner. After his removal to America he adopted other voices and styles, with the protean ease that had always been characteristic of him. But it was not yet the end of the Audenesque chapter in English poetry. . . .

[Bergonzi examines further the influence of 'the Audenesque' on poets in the forties and fifties. He cites examples from poems by Roy Fuller, Ruthven Todd, Keith Douglas, Herbert Corby and Randall Swingler, but notes differences in stylistic usage. For example: 'The use of definitive articles and adjectives, instead of projecting a conceptual map of the known and knowable, indicated a nightmare landscape, or a concrete and detailed but alien and threatening environment.' Bergonzi also notes how the Audenesque became 'absorbed into the diction or syntax of later poets', such as Kingsley Amis – Ed.]

SOURCE: extracts from ch. 2, 'Auden and the Audenesque', in Bergonzi's *Reading the Thirties: Texts and Contexts* (London, 1978), pp. 39–44, 47–9, 51–5.

NOTES

[Reorganised and renumbered from the original – Ed.]

1. A later writer – G. W. Turner, in *Stylistics* (Harmondsworth, 1973), p. 85 – has made a helpful addition to the discussion:

A whole book, and a very readable and interesting one, *The Tell-Tale Article* by G. Rostrevor Hamilton, has been written on the word *the* in modern poetry. A more technical discussion of the word *the* in Yeats's 'Leda and the Swan' by M. A. K. Halliday can be found in *Patterns of Language* by Angus McIntosh and M. A. K. Halliday. The word *the* is chosen, instead of *a* or a plural without an article, to refer to something known, either universally ('the sun', 'the Bible') or defined within the nominal group ('the point I want to make', 'the King of France', 'the Dover Road', and perhaps long-established London names like 'the Edgware Road') or the general context. When Auden records the mood of left-wing England during the Spanish Civil War, he mentions 'the boring meeting' and 'the flat political pamphlet', where plurals 'boring meetings' and 'flat political pamphlets' would have been the normal choice of earlier poets. Auden's use invites us to think 'Ah, yes, how well we know it all'. Indeed, the frequency of *the* in subsequent poetry, added to its falling intonations, tended towards a universal boredom. We all, like Tiresias, have seen it all. We are not childlike Romantics any more. The crowd of golden daffodils, the rainbow in the sky, the clerk of Oxenford also – none of them are new that way.

2. Edward Upward, *The Railway Accident and Other Stories* (Harmondsworth, 1972), p. 83.
3. Karl Shapiro, *Essays on Rime* (London, 1947), p. 40.
4. John Cornford, *Understand the Weapon, Understand the Wound* (Manchester, 1976), pp. 38–40.
5. C. K. Stead, 'Auden's "Spain" ', *London Magazine*, VII, 12 (March 1968), pp. 41–54.
6. Notably by George Orwell in 'Inside the Whale', *Collected Essays, Journalism and Letters*, vol. I (Harmondsworth, 1970), pp. 540–78.

SELECT BIBLIOGRAPHY

In addition to the complete studies from which extracts have been reproduced in this selection, and the works cited in the Introduction for further reading, the following books and articles are also recommended.

A. Alvarez, 'W. H. Auden: Poetry and Journalism' – ch. IV of his *The Shaping Spirit* (London, 1958). He takes a largely unfavourable view of aspects of Auden's poetry.

Clifford Dyment, *C. Day Lewis*, 'Writers and Their Work' series, no. 62 (London, 1955).

John Fuller, *A Reader's Guide to W. H. Auden* (London, 1970). This is the best general introduction to Auden's poetry; Fuller provides a penetrating discussion of individual poems and is judicious in the handling of the pre- and post-1939 Auden.

Richard Hoggart, *W. H. Auden*, 'Writers and Their Work' series, no. 93, revised edition (London, 1977).

Samuel Hynes, 'The Single Poem of C. Day Lewis' in D. Abse (ed.), *Poetry Dimension Annual, 5* (London, 1973), pp. 79–81. This is lucid and searching on the development of Day Lewis's poetry.

Randall Jarrell, 'Changes of Attitude and Rhetoric in Auden's Poetry', *Southern Review*, VII (Autumn 1941), pp. 326–49; reproduced in his *The Third Book of Criticism* (New York, 1969; London, 1975). Jarrell's view of Auden is in the main unfavourable.

Arnold Kettle, *Poetry and Politics*, Open University Course A306, Units 21–22 (Open University Press, 1976).

F. R. Leavis, 'Auden, Bottrall and Others', *Scrutiny*, III, 1 (June 1934), pp. 70–83. Leavis was perhaps the most powerful of the critics hostile to Auden and his associates.

F. R. Leavis, 'Retrospect 1950' – ch. VII of his *New Bearings in English Poetry* (first published in 1932) in its revised edition (London, 1950).

David Lodge, 'In the Thirties' – Part 3:6 of *The Modes of Modern Writing* (London, 1977). Stylistic and linguistic in orientation.

John Lucas (ed.), *The Nineteen Thirties: A Challenge to Orthodoxy* (Brighton, 1978); also available in its original form as an issue of *Renaissance and Modern Studies*, XX (1976).

William T. McKinnon, *Apollo's Blended Dream: A Study of the Poetry of Louis MacNeice* (Oxford, 1971). This contains much formalistic discussion and analysis, and also a useful review of critical studies on MacNeice, pp. 244–8.

Edward Mendelson, 'Introduction' to *W. H. Auden: Selected Poems* (London, 1979).

D. B. Moore, *The Poetry of Louis MacNeice* (Leicester, 1972).

Tom Paulin, 'Going North: *Letters from Iceland*', in John Lucas (ed.), op. cit., pp. 58–77.

Allan Rodway, 'Logicless Grammar in Audenland', in his *The Truths of Fiction* (London, 1970), pp. 206–19. Stylistic and linguistic in orientation.

Villas Sarang, 'Articles in the Poetry of W. H. Auden', *Language and Style*, VII, 2 (1974), pp. 77–90. Stylistic and linguistic in orientation.

Monroe K. Spears, *The Disenchanted Island: The Poetry of W. H. Auden* (Oxford, 1963).

Stephen Spender, 'The Theme of Political Orthodoxy in the Thirties', in his *The Creative Element* (London, 1953).

C. K. Stead, 'Auden's Spain', *London Magazine*, VII, 12 (March 1968), pp. 41–54.

The following are also useful for reference and background reading:

Edward Mendelson, *Early Auden* (London, 1981). This is now the definitive biography on Auden in the thirties.

Allan Rodway (ed.), *Poetry in the 1930s* (London, 1968).

Robin Skelton (ed.), *Poetry of the Thirties* (Harmondsworth, 1964).

Stephen Spender, *World Within World* – autobiography (London, 1951).

Stephen Spender, *W. H. Auden: A Tribute* (London, 1974).

Stephen Spender, *The Thirties and After* (London, 1978).

Julian Symons, *The Thirties: A Dream Revolved*, 2nd edition (London, 1975).

A. F. Tolley, *The Poetry of the Thirties* (London, 1975).

EDITIONS

There have been several different editions of Auden's poetry in recent years. These are listed here with a brief note on contents and orientation. All are published by Faber.

1. *Collected Shorter Poems, 1927–1957* (1966); still very much the standard edition, containing the poems and texts Auden wished to have preserved.
2. *Collected Longer Poems* (1968); complete, largely unrevised, texts of the longer poems.
3. *Collected Poems* (1976), edited by Edward Mendelson; a compilation of all the poems Auden wished to have preserved. It covers all the volumes of verse published after 1939, together with a selection of poems from the pre-1939 period – some of which, as in the 1966 volume, are in their revised form.
4. *The English Auden: Poems, Essays and Dramatic Writings*, edited by Edward Mendelson (1977); this volume reproduces the original texts of Auden's Thirties poems, including 'Spain', the poems from *Letters to Iceland* and *Journey to a War*, some previously unpublished or uncollected poems, excerpts from the Auden-Isherwood plays, a chapter from an unpublished book, and entries from early journals. The book is a necessary complement to the Collected Poems.
5. *Selected Poems* (1968); a selection made by Auden himself of poems up to and including the volume *About the House* (1966).

6. *Selected Poems*, edited by Edward Mendelson (1979); a selection of 100 poems from all periods of Auden's career made by his literary executor. In all cases the original texts are used; the book contains a highly perceptive and challenging introduction to Auden's poetry.

BIBLIOGRAPHICAL STUDIES

C. M. Armitage and Neil Clark, *A Bibliography of the Works of Louis MacNeice* (London, 1973).

B. C. Bloomfield and E. Mendelson, *W. H. Auden: A Bibliography*, 2nd edition (Charlottesville, Va., 1972).

Martin E. Gingerich, *W. H. Auden: A Reference Guide* (Boston, Mass., 1977).

G. Handley-Taylor and T. D'Arch-Smith, *C. Day Lewis: A Bibliography* (London, 1968).

A. T. Tolley, *The Early Published Poems of Stephen Spender* (Carlton, Ottawa, 1967).

NOTES ON CONTRIBUTORS

W. H. AUDEN (1907–73): poet, critic, translator, librettist and dramatist. He went to the United States in 1939 and became an American citizen. Professor of Poetry at Oxford, 1956–61, he returned to live there shortly before his death.

BERNARD BERGONZI: Professor of English, University of Warwick; his numerous publications on Victorian and twentieth-century literature include *Gerard Manley Hopkins, Reading the Thirties* and *The Situation of the Novel* (now in a revised edition).

TERENCE BROWN: Lecturer in English, Trinity College, Dublin; his special interest is in Anglo-Irish literature, and he has published widely on MacNeice and on Ulster poets.

C. DAY LEWIS (1904–72); poet, critic, novelist and translator; Poet Laureate, 1968–72, and Auden's predecessor (1951–56) as Professor of Poetry at Oxford. His criticism includes *The Lyrical Poetry of Thomas Hardy, The Poetic Image* and *The Lyric Impulse*. His autobiography, *The Buried Day*, was published in 1960. He wrote detective fiction under the pseudonym of 'Nicholas Blake'. The standard edition of his poetry is *The Poems of C. Day Lewis, 1925–1972* (London, 1977), with an Introduction by Ian Parsons.

MARTIN DODSWORTH: Lecturer in English, Royal Holloway College, University of London, and currently editor of the journal, *English*; his publications include edited volumes on Mrs Gaskell's *North and South* and *The Survival of Poetry: A Contemporary Survey* (collected essays by various hands), and numerous studies on twentieth-century poetry.

GEORGE S. FRASER (1915–80): poet and critic; from 1958 to 1979 Lecturer, and then Reader, in English Poetry, University of Leicester. His literary criticism includes the widely read *The Modern Writer and His World* and *Essays on Twentieth-Century Poetry*; he edited the Casebook on Keats's *Odes*.

BARBARA HARDY: Professor of English, Birkbeck College, University of London; her many studies in nineteenth- and twentieth-century literature include *The Appropriate Form*, *The Moral Art of Dickens*, *Tellers and Listeners: The Narrative Imagination* and *The Advantage of Lyric*.

RICHARD HOGGART: Warden of Goldsmith's College, University of London, and previously Professor of English, University of Birmingham, and Assistant Director General of UNESCO. In addition to his work on Auden, his publications include *The Uses of Literacy*, *Speaking to Each Other* and *Only Connect* (Reith Lectures of 1972).

FRANCIS HOPE: poet, critic, historian, and former Fellow of All Souls', Oxford; he contributed to *New Lines 2* and his verse publications include *'Instead of a Poet' and Other Poems*. For many years before his death he was a frequent contributor to the *New Statesman*.

GRAHAM HOUGH: Professor of English at Cambridge, 1966–75; his publications include *The Last Romantics*, *The Romantic Poets*, *The Dark Sun* (on D. H. Lawrence), *Image and Experience* and *Style and Stylistics*; his *Selected Essays* were published in 1978.

SAMUEL HYNES: Professor of English, Princeton University; his publications include *The Pattern of Hardy's Poetry*, *Edwardian Occasions* and *The Auden Generation*.

CHRISTOPHER ISHERWOOD: dramatist, novelist and critic, and collaborator with Auden in the 1930s on a number of poetic dramas; he is chiefly renowned as a novelist (notably for *Mr Norris Changes Trains*, *Goodbye to Berlin*, *A Single Man* and *A Meeting by the River*). He went to the United States in 1939, became an American citizen in 1946, and has held university appointments there. His autobiography, *Christopher and His Kind*, was published in 1978.

LOUIS MACNEICE (1907–63): poet, critic and dramatist; after lecturing in Classics at Birmingham and London universities, he worked for most of his professional life at the BBC, as producer, features writer and radio dramatist. His criticism includes *Modern Poetry*, *The Poetry of W. B. Yeats* and *Varieties of Parable*; and his autobiography, *The Strings are False* was published in 1965. The standard edition of his poetry is *The Collected Poems of Louis MacNeice* (London, 1966), edited by E. R. Dodds.

D. E. S. MAXWELL: Professor of English, Winters College, York University, Ontario; among his many publications are *The Poetry of T. S. Eliot*, *American Fiction* and *Herman Melville*.

MICHAEL ROBERTS (1902–48): teacher, poet and critic; editor of the influential anthologies *New Signatures* (1932) and *New Country* (1933), and also of *The Faber Book of Modern Verse* (1936). His criticism includes the *Critique of Poetry*.

JUSTIN REPLOGLE: Professor of English, University of Wisconsin; he has published widely on poets of the 1930s and on aspects of Auden's Marxism and Christianity.

FRANCIS SCARFE: editor, poet, novelist, critic and translator; Professor of French, University of London, and Director of the British Institute in Paris until 1978. In addition to *Auden and After* and *W. H. Auden*, his publications include editions of André Chénier and Baudelaire.

STEPHEN SPENDER: poet, critic and editor; Professor of English, University

College, London, 1968–73. He co-founded and was a co-editor of *Horizon* and *Encounter*. His *Collected Poems* were published in 1955 and this was followed in 1971 by a further collection, *The Generous Days*. Among his several books of criticism are *The Destructive Element* and *The Struggle of the Modern*. His autobiography, *World Within World*, appeared in 1951.

GEOFFREY THURLEY: Lecturer in Literature, University of Essex: he previously taught at the University of Adelaide. His publications include *The Ironic Harvest* and *The American Moment: American Poetry in the Mid-Century*.

ACKNOWLEDGEMENTS

The author and publishers wish to thank the following who have given permission for the use of copyright material: W. H. Auden, extract from essay 'Psychology and Art Today' in *The Arts Today*, edited by Geoffrey Grigson, from *The English Auden: Poems, Essays and Dramatic Writings 1927–1939* by permission of Faber and Faber Ltd. W. H. Auden, Introduction to *Selected Poems of Louis MacNeice* (1964) by permission of Faber and Faber Ltd. W. H. Auden, Introduction to *The Poet's Tongue* (1935), edited by W. H. Auden and John Garrett, by permission of Bell & Hyman Ltd. Bernard Bergonzi, extracts from Chapter 2 in *Reading the Thirties*, by permission of A. D. Peters & Co. Ltd. Terence Brown, extract from 'The Poet and His Imagery' in *Louis MacNeice: Sceptical Vision* (1975), by permission of Gill and Macmillan Ltd. Martin Dodsworth, essay 'Bernard Spencer' by permission of the author. G. S. Fraser, extracts from 'Evasive Honesty: The Poetry of Louis MacNeice' in *Vision and Rhetoric: Studies in Modern Poetry*, by permission of Faber and Faber Ltd. Barbara Hardy, extract from essay 'The Reticence of W. H. Auden' in *The Review* (1964), reprinted in her *The Advantage of Lyric: Essays on Feeling in Poetry* (1977), by permission of The Athlone Press Ltd. Graham Hough, article 'MacNeice and Auden' in *Critical Quarterly*, 9, No. 1, 1967, by permission of the author. Richard Hoggart, extract from *Auden: An Introductory Essay* (1951) by permission of Chatto and Windus Ltd. Francis Hope, essay 'Then and Now' by permission of Mrs Mary Hope. Samuel Hynes, extracts from *The Auden Generation* (1976) by permission of The Bodley Head. Christopher Isherwood, essay 'Some Notes on Auden's Early Poetry' from *Exhumations* (1966), by permission of Curtis Brown Ltd. C. Day Lewis, extracts from *A Hope For Poetry* (1934) and from Preface to *Oxford Poetry* (1927) published by Basil Blackwell Ltd. and reproduced by permission of A. D. Peters & Co. Ltd. Louis MacNeice, extracts from *Modern Poetry: A Personal Statement* (1938), *The Poetry of W. B. Yeats* (1941), and *New Verse* (1937 and 1938) by permission of David Higham Associates Ltd. D. E. Maxwell, extracts from *Poets of the Thirties* (1969) by permission of Routledge & Kegan Paul Ltd. Justin Repogle, extracts from *Auden's Poetry* (1969), by permission of Eyre Methuen Ltd. Michael Roberts, extract from Preface to *New Signatures* (1931), and from 'Aspects of English Poetry, 1932–1937' in *Poetry*, No. 49, 1937, by permission of Mrs John Carleton. Francis Scarfe, extracts from *Auden and After* (1941), by permission of Routledge & Kegan Paul Ltd. Stephen Spender, articles in *Poetry* No. 78 (1951), *Fact* No. 4 (1937) and *The Review* (1970) by permission of A. D. Peters & Co. Ltd. Stephen Spender, article 'The Brilliant Mr MacNeice' in *The New Republic* (157 No. 4, 1967), by permission of The New Republic Inc. Geoffrey Thurley, Chapter 5 from *The Ironic Harvest: English Poetry in the Twentieth Century*, by permission of Edward Arnold (Publishers) Ltd.

Every effort has been made to trace all the copyright holders but if any have been inadvertently overlooked the publishers will be pleased to make the necessary arrangements at the first opportunity.

INDEX

This is a select, not a comprehensive, index. References to Auden, Day Lewis, MacNeice and Spender are confined to critical excerpts by them and to titles of texts for which there is a measure of textual discussion. Only texts by these authors are cited here. **Bold** type denotes essays or excerpts in this Casebook.

OCTOR
MONSTER OF THE DEEP

BY ADAM BLADE

ORCHARD

EMERGENCY TRANSMISSION FROM SELLIUS, INVENTOR AND MECHANIC

LOCATION: SOMEWHERE IN THE LOST LAGOON

Is anybody out there?

I am locked in the hold of a pirate ship with only my robodog Rusty for company. It's so dark in here! I've nothing to eat but scraps of seaweed. Nothing to drink but stale grog.

I fear it is too late for me. But if you have received this transmission… beware! The cruel pirate captain has forced me to create a Robobeast for her. And soon this deadly creature will be unleashed on the innocent people of the Lost Lagoon.

I do not know what the captain is planning. All I know is that the beast I have made is unstoppable — a terrible monster of the deep.

Forgive me, for I had no choice…

STORY 1:

A SURPRISE FROM CORA BLACKHEART

CHAPTER ONE

THE MESSENGER

Max grinned, his stomach bubbling with excitement as he reached a hand towards the sleek body of the swordfish floating before him. Her name was Silvertail, and she looked as fast as Max could have hoped for his first solo swordfish ride.

Click click click click click! Silvertail scolded, swinging her sword around and almost poking Max in the eye.

"Whoa!" Max snatched his hand back.

Beside him, his dogbot Rivet let out a growl. Silvertail stared back fiercely.

Lia giggled, and Max shot her a look. "I'm glad you're finding this funny," he said. They were visiting Lia's father Salinus, the Merryn King of Sumara, and Lia was giving Max his first swordfish riding lesson in the palace grounds. Her eyes were shining with amusement as she watched from the back of her own swordfish, Spike.

"She won't bite!" Lia said. "Try scratching her like this." Lia reached out her webbed fingers and gently scratched the swordfish behind its dorsal fin. The creature lifted its head and made a soft chattering sound. Max followed suit. To his surprise Silvertail closed her eyes, purring with pleasure.

"Right," Lia said, "now that you're friends, you'd better get on. You've got a lot to learn!"

"Not safe, Max!" Rivet barked.

"Don't worry, Riv," Max said. "I've ridden Spike with Lia hundreds of times. And it can't be harder than riding an aquabike!" Max swung himself onto Silvertail's back and gripped her dorsal fin.

"Good," Lia said. "Now squeeze gently with your knees and she'll start to swim. Push her dorsal fin to steer. If you want her to stop, pull back."

"Got it!" Max said, pressing his knees into the swordfish's sides.

Silvertail shot forwards. Max's stomach flipped as colourful seaweed streaked past. He tightened his grip, clinging with his knees, but Silvertail surged on even faster than before. Water rushed past, snatching the breath from Max's gills, and almost tearing him from Silvertail's back.

"Pull back!" Lia cried.

Max tugged hard on Silvertail's fin.

Silvertail angled her body in the water and stopped abruptly.

"Whoa!" Max lost his grip and flew off her back, spinning head over heels in the water. Finally, he hit a column of coral and stopped. He shook his head and righted himself as Lia swam over on Spike.

Lia raised an eyebrow, smiling. "Not as

easy as it looks, is it?" she said.

Max rubbed a sore elbow, his pulse still racing. "Give me an aquabike any day!" he said.

"No can do," Lia said. "Not if you want to play oceanball. It's a strictly tech-free game. Ready for another try?"

Max nodded. Lia gazed towards Silvertail, who was zipping in and out of a shoal of fish in the distance. Silvertail's head came up instantly, and she darted back over to join them, swimming a neat figure of eight on the way.

"See," Lia said. "She's as good as gold. She does exactly what you tell her."

"Yeah, if you happen to have telepathic Aqua Powers," Max muttered. Silvertail lifted her pointed nose, her eyes glinting with mischief. Max frowned. *I don't trust you at all!* he thought.

Suddenly, Lia's eyes went wide as she stared at something behind him. Max turned to see the shimmering lines of a translucent fish, flickering in and out of view.

"What species is that?" he asked.

"A shadowfish!" said Lia. "It's said they're the only creatures that can cross over to Nemos from the Lost Lagoon." She gasped. "It's talking to me… Oh no!"

Max's stomach churned. "What's wrong?"

"We'd better go and talk to my father," Lia said. "I'll explain then." She glanced at Silvertail who was busy turning somersaults beside them. "I think you'd better ride with me," she told Max.

Max grinned. "Good plan," he said. "I'm done with falling off fish for one day." He beckoned Rivet, and leapt onto Spike's back behind Lia. Spike flicked his tail, and they all surged off towards the palace with the shadowfish flickering along beside them.

Before long, the high coral walls of the palace rose up before them. Two Merryn warriors saluted and moved their spears aside as Lia approached the entrance. Max and Lia swooped past them, down a picture-lined passageway and through a curtain of seaweed that led into the throne room.

Inside, King Salinus sat high on his white throne, studying a stone tablet.

He looked up, frowning, as Max and Lia entered. When his eyes fell on the shadowfish beside them, his frown deepened. "I see you bring a visitor," he said.

"He's a messenger from the Lost Lagoon, Father," Lia said. "He needs our help." Lia crossed to a chest by the throne and drew out a long trumpet-shaped shell, positioning it before the shadowfish's mouth.

The fish began to speak in a strange musical voice that drifted in and out of hearing.

"I bring an urgent message from the explorer Piscanias," the shadowfish said.

Its words echoed from the shell, translated into Merryn. "He requests the assistance of Princess Lia and the Aquoran boy Max. The Lost Lagoon is under pirate attack."

Max's heart thumped. Last time he and Lia had been sucked into the Lost Lagoon, they had barely escaped with their lives. "It must be Cora Blackheart!" he said. "I thought she

wouldn't be able to cause any trouble in the Lost Lagoon, but it looks like I was wrong!"

King Salinus nodded. "I shall send my finest warriors!" he said.

Max bowed low before the King. "I beg your pardon, Your Majesty," he said. "But it was Lia and I who trapped Cora in the Lost Lagoon. It's our duty to return and face her."

King Salinus rubbed his chin, watching Max thoughtfully.

"I believe you are right," he said. "And you have proved yourselves in many Sea Quests before now. You may go. But be careful."

"We will be," Max said. But as he spoke, a tingle of fear stirred in his stomach. The Lost Lagoon was a strange and dangerous place. And Cora wasn't exactly a pushover either. *I just hope I'm doing the right thing turning down the King's help*, he thought. *Otherwise, this Sea Quest could be our last.*

CHAPTER TWO

WATERWOLVES!

Max looked though his hydrodisk's watershield at the bustle of Sumara's main square. Merryn men and women were buying seaweeds and mosses from market stalls, while children played tag alongside fish and other sea creatures. The sight had once seemed alien to Max. Now it was as comforting and familiar as his old home back in Aquora. Especially now he was about to leave it all behind for the underwater volcanoes and spider-web cities of the Lost Lagoon.

"Have you got the compass?" Lia said, her voice reaching him through his headset. She was swimming at his side on Spike. Max patted his deepsuit pocket, feeling the familiar weight of the compass that he and Lia had made on their last visit to the Lost Lagoon. It was constructed from four rare metals: Galdium, Rullium, Fennum and Barrum. Without it, Max knew they might never escape from the Lagoon.

"Got it," Max said.

"Then let's go." Lia put her fingers to her temples and gazed at the shadowfish. It turned a shimmering eye towards her, flicked its tail and darted away.

Lia leaned over Spike's back and swooped after it. Max threw his hydrodisk into gear.

"Come on, Riv!" he said, hitting the accelerator and surging through the coral arch that led out of the main square.

"So, what do you think we're looking for?" Max asked Lia through his headset as they zoomed into the open ocean.

"I don't know," Lia said. "The entrances to the Lost Lagoon are almost invisible, remember, and always moving."

"Hmm…an invisible moving doorway," Max said. "I'll keep my eyes peeled."

Lia grinned. "Apparently the shadowfish can track the portals," she said, swimming down into a patch of kelp. It billowed up all around them, cutting out the light and licking at the hydrodisk's windows. Max flicked on his main beams, as Spike nosed through the long strands. Max could just make out the shadowfish up ahead.

They swam on through the dense forest for most of the morning, keeping their speed low. Every now and then, they lost their guide in the darkness, and Lia had to use her Aqua Powers to find him.

"Nearly there yet, Max?" Rivet barked.

"I hope so, Riv," Max said.

"Me too," said Lia. "This isn't a part of the ocean we Merryn often visit."

"Well, it looks like we're reaching the edge of this forest," Max said, spotting a faint sheen of light in the water ahead. Sure enough, the shadowfish led them through a final curtain of weeds, and out into deep blue water. On either side were towering rock formations pitted with huge holes. Rivet let out a throaty growl as they entered the canyon.

"Oh no…" Lia said.

"What?" Max asked.

"Those holes…" Lia's eyes were wide as she glanced at the rocks all around them. "I think I know what made them." Her face was very pale. "Waterwolves," she whispered. "They make dens with their teeth, and hunt in packs. And they're always hungry."

Max ran his eyes along the high, craggy walls of the canyon. There was no way out except onwards. He let out a shaky breath. "Then we'd better keep a low profile," he said, killing the lights on his sub and silencing the engines.

"As long as we're quiet we should be OK," Lia said. "Waterwolves hate the sun. They sleep during the day. We'd just better hope they don't smell us."

As they followed the shadowfish past the first of the gaping holes, Max felt a creeping dread. Beside him, Rivet's ears were flattened back against his metal skull, and his sharp teeth were bared. Suddenly, Rivet snarled, and the hairs on Max's arms stood on end. A pair of glowing yellow eyes had appeared at the dark entrance to each den.

"We have to get out of here now!" Lia cried, leaning low over Spike's back and shooting

ahead. Max gunned the hydrodisk's engines and raced after her, just as the water around them erupted in a frenzy of snapping white teeth. Spiny black fish with fangs as long as Max's arm were pouring from the holes. Their yellow eyes blazed as they charged towards Max and Lia. Spike swooped between the thrashing forms, dodging their ravenous mouths. Max steered left and right as teeth snapped shut all around him.

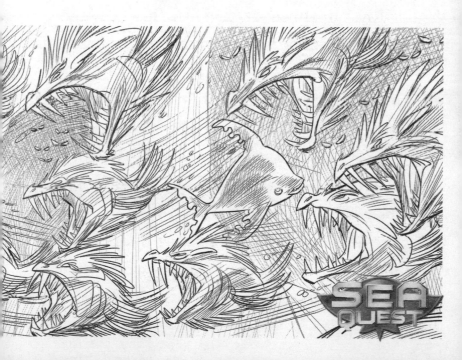

"Grrrrr! Bad fish, Max!" Rivet barked. Max looked back to see his dogbot's propellers spinning as he powered into the midst of the bristling fish, metal teeth bared.

"Rivet! No!" Max cried, but the dogbot wasn't listening. *His canine programming's too strong!* Max realised.

Rivet was barking madly. The waterwolves abandoned their chase of Max and Lia and quickly surrounded the dogbot.

Rivet snapped at the fish, his red eyes flashing. But he was seriously outnumbered. The waterwolves snatched at his legs and tail and dragged him towards their dens.

Lia gasped. "They'll rip him apart!"

Max was already spinning his hydrodisk around. "I don't think so!" he said. He could just see the glint of Rivet's robotic body between the spiny fish as they disappeared into a hole, leaving churning water in their wake. Max frowned as he sized up the hole. It was going to be tight, but he had no choice. He angled his speeding sub towards the narrow gap.

Screeech! The body of his hydrodisk juddered as it scraped its way through the hole and burst into a dark cave beyond. Max flicked on his headlights and swung them through the darkness.

The long beams cast white circles onto the craggy cavern walls. Max could hear frenzied snarling and snapping. He turned his beams towards the sound.

The waterwolves tugged at Rivet, their teeth glinting white in Max's headlights. Max gasped in horror. There were at least fifty of them. *I've got no chance against so many. We're going to be shredded!* Max thought.

URGENT REPAIRS

Max studied his hydrodisk's controls. His eyes fell on his sub's yellow SOS button. *Waterwolves don't like bright light...*

He stabbed his finger downwards, activating the emergency flare. *This has to work!*

There was a fizzing sound, then with a bang the whole cavern lit up in a flash of dazzling light. Max narrowed his eyes against the brightness. The waterwolves' tails and bodies thrashed wildly. They snarled and dropped their prey, darting away through narrow passages at the back of the cave. Max flipped the lid of his hydrodisk, jumped out and dived towards his dogbot. He snatched Rivet up and dragged him back to the sub.

Once they were safely inside, Max checked Rivet for damage. There were scratches, but nothing Max couldn't polish out. Rivet wagged his tail, his eyes glowing brightly.

"Rivet scared bad fish, Max!" the dogbot said proudly. Max shook his head in exasperation.

"Of course you did, Riv," he said, patting Rivet's head. Then he threw his hydrodisk around, and sped back out of the cave.

"Did you get him?" Lia asked anxiously as Max pulled up at her side.

Max glanced at the seat beside him. Rivet was still staring back towards the caves, growling and wagging his tail.

"Yup," Max said. "But we'd better get out of here before he decides to go back for another attack."

"Um, Max?" Lia said, frowning at something in the water beyond him. "Is yellow stuff supposed to be pouring from the side of your sub?"

Max glanced through the rear window to see a stream of yellow fuel snaking out into the water. "Oh no!" he said. "The tank must have ruptured when I forced the hydrodisk into that cave. Once we get away from here, tell the shadowfish to stop. I need to check the damage."

Almost as soon as the rocky home of the waterwolves dipped out of sight behind a sandy dune in the ocean floor, Max's hydrodisk gave a splutter, and the engines died. Without power, the sub drifted down to the seabed. Max climbed out.

Lia swam to his side on Spike with the shadowfish close behind her. Max ran his finger along a jagged gash in the metal of his fuel tank. "I might be able to patch it," Max said. "But I'm out of fuel. We need to find a source of Celerium, fast."

"Or you could just ride with me on Spike," Lia suggested.

Max shook his head. "We'll have a better chance of defeating Cora in the Lost Lagoon if we've got my weapons and tech."

"But how are you going to find one of the rarest and most flammable substances in Nemos out here in the middle of the ocean?" Lia asked.

Max grinned. "Watch," he said. "Here, Rivet!" Rivet swam over to Max, his eyes glowing expectantly. Max flipped a panel in his dogbot's side, tapped in a command, then closed the panel. Rivet lifted his nose and started sniffing and turning about. Suddenly he stopped and his eyes flashed red.

"Upsilon-7 that way!" Rivet said.

"Perfect!" Max said. "Upsilon-7 is one of Aquora's Celerium-harvesting outposts. But we'll have to tow my sub there." He ducked back inside the hydrodisk and drew out four metal cords, then clipped two to each wing of the vehicle. He passed the other end of one cord around Rivet's middle, and made the end of another into a harness for Spike.

He handed the third cord to Lia, and took hold of the last one himself.

"Right, on the count of three!" Max said. "One, two, three!" Max swam forward, kicking his legs hard to pull his cord taut. Rivet's propellers churned and Spike's tail flicked. They all surged forward, pulling Max's sub up from the ocean bed and tugging it along behind them. Rivet led the way while the shadowfish dropped back, swimming nose to tail with Spike.

"You seriously need to learn to ride a swordfish," Lia said, frowning with the effort of pulling the sub. "You wouldn't catch Silvertail running out of fuel and needing to be tugged halfway across the ocean."

"No," Max said, gritting his teeth against

the weight of the sub. "But then, I don't remember my hydrodisk ever deciding to throw me, either."

As they towed the hydrodisk onwards, the seabed rose, and sunlight dappled the shallower waters. Soon Max spotted patches of velvety red on the rocks below.

"That's what we're looking for," Max said, pointing to the scarlet patches. "It's a special kind of algae, and it gives off Celerium as a waste product. Robots collect the Celerium, so we can use it as a fuel. Pretty clever, huh?"

Lia shrugged her shoulders. "The algae makes the fuel. Your robots just scoop it up. I don't see what's so clever about that."

Max sighed. "No, I suppose you wouldn't," he said.

In the red-tinged waters ahead they could see a huge elephant-like robot with a corrugated pipe hanging from its face like a trunk, reaching down to the ocean floor. The robot gave off a blue sheen, as if its metal body was glowing.

"A harvester robot," Max said, pointing. "We must be almost there."

Soon the seabed around them became crowded with robots, all humming softly while they hoovered up algal waste. Lime green fish swam alongside them, darting

in and out of the red sediment the robots disturbed as they moved.

Ahead, Max could see a square platform floating on the surface of the water. It was as big as a cruise ship, and had the same sheen as the robots.

Lia slipped on her Amphibio mask so she could breathe out of water and they all headed up towards the outpost, dragging the

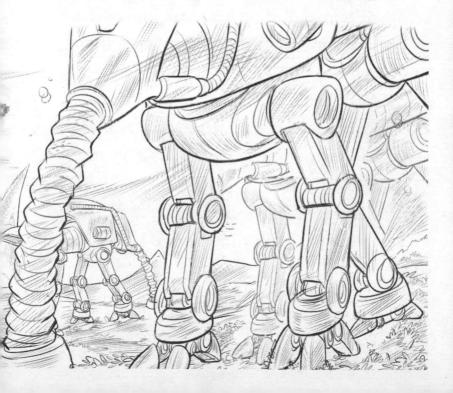

hydrodisk behind them.

Max broke the surface and blinked in the dull grey light of an overcast afternoon. The huge structure of the Celerium outpost towered above him, an ugly mass of metal beams and flat-roofed concrete buildings. He spotted a row of metal jetties along the edge of the rig with ladders connecting them to the higher platform above. Lia surfaced beside him, pulled on her mask, and pushed her wet hair back from her face. Rivet shook himself.

"We'd better be quick," Max said. "If someone sees us, we'd have some awkward explaining to do. These outposts are strictly military only."

Lia slipped from Spike's back. "Spike, stay here with the shadowfish," she said. "We'll be back soon."

Max, Rivet and Lia towed the hydrodisk

into the dock. Max pulled himself out of the water and crossed to the repairs shed. He found a welding gun, and a metal patch big enough to mend his damaged fuel tank.

"Rivet, keep a lookout while I fix the sub up," Max said. "Lia, can you hold this in place?" Max positioned the sheet of metal over the gash in his sub, and showed Lia where to put her hands. Then he fired up the welding torch, sending a jet of blue flame towards her.

"Hey!" Lia cried in alarm. "I happen to like having hair."

"Sorry!" Max said. He aimed the torch, and carefully welded the new section of metal into place. Once he'd finished, he screwed the nozzle of the Celerium pump to his sub's fuel inlet and filled his tank.

"All done!" Max said, satisfied. "Next stop, the Lost Lagoon."

There was a sudden clatter of heavy boots from the platform above them.

"Soldiers, Max!" Rivet barked, as a troop of uniformed men appeared at the guardrail of the platform, and aimed blasters down towards them.

Max shielded his eyes and looked up at the men. His stomach sank. Staring back at him, with his thin moustache twitched into a superior smile, was Lieutenant Jared, the officer who had imprisoned Max and his parents back on Aquora.

"Well, well, well," Jared said, eyeing Max and Lia smugly. "Look what the tide dragged in."

CHAPTER FOUR

RACE AGAINST DEATH

A wave of irritation hit Max as Jared ran his greedy eyes over the newly repaired sub. Max could see the lieutenant calculating just how to make his life as difficult as possible.

"So good of you to pay me a visit," Jared said. "Although I suppose it's the least you could do after getting me sent to this dreary patch of nothing in the middle of nowhere."

Lia narrowed her eyes. "It wasn't Max's

fault you ran away from your duty!" she said. "If you'd helped us fight Drakkos with the rest of your fleet you'd still be in Aquora now."

"Is that right?" Jared replied, eyeing Lia's webbed hands and gills with distaste. "Well, you two will only have yourselves to blame when I arrest you for trespassing and theft!"

"Lieutenant, you can't!" Max said. "We're on a rescue mission. I needed to repair my sub to reach the Lost Lagoon –"

"Ha!" Jared laughed. The heavyset soldiers beside him joined in, nudging each other and chuckling. Jared suddenly stopped laughing, his eyes turning as cold as ice.

"Don't think you can make a fool of me again, boy," Jared said. "The Lost Lagoon? Keep your fairy stories for kids your own age." He turned to the guard beside him. "Sergeant Seawell, search that sub. These two have got a reputation, and I mean to find out why they're here."

Max could feel his irritation swelling to anger as the sergeant climbed down the ladder towards them. *We don't have time for this! Cora could be up to anything!* Max rubbed his hands over his face, forcing himself to stay calm. "We've got to get out of here!" he hissed to Lia. "Can you create a distraction?"

A slow grin spread across Lia's face. She pressed a hand to her temple for a moment. Just as the soldier reached the bottom rung of the ladder, Lia lifted her arms and let out a terrible screech, so loud that it made even Max jump.

"You have angered the spirit of the sea!" Lia cried, letting her eyes roll back in her head and clawing at the air. "I call on the creatures of the deep. If you harm us or our

property, they will turn you all into fish!" At
that moment Spike shot up out of the water
behind Lia, a cloud of green fish flipping and
tumbling all around him.

Nice one, Lia! Max thought.

The sergeant's face drained of colour and

he turned and scrambled back up the ladder. The other men were turning from their posts at the railing too. Jared stood and stared for a moment, his eyes wide and his thin lips working.

"Men! Take cover!" he cried to his retreating troops. "The girl's a sea witch!" He turned to Lia and Max. "Don't think you'll get away with this!" he said, then sprinted away after his soldiers.

Lia giggled. "That was way too easy!" she said.

Max grinned. "Jared will work out our bluff soon enough. He's a coward, but he's not stupid." He leapt into his hydrodisk. "Come on, Riv!" he called, patting the passenger seat beside him. Rivet jumped aboard, and Max closed the lid as Lia slipped off her Amphibio mask and dived beneath the waves.

Max felt a twinge of apprehension as he

powered up his sub. *I hope my repairs have worked!* But then the sub hummed into life, and Max gave a whoop of triumph. He hit the accelerator, and zoomed after Lia as she and Spike darted through the red-tinged water with the shadowfish shimmering ahead of them.

From the platform behind him, Max heard the throb of engines starting up. He

glanced back to see four sleek, black stealth subs powering after him.

"Torpedoes, Max!" Rivet barked. Sure enough, each of the four subs had dropped a fat, pointed torpedo into the water below them.

Vroom! The torpedoes trailed bubbles as they made a beeline straight for Max.

Max thrashed his engines, squeezing

every bit of power from his sub. He could hear the drone of the torpedoes behind him. He steered hard left, then right, trying to lose them. Each time he swerved, he looked back to see the torpedoes veering after him. They were gaining fast. Max swallowed hard. *They must have a lock on me!*

"Lia!" Max cried. "I can't outrun those torpedoes!"

Suddenly the shadowfish flashed and vanished.

"Where did it go?" Max asked, urgently.

"I don't know," Lia said. "Hang on! I can see a patch of –" Suddenly Lia's words were cut off as she too flashed and vanished before Max's eyes.

"Gone, Max!" Rivet barked. Max glanced behind him to see the stubby nose of a torpedo almost at his back. His heart hammered as he willed the powerful sub to go faster. He tensed his muscles and gritted his teeth, expecting an impact from behind at any moment.

CHAPTER FIVE

DEVASTATION AND RUIN

Bam! There was a jolt, and Max felt a tug in his stomach. The water around him melted into a shifting rainbow dance. The air in the sub hummed and Max's vision filled with dark spots.

He shook his head and blinked to clear his senses. When he opened his eyes, he was looking out into deep, slate-grey water, broken by shadowy patches of craggy rock. He glanced behind him. The torpedoes were gone. Max let out a huge sigh of relief. *We must have made it to the Lost Lagoon!* he thought. Lia and Spike were floating in the dark blue water nearby. Lia was rubbing her arms and shivering. Max pulled up beside her and shut off his engines.

"The shadowfish has vanished," Lia said through chattering teeth.

"Well, it got us here and that's the main thing," Max said.

Lia pulled her seaweed tunic close about her. "I'd forgotten how cold it can get here!"

Max could feel the chill of the place creeping into his sub. "Maybe we're near the ice land of the Colossids. Let's head up to the surface and take a look."

Lia slipped on her Amphibio mask, and together they pushed upwards through the freezing waters of the Lagoon.

When Max's hydrodisk broke the surface,

he blinked in the silvery sunlight pouring
through his windows. Beside him, Lia was
shielding her eyes and scanning the horizons
of the huge lagoon. She pointed towards a
wooden structure in the distance.

"The city of Ur," she said. Max squinted,
and recognised the low huts and wooden
walkways of the floating city, glittering with

a sheen of frost. It must have floated closer to the land of the Colossids.

"Let's get a closer look," Max said. "Maybe the Ur-folk can tell us why we're here."

"Or maybe they'll just string us up and try to kill us like they did last time," Lia said. "I'm thinking we should leave your sub behind. They're not too keen on tech."

Max looked again at the floating city. Between him and Ur, nothing stirred. The choppy grey waters of the lagoon were empty, and apart from the lonely keening of the wind, the air was eerily quiet. An uneasy feeling settled in Max's stomach.

"Something's not right," Max said. "I'm taking my sub. I've got a feeling we're going to need it."

As Lia gazed out over the water, Max saw a shudder run through her body. She turned to him and nodded.

There were no boats in the water around Ur and no one appeared to greet them.

"Max," Lia suddenly gasped. "Look at the huts!" Max followed the line of her finger, and saw what she had noticed. The outlines of the wooden structures were jagged, and some were tilted at an angle.

As they drew closer to the city, it was clear even from the water that the Ur-folk would be no help to them at all. The wooden streets and buildings were deserted, and the huts bore pale gashes and splintered edges where beams had been hacked apart.

"Cora?" Lia said, frowning. "So what do we do now?"

Max scanned the deserted skyline, chewing his lip. "Last time we followed the ice-birds to the lighthouse of Piscanias," he said. "But now there aren't any birds at all, and everything's moved. Rivet – can you do a scan of the coastline and see if you can locate the Fennum Lighthouse?"

Rivet's ears pricked up, and a faint humming came from deep within his body as he engaged his electromagnets. Suddenly his eyes flashed red. "That way, Max!" Rivet barked, pointing to a spot on the horizon with his nose.

"Good boy, Riv!" Max said. "Full speed to the Fennum Lighthouse."

Max turned away from Ur, and towards the southern horizon. Lia's silver hair streamed behind her, glittering in the sun as they raced into the icy wind.

At last, the tall silhouette of the Fennum Lighthouse came into view. Max felt a heavy stone of dread settle in his stomach. Lia let out a cry of dismay. The once shining metal tower was tarnished all over and pockmarked with soot-tinged blaster holes. Where it used

to stand like a golden beacon, reflecting the
sun all around it, now it was dull and broken.
The squabbling, swooping ice-birds that had
filled the sky were gone.

Max cut his engines and eased the hydrodisk towards the rocky shore where the lighthouse stood. As he stepped out onto the stones, he could see the full extent of the damage to the tower. Great sections of Fennum swam with oily colours, outlined by charring, as if someone had tried to set it alight. The rocks that surrounded the lighthouse were charred too, and the lighthouse windows were shattered.

"Wait here," Lia told Spike, sliding from his back and pulling herself up onto the shore beside Max. Rivet kept close to Max's side as they approached the lighthouse, his eyes narrowed and his nose twitching as he sniffed the chilly air.

The door had been blasted into splinters which littered the entrance hall inside, along with fragments of Piscanias's driftwood and seashell furniture.

"Hello?" Max called up the spiral staircase that wound around the wall of the tower. His words echoed back towards him, but there was no answer from above.

Max and Lia exchanged a worried glance, then started up the steps. As they climbed, the clatter of their footsteps rang harshly in the silent air.

"Danger, Max!" Rivet barked.

Max nodded. "A terrible battle must have happened here. I hope Piscanias survived." Eventually they reached the door to Piscanias's observation room. Pale cuts scored the wood of the door, but it was all in one piece, and shut. Lia looked at Max, her eyes wide and anxious.

Max shrugged, but his own heart was hammering fast. "Here goes," he said, pushing the door.

"Oh, for Thallos' sake!" came a gruff,

croaky voice from inside. "I credited you two with more sense!" Max gaped in confusion at the sight of the wrinkled old Piscanias, tied roughly to the chair of his huge telescope. He was glaring crossly back at them from over the top of his Amphibio mask.

Lia put her hands on her hips. "Well, that's no way to thank us for coming to your rescue," she said.

Piscanias puffed out an exasperated breath.

"Idiots. Anyone with half a brain would have seen this was a trap!"

Max's pulse quickened. *What does he mean, a trap?*

There was an evil chuckle from above, and Max looked up to see cold eyes watching him through a gap in the lighthouse's domed roof. "I couldn't have said it better myself," a familiar female voice said. There was a grating sound and the dome opened wider, revealing the grinning face of Cora, surrounded by a host of pirates.

CHAPTER SIX

CORA'S SURPRISE

Cora leapt lightly through the hatch in the ceiling and dropped to the floor, her blaster aimed and ready. She stood before them grinning wickedly, dressed in a long black coat trimmed with fur. Her electric cat-o'-nine-tails was strapped to her side, and her gold jewellery jangled as she moved.

Rivet growled and leapt towards her, but Cora bared her teeth and snarled, stamping her shiny robotic leg at him. Rivet scampered behind Max and Lia as Cora cackled, then met Max's eyes, her evil smile back in place.

"I wasn't expecting you to come running so quickly," she said. "Once I convinced our friend Piscanias to send my message, I thought I'd be in for a wait. But your sweet, innocent faces are a most welcome sight. I've

plundered everything worth having in this hole and still don't have what I need to make a compass and get out of here." Cora's smile broadened. "But now I can just take yours." Max opened his mouth to protest, but Cora drew her cat-o'-nine-tails from her belt and flicked it on, cracking its electric strands.

Max cringed as Cora came near, lifted her other hand and ran the point of one black fingernail down his cheek. "You won't be needing your compass any more. Not once you've seen my surprise." Cora reached into Max's pocket and took out the compass, then stepped back and cracked her whip again. A spider-like Colossid with eight shiny legs dropped through the hatch in the ceiling and landed beside her, wielding a hyperblade cutlass. He was quickly followed by a fur-clad Ur-man, his broad, scarred face covered in blue war paint. Max could see more pirates waiting above.

"Clobber! Fangs!" Cora shouted. "Tie this pair of pasty bilge-rats up, along with their whining mutt, then take 'em to the boat! It's time to have some fun."

The two pirates lunged towards Max and Lia. Max balled his fist and swung for the Colossid, but a spindly leg whipped out and knocked his blow aside. Two more legs wrapped around his waist, and another swiped Rivet up from the ground. Max was heaved onto the creature's back and held in place by a strong, jointed limb.

"Get off me, you brute!" Lia cried, as the fur-clad Ur-man swept her up and bundled her over his shoulder.

"Much obliged for your hospitality," Cora called to Piscanias as she started down the spiral staircase.

"Then maybe you could untie me?"

Piscanias growled.

Cora lifted her head and laughed. "I could," she said, "but I'm not going to." She continued down the steps, still cackling to herself.

Max's final view as he was carried down the stairs was of the old explorer sitting back in his chair with a grunt.

The pirates hefted Max, Lia and Rivet down the stairs and out into the cold wind. Cora stalked ahead, leading them over rocks to the back of the lighthouse. Max saw a motorboat moored by the rocks, and beyond that, hidden from the rest of the lagoon, a tatty-looking pirate ship made of scraps of wood and metal. *She must have built it here*, Max thought. *If we'd searched the island before, we would have spotted it!* he realised, gritting his teeth at his own mistake.

Cora stopped before she reached the

motorboat, and swung around, smiling.

"Now Max, you'll never guess what your clever-clogs of an uncle left behind on my ship when he got himself arrested," she said. "Only some rather interesting blueprints. So, I had that old squid mechanic Sellius take a look… I believe he's a friend of yours?" Max remembered the cheerful mechanic who had sold him Barrum last time they were in the Lost Lagoon, and hoped Cora hadn't hurt him too much.

"Anyway," Cora went on, "Sellius has done rather a neat job of creating my very own Robobeast, Octor. He's a fire flinger." Cora frowned. "Or at least, he will be when he's fully powered up. But I think he's ready for a test. And who better to try him out on than my old chums, Max and Lia?" She turned to her band of pirates and lifted her whip. "Chain 'em up!" she snapped, gesturing to a rock with her thumb. "And bring over the girl's pet fish."

Max struggled against the Colossid's iron grip as the creature scuttled towards the rock at the edge of the lagoon. It was useless. Each time he strained he felt the spindly legs grip him harder. Beside him, Lia was squirming

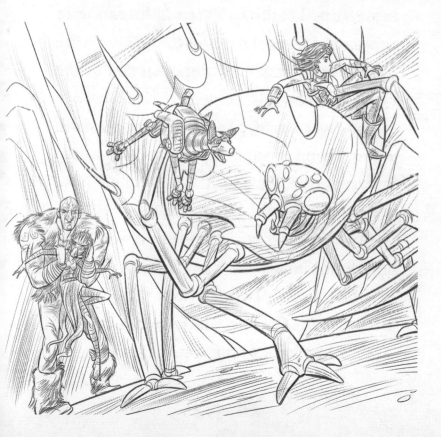

in the arms of the Ur-man, but he was at least three times her size.

When they reached the edge of the water, the Colossid threw Max down onto the rock, pinning him there with two pointed feet. Another pair of limbs slammed Rivet down beside him. A huge, boulder-like Grundle heaved a coil of thick rope from his shoulder and started to tie them down.

Cora has marshalled all the species in the Lost Lagoon to work for her!

There was a loud, panicked clicking sound, and a second Grundle appeared with a net. Spike thrashed inside it, his pointed nose poking through the loops.

"Spike!" Lia cried. "He'll die if you keep him out of water."

"Oh, stop whimpering," Cora said. "Tie the fish below the tideline," she told the Grundle. "It'll be much more fun watching Octor rip him to pieces."

Soon, Max, Lia, Rivet and Spike were all tied fast to the rock. Cora ran her eyes over them approvingly.

"I hope you enjoy my surprise!" she called, smiling brightly. Then she lifted a hand in farewell and strode towards her waiting motorboat.

As the Colossid who had carried him turned to go, Max suddenly remembered something. *Colossids love watching fights!*

"Psst!" Max called. The Colossid turned, his black eyes glittering.

"If you want to see a real Robobeast battle," Max said, "you've got to give us a chance. We're just dinner on a plate like this."

The Colossid glanced towards Cora and the other pirates boarding the motorboat. Then he slipped a knife from his belt and pressed the handle into the palm of Max's hand. Max shifted his grip on the knife as the Colossid scuttled away. The blade was small, more like a dinner knife than a weapon. *But a small chance is better than none.*

Max heard the motorboat engine growl into life and watched as it shot out into the lagoon, trailing a white V of foam as it raced towards Cora's ship.

He turned his head to glance at Rivet who was struggling to get his jaws around his ropes. Beside Rivet, Lia was staring out over the water.

"There's something coming," Lia said, her voice low and urgent. "Something terrible. I can sense it."

Max felt the icy water lap at his legs. He glanced across the lagoon to see circular waves rippling towards him from a bubbling mass at their centre. Something poked up from the surface: a long, blue tentacle, covered

in suckers. It rose from the waves, as thick
as a tree, and reaching up almost as high.
On the end of the tentacle, Max could see
something shimmering with a strange blue
light. It looked worryingly like a circular saw.
Another tentacle broke the waves, tipped
with a razor-sharp spike. Max swallowed
hard.

Octor had arrived.

CHAPTER SEVEN

OCTOR ATTACKS

Max lifted the knife and started to saw frantically at the cords that circled his chest, binding him to the rock. Rivet sank his teeth into his own ropes. There was a grating, electric whir, and Max glanced up to see Octor's circular saw glinting as it powered towards them on the end of a writhing tentacle. Beneath the surface, Max could see an immense shadowy form gliding through the water. Spike lifted his nose from the shallows near the rocks and let out a flurry of terrified clicks.

"Hurry, Max!" Lia cried.

Max hacked through the last loop around his chest just as Rivet gnawed his way free and leapt into the lagoon.

"Rivet free Spike!" the dogbot barked, and ducked below the waves. Max turned and sliced through Lia's bonds as the whirring saw swooped closer. More shining tentacles of muscular flesh broke the water all around it, shimmering as they changed colour from blue to white to green. The water of the lagoon seemed to boil with movement.

Rivet surfaced, a frayed rope hanging from his jaws. Spike lifted his nose and clicked at Lia. Then Rivet let out a strangled bark and disappeared, a coil of glistening flesh wrapped around his neck. Spike vanished at almost the same moment, seized by another tentacle.

Lia screamed as a third coil curled around her ankle, dragging her into the lagoon. Max lifted his knife and glanced towards the mass of twisting, gliding limbs tipped with shining weaponry. The knife in his hand felt smaller than ever, but he took a deep breath and dived.

Beneath the surface, the water of the lagoon was in turmoil. Tentacles whipped about in every direction, trailing bubbles and throwing up clouds of silt. Max could feel the currents they created tugging at his body.

Each tentacle was tipped with the same blue metal cladding as the harvester robots around Upsilon-7, and each wielded a different, lethal-looking weapon.

The creature was huge. Max could just make out its giant balloon of a body at the centre of all the chaos. It was speckled all over, and

changed colour to match its surroundings as it moved. *Cora must have found the octopus in the lagoon and forced Sellius to modify it!* Max thought. He heard a scream, and turned to see Lia being tugged through the water, wrapped tight in a thick coil.

Max darted forwards, knife ready to strike. Then something grabbed his leg. He tried to kick free but the tentacle was too strong. He swung back his arm to slice at the coil, but a

cold pressure wrapped about his wrist then squeezed. His leg was tugged in one direction and his arm in another. Max gasped in agony. His arm and leg muscles burned and he could feel his shoulder wrenching from its socket.

"Rivet save Max!" The dogbot barrelled through the water towards him and fastened his metal teeth around the tentacle holding Max's arm.

Thank goodness Rivet got free! Max thought.

The pain was starting to blur his vision. Rivet growled, snapping at the limb.

Suddenly, a glinting spike surged through the water towards Rivet.

"Watch out!" Max tried to shout, but his voice was weak from the agony that tore through his body.

This is it! Max thought as the spike jabbed towards Rivet. *We don't stand a chance!*

Zap! Suddenly the water of the lagoon flashed red. An energy bolt whizzed towards Max and smashed into the tentacle around his leg. Octor's sinuous limbs all flexed and uncoiled at once. Max swam free, dizzy with relief, as Rivet powered to his side. Octor's tentacles were rippling away across the lagoon behind his gigantic spotted body. Max glanced about, looking for the source of the energy bolt that had freed him.

"Max, look!" Lia cried, joining him on

Spike and pointing at the water behind them. Max turned to see the shimmering outline of a stealth sub zooming towards them. Through the window, he could see Lieutenant Jared frowning.

"He must have slipped through the portal behind us when we entered the Lost Lagoon!" Lia said, rubbing at a line of red sucker marks on her arm.

"I hate to admit it," Max said, "but I think he just saved our lives."

"Drop your weapon!" Jared shouted at Max and Lia, his voice tinny over his sub's intercom. "You are all under arrest!" Octor's shadowy form was already circling back towards them. Max could see the glint of metal weapons slicing through the water, but the creature's skin had turned a deep, shadowy blue and was next to invisible.

"I said drop your weapon!" Jared cried.

"Lieutenant!" Lia cried. "There's a giant armed octopus coming to kill us! And you're worried about a tiny knife?" Max glanced towards Octor and his heart gave a jolt. The creature was almost on them, and its bulging eyes were fixed angrily on Jared's sub. Max could hear the whizz of Octor's circular saw. He could feel the current of the creature's movement flowing around him.

"Jared, we have to go. Now!" Max cried, pointing at the monster. Jared followed the line of Max's finger, and the colour drained from his face. He started scrabbling at his controls, his eyes wide with terror.

Max kicked his legs and darted away through the water. Rivet's propellers whirred beside him, and Lia and Spike surged past. Max heard a metallic clang and felt a terrible sinking feeling. He glanced back to see one of Octor's metal appendages bounce off the

surface of Jared's sub.

Jared was still fumbling with his controls, staring in horror as Octor pulled back his shadowy tentacle for another blow.

"We have to help him!" Max told Lia.

"How?" Lia said. "We have a table knife and Spike's sword. We can't beat that thing." There was a hideous grating sound as Octor held the edge of his rotating saw against Jared's sub.

"Get it off me!" Jared screamed. Max

could hear the sub's engines whining as Jared tried to escape, but Octor's thick limbs were wrapped around it.

"Watch my back!" Max told Lia. Then he grabbed Rivet around the waist. "Full speed, Rivet!" Max cried.

Rivet whizzed forwards, and Max kicked his legs out behind them, adding his power to Rivet's to increase their speed. Jared was banging on the window of the sub as it filled with water. His eyes were wide with terror but Max was glad to see that at least he'd managed to strap on his breathing mask.

"I can't get out!" Jared cried. "The hatch is stuck!" The metal of the sub was creaking and buckling as Octor squeezed it. Max could see that the door in the roof was bent out of shape.

He let go of Rivet, thrust himself towards the top of the sub and hit the emergency catch. The hatch flew open and Jared shot out. His arms and legs scrabbled clumsily in the water as he tried to flee the Robobeast. Max grabbed his arm and pulled him through the water, expecting to feel the grip of Octor's tentacles around his ankle at any moment.

Lia caught hold of Jared's hand as they approached and helped him swing up onto Spike's back. Max turned, knife in hand, to face the giant octopus.

To his surprise, Octor was swimming away towards the surface, his long tentacles flowing out behind his massive dome of a body.

"Where's he going?"

Lia pulled on her Amphibio mask, and they all swam upwards, emerging from the water into the chilly sun. In the distance, Max could see the dark silhouette of Cora's retreating ship with Octor swimming behind it.

"Enjoy your retirement to the Lost Lagoon," Cora's voice rang out across the waves, distorted through a megaphone. "Octor's coming to Nemos with me," she called, "and once I've got his flame-throwers powered up, nothing'll stop us. Especially with you two gone!"

"She's going to use your compass to escape!" Lia said.

Max nodded, feeling suddenly tired and heavy with defeat. "We'll never catch her now," he said. "Which means we're stuck here until we can make another one."

Lia bit her lip. "If Cora couldn't find what she needed, that's not going to be easy," she said.

"No," Max said. He took a deep breath, forcing his tiredness aside. "But we have to catch up with her, and fast. Let's try Piscanias. He didn't give us his compass last time we asked, but we have to try. That Robobeast's the most dangerous we've faced. If he's let loose in Nemos..." Max trailed off, and exchanged a worried look with Lia. He didn't need to say what he was thinking. Things had never looked so bad.

But we haven't failed on a Sea Quest yet, Max thought, balling his fists. *I'm not about to now!*

STORY 2:

THE BATTLE OF UPSILON-7

CHAPTER ONE

TRAPPED IN THE LOST LAGOON

A cold wind shrieked across the surface of the lagoon, throwing up choppy waves. Max could feel it buffeting against his sub as he raced towards the Fennum Lighthouse. Spike was cutting through the water alongside him, with Lia on his back. Jared scowled into the wind, clinging tight to Spike's back behind Lia. The pockmarked silhouette of Piscanias's home rose up ahead.

Max urged his hydrodisk onwards, anxiety bubbling inside him.

When they reached the scorched and silent lighthouse, Max docked his sub and leapt ashore with Rivet. Lia hopped up beside him and held a hand out to Jared, but the lieutenant ignored her and clambered awkwardly onto the dock, shivering and dripping water. They traced their steps back to the lighthouse and climbed the winding stairs.

When they reached the top, they found Piscanias snoring gently, a string of drool hanging from the chin of his Amphibio mask.

"You expect to get help from that?" Jared asked, scowling scornfully at the sleeping Merryn.

Max shot Jared a warning look. "I'm going to do whatever it takes to get us out of here and defeat Cora!" he said.

"Ruff!" Rivet barked in agreement. The old Merryn snorted at the sound, and his eyes flickered open. When he saw Max and Lia, he grimaced.

"You again!" he said. "Well, I hope you've not come looking for an apology, because I didn't have any choice!"

Lia sighed and rolled her eyes, but set about untying the old man from his chair.

"Cora's escaped to Nemos," Max told Piscanias. "She stole my compass to get there, and she's taking along a Robobeast with enough weaponry to destroy Sumara. Lia and I are going to stop her, but we need to borrow the compass you used in your old exploring days."

Piscanias rubbed at the red marks on his wrists and glowered at Max. "If you must know," Piscanias said, "I swapped it for some seaweed cakes years ago. They reminded me of home."

Max felt his temper flaring.

"Well, how about getting us a shadowfish?" he said. "You managed to trick us into coming here with one."

Piscanias sighed. "If there was any way I could get rid of you, believe me, I would. But shadowfish don't just grow on kelp, you know. I have no idea what Cora did to make one do what she wanted, but I don't suppose it was nice. Now, if you don't mind, I have a lighthouse to repair. Do you think you could leave me in peace?"

"It would be our pleasure," Lia said, tossing her head. She started down the stairs. Max followed close behind her, with Rivet at his heels, and beckoned for Jared to follow.

"Wait a minute," Max said, turning back to Piscanias. "Do you think we could have some Fennum?"

"Take what you need," said Piscanias, with a wave of his hand. "There's enough of the stuff lying about on the rocks."

So Max did – he joined the others at the bottom of the stairs and picked up a sliver of the metal cladding which had been blasted from the lighthouse's walls. "Just three metals to get," he said. "We'd better head to the Underwater Market. They had what we

needed there last time. With any luck, we'll be able to make ourselves a compass and catch up with Cora before she does any serious damage."

"Agreed," Lia said. Max led the way down to the dock where his hydrodisk was moored. Spike surfaced, and Lia leapt onto his back. Jared watched from the rocks, looking cold and wet and miserable.

"You can ride with me if you want to," Max said, patting the passenger seat of his sub. Jared ran his eyes over the hydrodisk and scowled.

"I suppose that's another stolen vessel I have to add to your list of felonies?" he said.

"Actually," Max said, "this sub's far better than anything the Navy can offer. I built it myself. Now, you can either ride with me, or with Lia." Max started to close the lid.

"Wait!" Jared said. His thin lips were

pressed together, but he scrambled into the passenger seat beside Max. Rivet hopped into the footwell, and Max closed the hatch.

Spike and Lia dived below the surface of the lagoon. Max revved his engines, and plunged after her, hitting the accelerator hard. His stomach flipped as the sub plummeted through the dark water. Jared gasped and grabbed the dashboard. Max couldn't help grinning at the panicked expression on the lieutenant's face. He levelled his hydrodisk and swooped after Lia.

It wasn't far to the market, and as Max peered through the clear, deep water he expected to see lights up ahead any moment. But there was nothing. *It's just one of the quirks of the Lagoon*, Max told himself. *Nothing's where you expect it...* But even so, he felt uneasy.

Eventually, tall pillars loomed before them,

black shadows in the darkness. Lia slowed Spike, and Max drifted to her side. As they got closer Max could clearly make out the tall rocky columns and interconnected floors of the Underwater Market. But the rock was pockmarked just like Piscanias's lighthouse, and covered in tangled sea-moss.

"Some market," Jared snorted.

"Where is everyone?" Max said, cold dread prickling his skin. The last time he'd seen the

market it had been busy with sea folk. Now
there were no lights, no traders and nothing
to buy.

"We'd better take a look inside," Lia said,
her voice hushed and anxious as it echoed
through the sub's speakers.

"In there?" Jared said, peering into the
gloom. "The place should be torn down."

"We don't have any choice," Max said. He
surged forwards with Lia and Spike, using

his headlights to search the dark interior for any sign of life.

He found stalls cluttered with junk and half barricaded with buckled pillars. There were broken barrels, silt-covered tables and piles of old shells left behind from the market. But nothing else.

Suddenly, something fast and shiny broke through the beams of his headlights. *A shadowfish!* And there was another. A stream of flickering translucent forms whizzed past, churning up clouds of silt.

"After them!" Max said. He gunned his engines and Spike flicked his tail, surging after the racing forms. The fish slalomed between broken pillars then swerved upwards through a crack in the ceiling. Spike darted through with Lia, and Max pulled on his controls, steering sharply upwards.

"Hurray!" A chorus of gruff cries rang out

as Max and Lia arrived in the upper floor of the market.

The shadowfish were pouring, one after another, through a series of glowing hoops in the middle of the room. Beyond the shadowfish, a group of human-like creatures in dark cloaks huddled near the far wall. They were holding glowing lantern-fish that cast long shadows beneath them. Max saw the glint of gems changing hands as the creatures muttered and laughed.

"You were lucky that time," Max heard a familiar voice say from within the group. "I will bet you two golds and a blue that my beautiful Imogen will outrun your fish next time." Max grinned. *Sellius!* He opened the lid of the hydrodisk and swam out with Rivet. Jared followed, wearing his breathing mask.

"A race!" Lia said. "The shadowfish were

racing. And Max, look!" She pointed to a squat, square form darting through the shoal of shadowfish, wagging a stumpy tail. *A dogbot!* It was a little rough round the edges, but Max would have recognised the design anywhere. It was clearly based on Rivet.

Max's pet wagged his tail. "Play, Max?" Rivet barked, watching the other dogbot.

"That's no game," Jared said. "It looks like a highly illegal betting ring to me!"

"Stop right there!" came a gruff voice from behind them. Lia gasped and turned, and Max spun around too, to see a huge, bleary-eyed walrus-like creature glaring at them down the barrel of a blaster cannon.

CHAPTER TWO

SHADY DEALINGS

"What's yer business here?" the walrus-man growled, scowling as he turned his blaster slowly from Max and Jared, to Lia on Spike, and then back again.

Jared cowered away from the gun, suddenly very quiet. Max urgently scanned the features of the cloaked figures by the far wall. Relief flooded through him as he spotted the huge dark eyes and cheerful squid-like features he'd been looking for.

"We're here to see the mechanic Sellius," Max said, pointing.

The walrus-like creature narrowed his eyes suspiciously, but slowly lowered his blaster.

"Oi! Squid-man," he shouted over his shoulder. "These foreigners are 'ere to see yer."

Sellius turned towards them, frowning, then his big eyes opened wide and his beak-like mouth curved into a smile.

"Max and Lia!" Sellius said, swimming towards them. "I never forget a face! You fixed my crab for some Barrum!" Sellius turned to the red-eyed walrus-man. "I will look after my young friends from here," Sellius said. The large, whiskered creature glowered once more at each of them in turn, then swam slowly away.

Sellius turned to Max and Lia and grinned. "I get so few customers these days!" he said. "You are most welcome. And let us not forget my dear friend Rivet!" Rivet's metal paws scrabbled excitedly at the trader's cloak as Sellius bent and patted him on the head. The other dogbot bounded over to join them.

"Rivet, meet Rusty," Sellius said, patting the other dogbot and offering each dog a rusted bolt. The two robots swam a short distance away and started to chew on their bolts happily. Sellius turned to Max and Lia.

"You see I have built a dog of my own," Sellius said. "And I think you will agree Rusty is a great success. I had to make some minor adjustments after he ate my poor old robocrab, Pinch, but since then, he's hardly nibbled anyone." Sellius smiled fondly at Rusty. "So anyway, what can I do for my dear friends?" Sellius asked.

"We came here to buy precious metals," Lia said. "But what happened? All the stalls are gone."

Sellius frowned sadly. "Cora happened," he said. "She swept through here like a tidal wave, turning everything upside down, looking for rare metals like you are. When I told her we didn't have any, she took me to her ship. Forced me to work on a giant octopus she had captured, giving it all sorts of strange appendages." Sellius's long tentacles flapped as he spoke. "I told her it was a big mistake. The finished creature was an abomination. A living war machine complete with camouflage," he said, "but she wouldn't listen. She said she'd kill me if I did not help."

"Octor," Max said, frowning. "Sellius, have you still got the blueprints Cora gave you to work from? That octopus is headed to Nemos, and we need to defeat it."

"That's right!" Jared snapped, stepping forward with his hands on his hips. "I insist you hand the blueprints over this minute, or I'll have you prosecuted for withholding evidence."

Sellius stepped back sharply, his tentacles quivering. "Max!" he hissed, glancing nervously about him. "Why does your friend talk this way? He will get us in big trouble."

"Oof!" Jared bent double as Lia jabbed him in the ribs with her elbow.

"Don't worry, Sellius," Lia said. "Jared thinks he's in charge, but I promise I'll keep him under control." She glanced towards the other traders, who were ready to start the next race. Two cloaked figures had broken away from the group, and were heading towards them. One was tall and thin, and wore an eye patch on an otherwise plain-looking face, while the other was so fat he was almost round. His eyes bulged, and his skin was mottled and green. He reminded Max a lot of a toad.

"Sellius!" the fat creature croaked, suddenly leaping forwards and grabbing the mechanic by the tentacles. "You'd better hope Imogen wins this race. You owe me, and if you don't pay up, it'll be time for me to give you that trim." The slim, featureless creature at the toad's side silently drew out a knife. Max barged past it, anger flaring inside him. Sellius's eyes were round with horror as he tried to twist out of the toad-creature's grip.

"Let him go!" Max cried, putting his hand on the hilt of his hyperblade and glaring angrily at the toad.

The creature let go of Sellius, and stepped back, his eyes bulging more than ever. "I'm not done with you, squid-man," he said. "You

pay up, or next time you're on your own…"
The fat creature ran a knobbly finger across
his bloated throat, then laughed hoarsely
and turned away.

Sellius was quivering all over.

"Don't worry," Lia said. "I have an idea. Tell
me which fish is yours, and I'll make sure it
wins the next race. That way you'll win the
money you need to pay your debts, and you
can give us Cora's blueprints in return."

Sellius glanced uneasily at Jared, but the
lieutenant was staring sulkily at his feet and
rubbing his side where Lia had jabbed him.

"Done!" Sellius said. "My fish is called
Imogen. She is the pretty one with the red
stripe." Lia shook Sellius's hand, then turned
her attention to the row of shadowfish lined
up at a starting point.

She put her fingertips to her head and
frowned in concentration as a bearded

trader lifted a trumpet-like shell to his lips and blew.

The shadowfish shot forwards all at once in a shimmering, dazzling cloud. The first darted through a glowing golden hoop. The rest flowed after it like a glistening silver stream. As the fish raced on, pouring through hoop after hoop, Max could hear the traders muttering names and numbers. Lia was frowning intently. The fish were so close together, Max couldn't tell which was which. Suddenly, a gap opened out at the front of the race. Max could see a small fish with blue-tinged fins in the lead. Next came Imogen, with a shimmering red streak on her back.

Lia leaned towards them, frowning, as they raced towards the final set of hoops.

Max could see her hands trembling as she pressed her fingers against her temples.

He turned his attention back to the race. The blue-tinged fish and Imogen were almost fin-and-fin as they soared towards the final ring, but the blue-tinged fish was still a whisker ahead. Then, just before the blue-tinged fish plunged through the glowing hoop, it flicked its tail and swerved aside. Imogen streaked through ahead of it, followed by the rest of the fish. A mix of cheers and growls went up from the assembled traders. Lia let out a sigh, her shoulders slumping with exhaustion.

"Ha ha!" Sellius cried, grabbing Lia by the hands and dancing her round in a circle. Then he pulled a small chip from his pocket and pushed it into Max's hand. "There are your plans," he said. "Now if you don't mind, I'm going to collect my winnings!" He made his way towards the other traders.

"So far so good!" Lia said. "But we still need to find a way out of the Lagoon."

Max pocketed the chip, frowning. He'd been watching Rivet and Rusty swimming in and out of the group of shadowfish, and it had given him an idea. He looked again, noticing how the shadowfish evaded the dogbots easily by flickering out of sight each time the dogs got close. They were crossing back and forth from the Lost Lagoon to Nemos.

Max turned to Lia and grinned. "I am way ahead of you," he said.

BACK TO REALITY

"Sellius!" Max called. "We need to ask you for one more favour!"

Sellius stuffed a handful of gleaming coins and gems into his pocket, then swam over to Max, grinning. "Anything, Max!" he said. "I have never had such a big win!"

"We need to borrow Imogen," Max said, "but I promise we'll send her back."

Sellius's usually broad smile vanished at that. "She is my livelihood, Max. Without her, I have nothing."

"We have to get to Nemos to stop Cora and the octopus you altered from killing thousands of people. If we can ask Imogen and the other shadowfish to make the crossing together, we should be able to follow in their wake."

Sellius frowned. "That does sound like it could work," he said. "And I would never forgive myself if that Robobeast hurt anybody…" Sellius thought for a moment, then nodded once. "You may borrow her!" he said.

"Great," Max said. "Lia, can you summon all the fish?"

"I just did," Lia said, grinning. "And they're more than willing. Apparently Cora is not their favourite person either."

"Let's go then!" Max said. "Rivet! Say goodbye to Rusty. We're going back to

Nemos in style."

Max swam over to his hydrodisk and he and Rivet hopped inside. Jared eyed the disk warily. "Do you think you can go easy on the throttle this time?" he asked.

Max grinned. "You're welcome to stay here if you like." Jared glanced around the gloomy market where the traders were setting up the next race. He shuddered, then hopped into the hydrodisk. Lia gazed towards Imogen, waiting ready at the starting line. The red-striped fish glanced at Lia, her eyes sparkling merrily. Then the bearded trader blew a note on his shell, and the shadowfish raced away.

Lia swooped ahead, following the flickering stream. Max's stomach leapt as he rocketed through the half-darkness. He could hardly see a thing. He kept his eyes fixed on Lia's back and steered, ignoring the yelps and gasps from Jared beside him.

The shadowfish climbed through the water towards the sun-dappled surface of the lagoon. Just when Max was sure they were going to shoot straight into the air, Lia let out a cry.

"They're making the crossing!" she said. The shadowfish disappeared one after another, leaving a cloud of rainbow

ripples dancing in the water. Lia went next, vanishing as she reached the patch of glimmering colours. Max didn't even have time to hold his breath before his sub hit the portal. He felt a whooshing shift of speed that snatched his breath away. All around him colours pulsed and trembled. Then, with a tremendous flash of blinding light, they were through. The hydrodisk slowed suddenly, throwing Max and Jared forwards in their seats and sending Rivet flying.

Max blinked, trying to make sense of the dull, flat colours all around him. He shook his head, and gradually, everything shifted back into focus. He was home. Back in the ocean of Nemos.

"We did it!" Lia cried, sending Spike in a loop-the-loop.

"Thanks to you!" Max said, grinning. Beside him, Jared wiped a film of sweat from his forehead. Max took the chip that Sellius had given him from his pocket, and slipped it into a slot on his dashboard. A screen in front of him lit up with a set of glowing blue diagrams.

"Lia, come and take a look at this," Max called into his headset. Lia turned to the shoal of shadowfish and raised a hand in farewell, then swam over to the hydrodisk window. The shoal glowed brightly, then vanished.

Max turned to the diagrams before him. He traced the wiring, and inspected the Robobeast's fearsome weaponry. "It's a plasma gun!" Max said, reading the neatly printed words next to one of Octor's weapons.

Lia peered through the window, and rolled her eyes. "Fantastic!" she said. "And you still think tech's a good thing!"

"That gun will be powered by Celerium," Jared said, pointing at the diagram. "It's the only fuel that could work. If Cora wants to use that gun, she'll be headed to a harvesting outpost."

Rivet's ears pricked, and his eyes flashed. "Upsilon-7 that way!" he said, pointing through the sub's window with his nose.

"Good boy, Riv!" Max said. Then he remembered something. Octor's weapons had the same strange blue sheen as the harvester robots at the outpost. "Octor's weapons must be made of Tinactium," he said.

"Makes sense," Jared said. "Nothing else would contain the fuel. Tinactium can withstand any temperature. It can also be magnetised. That's how we call the robots back in when they're finished harvesting."

Lia cleared her throat loudly outside the sub. "I hate to interrupt this fascinating technical discussion," she said, "but there's a huge octopus on the loose that's about to become a flame-thrower. If we're going to stop Cora, we need to get moving. Now!"

Max ran his eyes once more over the range of terrifying weapons on the blueprints, then closed the diagram app. "All right," he said. "Hold on, Jared. We're taking you back to Upsilon-7 to defeat that Robobeast."

CHAPTER FOUR

BATTLE OF UPSILON-7

"Rivet!" Max said to his dogbot, as they whizzed towards Upsilon-7. "I need you to take a message to Dad in Aquora – warn him that Cora is on the loose with another Robobeast."

"No battle, Max?" Rivet barked, his metal ears drooping with disappointment.

"Not yet, Riv, but this is important," Max said. "Octor's the most dangerous Robobeast we've faced yet, and with a ship full of pirates to tackle as well, we might just need some backup. And as Head of Defence in Aquora, Dad needs to know what Cora's planning."

"Right, Max!" Rivet said, his ears pricking and his tail wagging. Max opened the sub's escape hatch, and Rivet leapt through. His propellers spun as he shot off towards Aquora, using his stumpy tail to steer. Max felt a twinge of sadness as he watched his dogbot go, but he knew there was no choice.

Before long the water ahead turned a deep shadowy red, and Max spotted scarlet algae on the rocks below. They raced past a herd of harvesting robots, until the floating blue platform of the outpost came into view.

"Any sign of Octor or Cora?" Max asked, scanning the ocean around the rig.

"Not yet," Lia said. "The portal from the Lost Lagoon Cora used must have been further from the platform than ours. But we'd better hurry or…" Lia broke off suddenly, and pointed. In the distance, beyond the platform, Max could just make out a dark blot the size of a ship on the surface of the water above. It was moving towards the platform, fast. And beneath it, Max could see the glint of silvery blue metal flitting along the seabed. *Octor!*

"They're coming!" Max cried. "Jared, go to the outpost and raise the alarm. Lia and I will tackle Octor while you and your men fend off Cora."

Jared narrowed his eyes. "Since when do you give the orders?" he asked.

"Fine!" Max said. "You battle Octor. We'll go and raise the alarm."

Jared's face went pale. "I'll go," he said. Then his superior smile returned. "After all, we'll need an experienced commander on the base if we're going to capture Cora."

Then it's a shame they'll have to make do with you, Max thought. He steered his sub towards the outpost. When they reached the shadow of the metal structure, Max surfaced and climbed out. Jared jumped out onto the platform. He ran along the jetty and clattered up the ladder, hitting a big red button on the way.

Honk! Honk! Honk! An alarm sounded right across the base, and red lights flashed. Max heard running, booted feet as men wearing black combat suits wielding blasters appeared along the guardrail of the rig.

"All men at the ready!" Jared's voice blared through a tannoy. "We're under attack!"

Max glanced towards Cora's ship as it cut towards the outpost. A tattered skull-and-crossbones fluttered from its mast, and a row of huge cannons poked through its patchwork hull. As Max watched, the cannons all jolted at once, flashing red.

WHIZZ! Energy bolts soared through the sky.

BOOM! They smashed into the platform, making it judder. More sizzled into the sea nearby, throwing plumes of water up high.

Max turned to Lia, who had surfaced beside him. "Let's find Octor," he said. Lia nodded, pulled off her Amphibio mask, and dipped below the waves. Max closed the hatch of his hydrodisk, and angled it after her.

Beneath the water, Max could hear the muted sounds of the gun battle above. Red spears of energy sliced through the water as cannon fire rained down.

"Max! Over there!" Lia cried. Max turned to see something stirring among the red boulders on the seabed ahead. It almost looked like a mirage. But in the shifting patterns, Max could just make out the rippling movement of long limbs and the glint of shining blue weapons sliding between the rocks.

Suddenly, Max felt a vibration in the water and heard the quiet hum of engines behind him.

Tak-tak-tak! Two ray-shaped Aquoran stealth subs shot past from Upsilon-7, firing rapid blasts of energy towards the camouflaged octopus.

"They must have spotted him on the outpost's radar!" Max told Lia. "Let's give them a hand!"

Lia angled Spike towards the Robobeast, and they sped after the firing subs.

As the sub's energy blasts hit Octor, the creature loomed up from the seabed, changing colour in an instant from dusky red and grey to bright, glistening white with livid scarlet spots. Two of his limbs snaked upwards, each tipped with a glinting spike. Max aimed his blasters as he raced towards the giant octopus, but with the stealth subs speeding ahead, he couldn't risk firing.

The stealth subs let fly again, and more blasts stabbed towards Octor. The creature's snaking limbs snapped out like striking cobras, deflecting the energy bolts. Then they lashed around the subs themselves. *I have to help those men!* Max thought, looking for a clear shot. But before he could get a lock on Octor's mighty limbs, they slammed together, smashing the subs into each other with tremendous force.

"No!" Lia cried as the hideous thunk of

metal hitting metal rang through the water. Max's skin tightened all over with horror as two broken stealth subs dropped from Octor's tentacles down to the seabed below. They were completely crushed. There was no way anyone inside could have survived. But then Max spotted two black-clad forms swimming quickly away, trailing bubbles from breathing gear. Max let out a sigh of relief. *Thank goodness they ejected!*

Max turned his attention back to the Robobeast. Octor's round eyes swivelled towards him, glinting coldly as one giant limb silently lifted and uncoiled. On the end was the deadly plasma cannon Max had spotted on the blueprints.

"He's going to fire!" Lia cried.

He can't! Max thought. *He isn't powered up.* But then he glanced towards the seabed. Another of Octor's limbs, tipped with some sort of pipe, was attached to the snaking hose of a harvester robot. Then Max noticed transparent tubes running the length of Octor's tentacles, swelling and turning yellow as they filled with fuel. Octor's eyes flashed with triumph as the fuel flowed towards the plasma cannon.

"Lia!" Max cried. "We have to disable him

fast! If Upsilon-7 takes a hit, it will go up like a torch. Everyone will be killed."

FSSSSSHHH! Max's heart stopped still as a burst of orange plasma flared from Octor's gun, straight towards him and Lia.

CHAPTER FIVE
OCTOR ATTACKS

Max slammed his sub into reverse, his heart thumping. Even through the walls of his hydrodisk he could feel the searing heat of the blast as it jetted towards him, superheating the water in its path.

"Ahhhh!" Lia screamed as she and Spike fled the burning plasma. The water around them was bubbling with steam and Lia grimaced with pain as they swam ahead of the orange flare, keeping just out of reach.

At last, the spurt of plasma stopped, leaving

a mist of bubbles in the water and a bright after-burn in Max's eyes. Max swallowed hard and wiped the sweat from his face. *Octor will need to recharge that cannon before he can fire again*, Max thought. *This is my chance!* He swung his sub around, and aimed his blasters towards the tiny control box between the creature's bulbous eyes. Before he could hit fire, another limb whipped towards him, swinging a spiked mace. Max steered sharply

downwards, diving beneath the limb. He found himself surrounded by more tentacles and glinting weapons, whipping about in a frenzy.

Max's pulse raced as he tried to make sense of the chaos.

He could see Lia dodging Octor's blows as Spike thrust at the creature's limbs with his sword, but Octor was too fast, snatching his tentacles out of reach. Max swallowed, and his throat felt as dry as sand. *He's playing with us!* Max thought. He took aim with his blasters again as one of Octor's limbs rose up and pointed towards him. Then his stomach clenched with horror. He was looking straight down the gaping barrel of Octor's blaster cannon.

Max spun his sub around and gunned the engines, swooping towards the seabed.

FSSSSSSHHHH! Terror seared through

Max at the roaring hiss of Octor's plasma gun erupting behind him. The cabin of his hydrodisk lit up with a flickering orange glow. Max could feel the heat of the burning blast, and glanced back to see fiery hot plasma licking at his back window. Max leaned forwards, urging his sub to go faster. He scanned the seabed, desperately looking for somewhere to hide. *There!* One of the crumpled defence-subs was almost within reach.

As Max rocketed towards it, the water around his hydrodisk bubbled and steamed, throwing him forwards and making the air in the sub so hot he could hardly breathe. He dived behind the broken stealth-sub and hit the brakes, just in time to avoid a direct hit.

Max looked at the crumpled shell of metal that shielded him from the blast

and saw that it was folding in on itself and melting away. Max tensed all over, waves of fear pounding through his body. His sub was going to be engulfed by flames any moment.

Then the bright light cast by Octor's plasma blast suddenly flickered out. Max breathed a sigh of relief.

Clang! One of Octor's limbs slammed into the melting stealth-sub and dashed it aside. Max found himself looking straight into Octor's strange, alien eyes. He spun his sub around and gunned the engines. His whole body was sweating now, and he was gasping for breath in the heat. He couldn't bear to think what such hot water would do to Lia. He glanced behind him, hoping for a glimpse of her, but all he could see was a tangle of pale limbs coiling and swirling in the water and Octor's horizontal pupils gazing back at him along the barrel of the plasma gun.

Ahead, Max could see the elephant-like shape of a harvester robot, glowing cool blue in the red water. He veered towards it, aiming for the gap between the seabed and the robot's belly. When he reached the shelter of the robot, he hit the brakes and jolted to a stop.

The water above him lit up with a bright

flash of orange light as Octor fired again. Hot plasma spattered around the sides of the harvester robot, but the blue Tinactium robot seemed to be holding up to the blast. He was safe – for now.

But I can't stay here! Max thought. *Lia's out there. And I have to destroy Octor's controls before he turns on Upsilon-7.* Max waited for the bright light from the blazing plasma to fade, leaving him in shadow. Then he slowly manoeuvred his sub out behind the harvester and upwards. He peered over the top, using the robot as a shield.

What he saw made his stomach churn. One of Octor's tentacles was coiled tight around Lia's chest. The Merryn princess was beating at the pale flesh with her fists, her face contorted with pain. Spike was nearby, jabbing at the tentacle with his sharp sword, but Octor didn't even flinch.

Max flicked the switch to power up his blasters and aimed them towards the thickest part of Octor's tentacle, well away from Lia.

"Spike! Get back!" Max cried, waving his arm. Spike swerved away, and Max hit *fire*.

Nothing happened.

Max checked his dashboard, and saw a blinking red light. His weapons were down. *It must be the heat!* Max thought.

He looked up, and sick panic squeezed his guts. Octor's plasma cannon was aimed point-blank at Lia's head. Lia's eyes opened wide as she struggled in Octor's limb. She lifted her hands to shield her face.

"Help!" she cried. Max knew he only had moments to act. He didn't have any weapons. But he did have his sub. He steered sharply, lining his disk up towards Octor's tentacle, then hit the hyperspeed button.

The force on Max's body was tremendous. He felt like his body was being crushed by the sudden acceleration. The pale flesh of the octopus raced towards him. Max waited, judging the right moment. *Now!* He flicked his emergency eject switch. The hatch above him flew open, and Max was catapulted into the water.

CLANG! Max heard the sound of his

sub hitting the metal tip of Octor's limb. He slowed himself with his legs and arms, and watched as Octor's long limb uncoiled, stunned by the force of the blow. Lia swam free and Spike swooped beneath her, scooping her up onto his back. Then he flicked his tail and darted towards Max.

Octor's huge eye followed Spike's trail. And so did the plasma cannon. A fountain of searing energy shot towards Max and Lia.

CHAPTER SIX

A DANGEROUS PLAN

"**G**et on!" Lia shouted.

Max leapt onto Spike's back behind Lia. The swordfish flicked his tail and sped away from the superheated plasma that was jetting towards them. Max clung to Lia, his stomach lurching as Spike swooped down and dived behind a harvester robot. A shudder ran through the robot as the plasma hit, but its Tinactium cladding deflected the blast. Max turned to face Lia. He could see red marks on her arms where the hot water had scalded her skin, and her hair was streaked with soot. His own shoulders and back were stinging.

"There has to be a way to beat this thing!" Lia said. "But I'm running out of ideas."

"I just can't get past those weapons!" Max said. "They're too powerful and Octor's too quick." He thought back to the blueprints, remembering what Jared had told him about Tinactium. "But maybe we can disable them!" he said. "Lia, wait here, I'm going to try something."

Max peered over the top of the harvester robot. He could see Octor's huge eyes staring back, waiting for him to emerge.

"I've got to reprogram this harvester robot, but I'm going to need a diversion," he told Lia. "Do you think you can outrun that plasma beam one last time?"

Lia grinned and nodded. Spike lifted his sword and let out a trill. Then they darted out from behind the robot. Max watched Octor's vast body turn, then shoot after Lia, firing a jet of water behind it. *I hope she'll be okay!* Max thought as he leapt up onto the harvester robot's back.

There was a small panel behind the robot's head. Max flicked it open with the tip of his hyperblade, then ran his eyes over the circuits and wires. *This should be simple enough...*

Max heard a searing hiss and glanced over to see Lia and Spike narrowly dodge a flickering beam. He turned his attention back to the controls. His hands were shaking and his heart was thumping. His skin was smarting with burns. But he had to focus. He sliced through a wire with his hyperblade, took out a chip, and rejigged some circuits.

He looked up to see Lia and Spike swooping back in his direction with Octor gliding after them. The giant octopus's long tentacles were stretched out ahead of it, reaching towards Spike's tail. And on the end of one, a giant blaster cannon shone, white-hot from firing plasma.

"Lia! I'm almost done!" Max cried. "Hide!" Lia swerved towards him and dived behind the harvester robot. Octor's plasma cannon swung after her, until it was pointing straight at Max. Max could see Octor's eyes watching him coldly from behind the cannon. There was no time to lose.

"Max, hurry!" Lia screamed from her hiding place beneath the harvester.

Max leaned towards the control box and made the final connection.

The harvester robot beneath him started to shudder. The water trembled and a low hum throbbed through Max's body. He glanced up towards Octor, and saw at once that his plan had worked. The huge Robobeast's tentacles were all dragged out below it by the magnetic force on its weapons. The creature's glinting spikes and saws and guns all rushed towards Max at once.

Max somersaulted off the back of the robot and ducked under its belly beside Lia and Spike, adrenaline pulsing through him. The water around them turned dark as Octor's shadow cut out the light.

SMASH! Max felt the harvester robot shudder as Octor's weapons slammed against it. He swam out from under its belly. Octor was straining against the magnetic force that held his limbs to the harvester's back. His tendrils coiled and uncoiled. His huge body stretched and bulged, flickering through all the colours of the rainbow as his eyes rolled in rage.

Max watched until he was sure Octor wasn't going anywhere. Then he kicked his legs and swam upwards past the struggling octopus, keeping his distance from the creature's limbs. Above them, Octor's body was pulled long and taut, the skin rippling with a kaleidoscope of changing colours. His huge round eyes were filled with rage. Max climbed up onto the creature's head towards the small metal box tucked into the dip between its eyes and its elongated,

balloon-like body. He lifted his hyperblade and swung it forcefully.

SNICK! Max felt the wires that had enslaved the giant sea creature give way beneath his blade.

With a tremendous grating sound, Max felt the octopus below him start to rise, pushing him up through the water. Max kicked his legs and swam away from the giant beast. Then he turned and watched in awe as the huge creature rose up in a billowing stream of bubbles, leaving his metal weapons stuck to the harvester robot. Octor swirled around in the water. His body turned a cool, speckled green, then he shot away, his long tentacles

rippling after him.

Lia swam to Max's side on Spike. "He's free!" she said, raising her webbed hand for a high five and smiling. Max slapped her hand and grinned back.

"Am I glad that is over!" he said. "I've never come so close to being cooked in my life. But we haven't won yet. We still have Cora and her crew to defeat." As Max said the words, he realised he could still hear the thumps and bangs of a battle raging above.

Lia put on her Amphibio mask, and Max drew his hyperblade. They kicked up towards the surface, leaving Spike below the waves.

As Max broke the surface, he was immediately surrounded by the clash of weapons mixed with the sound of guns and angry shouts. Cora's tatty, patchwork ship was docked alongside the outpost, rope ladders trailing from its gunwale. Pirates were fighting soldiers hand-to-hand along the docks, while more soldiers fired down at them from the platform above.

Max and Lia swam to the nearest docking station where a knot of pirates and soldiers were hacking at each other with blades. They scrambled out of the water and Max flipped open a repair box and handed Lia a wrench. Lia weighed it in her hand, then nodded. "That will do nicely," she said. Max raised his hyperblade and together they dived into the fray.

A Colossid pirate scuttled around to face Max. Max recognised him at once as the one that had given him the knife. Two of his shiny legs were missing, but he was grinning manically as he swung his hyperblade. Max parried the blow, and stabbed for the creature's chest. From the corner of his eye he could see Lia driving an Ur-man towards the water, swiping at him with her wrench, while soldiers stabbed and thrust at others.

The Colossid caught Max's blade with his own. "You didn't let me down," the pirate said, the voice crackling out of a communications device at his neck. "That was a fine battle."

"Ready for more?" Max said.

"Always!" The Colossid lunged forwards, jabbing for Max's heart. The blow was

clumsy with exhaustion and Max dodged it easily. Max swung his blade again and again, steadily driving the pirate towards the end of the dock. Soon, there was nowhere left for the pirate to go. The Colossid dropped his cutlass and lifted his hands. "All right," he said, panting. "I surrender."

Max glanced about. The clang of metal and the thud of guns had fallen quiet. He could see that all of the pirates had either been knocked into the water, or driven back towards the end of the docks, their hands raised above their heads. All apart from Cora, who Max couldn't see anywhere. Jared seemed to have vanished too. *Probably safely inside!* Max thought.

Suddenly a scream of rage cut the air from the direction of Cora's ship. Max looked up to see Cora standing at the prow, cracking her electric cat-o'-nine-tails, her face purple with rage. "You lousy, pathetic, sorry bunch of worthless maggots," Cora cried. "You Lost Lagooners call yourself pirates? You've given up already!"

"The game's up, Cora," Max called back to her. "We've defeated Octor. We're bringing you in."

"Not likely," Cora sneered. "I've got my escape pod ready."

"Look around you, Cora," Max said. "You're outnumbered. We'll catch you in no time."

"Not if you want to save the sorry hides of everyone on Upsilon-7," Cora said. "I've rigged my ship up with a bomb, ready to explode. And Octor will have shown you what pretty fireworks Celerium makes." With that, Cora gave a hideous cackle, and jumped over the gunwale into an escape pod on the side of the ship. Max heard the engines rev, and the sub shot into the sea, leaving a trail of bubbles as it sped away from the outpost.

CHAPTER SEVEN

UNFINISHED BUSINESS

"Evacuate! Evacuate!" Max heard Jared's panicked voice blurting over the loud speakers. The pirates and soldiers on the docks were already scrambling about, climbing into escape dinghies and jumping into the sea.

Max spotted Lia through the commotion. "We need to get to Cora's ship fast and disarm that bomb!" he called. Lia nodded.

They both raced along the dock, dodging

panicked pirates and soldiers. When they reached Cora's ship, they scrambled up a ladder and jumped onto the deck.

"You check the cabins," Max said. "I'll search the hold. Call me if you find anything."

"Will do," Lia said, and streaked away. Max climbed through a hatch in the deck and down another ladder. His heart thumped as he dropped into the stinking hold of the ship. There were barrels scattered about, and boxes of rotten-smelling rations. Behind them, Max could see a wooden crate with something that gleamed resting on top of it.

He pushed the boxes aside, and clambered over to the crate. It was filled with blocks of explosives all wired together. His compass and a digital timer sat on the top. Max's stomach flipped when he read the timer. *1:59…1:58…1:57.* He had less than two minutes to disarm the bomb.

"Lia!" Max called. "I've found it!" Then he squatted down to examine the wires. The bomb was crudely made, as if someone had put it together in a hurry. *One wrong move and it'll blow*, Max thought, wiping his sweaty hands on his deepsuit. He took a deep breath to steady his nerves.

I haven't defeated the deadliest Robobeast I've ever encountered to be blown up on a pirate ship! he thought. Lia arrived, panting and wide-eyed, at his side.

She peered at the bomb. "A minute and a half!" she said. "Can you disarm it?"

"Here's hoping," Max said. "Keep an eye on the timer." Lia nodded, and Max set to work untwisting delicate wires.

It was fiddly and time-consuming, with no room for mistakes. From the corner of his eye, Max could see the blinking timer counting down.

"Less than a minute," Lia said.

Max worked on, beads of sweat tricking down his spine.

"Thirty seconds," Lia said. Her voice was firm, but Max could hear the tension in it.

Finally, there was just one single wire left connecting the compass to the timer.

"Ten seconds," Lia said, her voice definitely quivering now.

"Here goes," Max said. He heard Lia take a deep breath, and did the same. Then he leant in, and tugged the wire free. The timer blinked once more, and went dark. Max waited a long moment, still holding his breath.

Nothing happened. Lia let out a trembling sigh and Max ran a hand across his sweaty face. Then they looked at each other, and grinned.

"Let's go and let Jared know his outpost's safe before he loses the plot completely," Max said.

As they climbed back on deck, Max saw that the evacuation from the outpost was in full swing. The water surrounding the base was filled with dinghies crowded with soldiers, and pirates treading water to stay afloat.

"Can you see Cora?" Lia asked Max, shielding her eyes and scanning the horizon.

"No," Max said. "I expect she's long gone." But Max did see something else that made him grin. A fleet of Aquoran ships was heading towards the outpost, a small figure with glowing red eyes powering through the water ahead of them.

"Look!" Max said. "It's Rivet with Dad!"

Max and Lia hurried down the ladder of

Cora's ship, back onto the docks of Upsilon-7. There was an intercom near one of the fuel pumps, and Max flicked it into loudspeaker mode.

"Return to your posts," Max said through the intercom, his own voice echoing back to him magnified and distorted. "The bomb has been defused. Aquoran Defence ships are on their way."

A huge cheer went up from the sea around the post.

Max and Lia waited on the docks for the fleet to arrive. As Rivet spotted Max, his eyes flashed, and his propellers whirred even faster. When Rivet reached the docks, Max leaned down and lifted his dogbot from the water. Rivet barked and wagged his tail excitedly as Max set him down on the quay.

"Rivet got Callum! Good Rivet!" Rivet barked. Max and Lia patted him all over, and

Lia even let Rivet lick her face.

As the first of the Aquoran ships slid into the dock, Max spotted his father at the prow and lifted his hand, grinning. "Hey, Dad!" Max shouted. Callum smiled, and raised his hand in return, then turned to the crew on his ship.

"Get those pirates out of the water and round them up!" he said.

Max rushed forwards as Callum climbed

down the ladder of his ship and onto the quay.

"I see you've got things under control," Callum said, stepping towards Max with his arms spread wide for a hug.

Max heard a scuffle of boots on the ladder behind him, and then Jared swept past and saluted briskly.

"We have indeed, sir," Jared said. "It was good of you to come, but as you can see,

Upsilon-7 was quite safe from Cora with me in charge. I hope you'll agree I've earned a post back on Aquora."

Beside Max, Lia gave an outraged gasp and stepped forwards. "But you didn't –" Max grabbed her arm, cutting her off.

"Jared did save our lives," Max whispered. "And it was Jared who worked out that Cora was headed here. For once he's actually been pretty helpful. Maybe he deserves a second chance."

"Hmph!" Lia said. But then she shrugged. "I suppose you're right."

Max's father looked from Jared, who was standing with his head held high, to Max and Lia, and frowned. Max could tell his father knew there was more to the story than Jared was telling. But then Callum smiled.

"Lieutenant Jared," he said. "We have not always seen eye to eye, but it seems on this occasion you have acted bravely. I will speak to Chief Councillor Glenon, and recommend your assignment back to Aquora."

Max saw Jared's nostrils flare and his jaw flex as he gritted his teeth. "Thank you, sir," Jared said, almost spitting the words at Callum, before turning and striding away. Callum sighed and shook his head, watching Jared storm off along the quay.

"There really is no pleasing some people," he said mildly.

Suddenly, Spike poked his nose from the waves, and let out a flurry of clicks.

Lia grinned. "You're right, Spike," she said. "It is time we headed back to Sumara. I'm singed and frazzled and I ache all over. I could really do with a bubble soak." She turned to Max. "And you need to finish your swordfish-riding lesson," she said.

Max felt a tinge of anxiety at the thought

of riding Silvertail again. "Do I have to?" he said.

Lia laughed. "It should be a doddle compared to facing Octor," she said.

At the thought of the Robobeast and his deadly Celerium cannon, Max suddenly felt uneasy. Cora was still out there somewhere, and now she'd be even more desperate for revenge. But then he shrugged and smiled. Lia was right. If they could face a Robobeast like Octor, they could do anything. And that included defeating Cora!

Don't miss the next Sea Quest book,
in which Max faces

FLIKTOR
THE DEADLY CONQUEROR

Read on for a sneak preview!

CHAPTER ONE
A NASTY BITE

"Hey, Lia! Take a look at this!" Max called into his headset, his finger hovering over the trigger for his aquafly's acid torpedoes. Through the domed glass cockpit of his new lightweight craft he could see Lia floating in the ocean nearby, twirling her new Merryn spear in one hand.

Beyond her, Max's dogbot Rivet and Lia's pet swordfish Spike were swooping through the sea-grass that surrounded Aquora. Lia lifted her hand, and threw a ball of seaweed out onto the current. Spike and Rivet streaked towards it. Rivet got there first, snapping it up in his metal jaws and veering away as Spike swerved after him.

Lia waved her hand through the water,

washing off flakes of seaweed from her fingers, then spun to face Max, sighing theatrically. "What now?" she asked. "You know, I can only pretend to be interested in triple-luminosity headlights for so long."

Max grinned. "If that was you pretending to be interested, I'd hate to see you acting bored. Now watch this!" Max peered at his target, a rock with a cyrate's face projected onto it about fifty paces away, then pressed the red torpedo button.

Voom! The torpedo surged through the water and smashed against the rock, releasing a splat of sticky green acid. The acid bubbled and frothed, eating away at the rock behind the cyrate's face, then dripping down to leave a fizzing crater in the seabed.

"Wow. That's quite a mess you've made there," Lia said flatly.

"Exactly! Max said. "These torpedoes are

designed to completely annihilate cyrates."

Lia shrugged. "I prefer good old Sumaran coral, personally," she said, jabbing her spear in a powerful thrust. "But I suppose metal-melting weapons could be useful, given your cousin's strange obsession with making evil robots. Although I was kind of hoping we'd seen the last of Siborg."

"Me too," Max said, "but something tells me that's unlikely." His stomach twisted with a familiar pang of dread at the thought of his evil cousin, but Max shrugged the feeling away and focussed back on his sleek new sub. "Anyway," he said, "if you think my torpedoes are cool, take a look at my jets!" Max flipped the cockpit open, swam out and ran his hand along the bullet-shaped thrusters. "With these I can go as fast over the surface of the water as I can beneath it, and if I power them up, I can even fly through the air! I reckon I could get as high up as my apartment. But you can't overload the thrusters for long or…" Max trailed off, noticing that Lia's gaze had drifted back towards Spike and Rivet.

"What's that thing Rivet's found?" Lia asked. Rivet was powering towards them, a blue oval object clasped between his teeth.

Rivet stopped at Max's feet, wagging his tail. Spike stayed a few paces away, eyeing the capsule nervously.

Max reached out a hand for the object and Rivet released it. It was as long as Max's forearm, and the surface was completely smooth and slightly warm to the touch.

"Rivet found lots!" Rivet barked, nodding towards the sea-grass behind them.

"What is it?" Lia asked, leaning over to touch the object gently with a webbed finger.

"I've no idea," Max said, "but it doesn't look natural."

Suddenly Spike let out a flurry of warning clicks. Max turned and gasped. At least fifty more capsules had floated up from the seagrass and were drifting towards them on the current. They were all the same size, and the same uniform blue. As one floated close to Spike, he jerked away, giving a high-pitched clack of alarm.

COLLECT THEM ALL!

SERIES 6: MASTER OF AQUORA

FLIKTOR
THE DEADLY CONQUEROR

978 1 40833 480 5

TENGAL
THE SAVAGE SHARK

978 1 40833 481 2

KULL
THE CAVE CRAWLER

978 1 40833 483 6

GULAK
THE GULPER EEL

978 1 40833 485 0

www.seaquestbooks.co.uk

WIN AN EXCLUSIVE
GOODY BAG

In every Sea Quest book the Sea Quest logo is
hidden in one of the pictures. Find the logo in this book,
make a note of which page it appears on and
go online to enter the competition at

www.seaquestbooks.co.uk

Each month we will put all of the correct entries into a draw
and select one winner to receive a special Sea Quest goody bag.

You can also send your entry on a postcard to:

Sea Quest Competition, Orchard Books,
338 Euston Road, London, NW1 3BH

Don't forget to include your name and address!

GOOD LUCK

Closing Date: 30th September 2015

DARE YOU DIVE IN?

Deep in the water lurks a new breed of Beast.

If you want the latest news and exclusive Sea Quest goodies, join our Sea Quest Club!

Visit www.seaquestbooks.co.uk/club and sign up today!

IF YOU LIKE SEA QUEST, YOU'LL LOVE BEAST QUEST!

Series 1: COLLECT THEM ALL!

An evil wizard has enchanted the magical beasts of Avantia. Only a true hero can free the beasts and save the land. Is Tom the hero Avantia has been waiting for?

FERNO
THE FIRE DRAGON

978 1 84616 483 5

SEPRON
THE SEA SERPENT

978 1 84616 482 8

ARCTA
THE MOUNTAIN GIANT

978 1 84616 484 2

TAGUS
THE HORSE MAN

978 1 84616 486 6

NANOOK
THE SNOW MONSTER

978 1 84616 485 9

EPOS
THE FLAME BIRD

978 1 84616 487 3